THE ANTHROPOLOGY OF DISPLACED COMMUNITIES

First published in 2020 by
Sean Kingston Publishing
www.seankingston.co.uk
Canon Pyon

British Library Cataloguing in Publication Data
A catalogue record for this book is available from the British Library.
The moral rights of the editor and authors have been asserted.

Cover image: Izzbba refugee settlement, Khartoum (see chapter 2).
Photograph by Soheel Issam.

Hardback ISBN 978-1-912385-22-5

The Anthropology of Displaced Communities

Edited by Robert Layton

Sean Kingston Publishing

www.seankingston.co.uk

Canon Pyon

Royal Anthropological Institute

This book is largely due to the inspiration of George Appell, who has led the funding drive to ensure that the Royal Anthropological Institute's Urgent Anthropology Fund has continued to be supported over many years. The extraordinary results that have been obtained are here clear to see.

CONTENTS

A tribute to my father

Laura P. Appell-Warren

Only by knowing how peoples in other times, other places, and other cultures have experienced and interpreted the human condition can we truly understand what it means to be human and our place in the universe.
George N. Appell[1]

I had the great good fortune in September of 2010 to attend the two-day seminar at the University of Kent entitled 'New Directions for Urgent Anthropological Research'. During this seminar, I not only heard the results of the research sponsored by the Anthropologists' Fund for Urgent Anthropological Research, but also heard of the impact that the RAI Urgent Anthropology Fellowships Programme has had on the researchers and the communities in which they have worked. The passion for ethnography, particularly in areas undergoing rapid social change, was palpable and is a testimony to the continued significance of urgent anthropological research. Most importantly, it was clear that my father's vision, that the programme 'would contribute to anthropological knowledge and theory as well as provide indigenous peoples with the results of such research' (Appell this volume, p. 25), had been realized.

Growing up in the Appell household, those two themes, anthropological knowledge and theory, and indigenous rights, were a constant. Sloppy scholarship was never tolerated, and we would have extended conversations over the dinner table, and later as we grew up, over drinks, about research that he considered to be lacking in rigour or to be biased. My father strove always to maintain the highest standards of research in his own work, and his life as a researcher was an extended journey in search of culture-free, scientific methods for mapping the sociocultural systems of non-Western peoples. A journey that continued until his death.

Another common topic of conversation, and a focus of my father's work, was the rights of indigenous peoples. He was a passionate advocate of these, whether for the Native Peoples in our home state of Maine or for indigenous

---

1   www.firebirdfellowships.org/sabah-oral-literature-project.html.

people in other parts of the world, as is evidenced by his work in the 1970s and 80s with both Cultural Survival and Survival International.

My father's fascination with anthropology and his commitment to indigenous peoples had its roots in his childhood, when he read, voraciously, anything he could find about Plains Indian societies. While in his teens he was particularly impacted by the violations of the human rights of Native American peoples, and by the systematic theft of their lands and livelihoods. The cruel treatment of Native Americans – first by the settlers and the United States Government, and then by other American citizens – appalled and disgusted him.

After college, my father spent some time getting an MBA and then working in the family businesses in York, Pennsylvania. However, his passion for anthropology eventually steered him back to graduate school, first at Harvard, where he and my mother met, then later at the Australian National University, where he received his doctorate in 1966.

Having decided to focus his research on the Rungus Momogun of Sabah, in what was then British North Borneo, it was not long before he discovered that the District Officer (DO) perceived the forest lands where the Rungus lived to be under-utilized. The DO, who was clearly unaware of the land-tenure system of the Rungus, was bent on finding ways to exploit what he saw as unused land and resources. From the research perspective, this experience catapulted my father into finding 'a clear, precise, and culture-free system for the discovery of the incidents of land tenure and property relations, a system that would not be tainted by the cultural biases and prejudices of researchers and agents of change.'[2] From the personal perspective, this experience brought into sharp focus the need for the goal of anthropological research to be to help protect the rights of indigenous people.

In 1963 my father was called upon by then DO Colin Wood to act as an advocate and interpreter for the Rungus at the Cobbold Commission hearings.[3] At stake, in addition to the impact on the Rungus of Sabah joining the Federation of Malaysia, were issues surrounding Chinese settlement on the Rungus land that was perceived to be unused by the Westerners living in the Kudat region of Sabah. This willingness to stand up publicly for the land-tenure rights of the Rungus people came at great personal cost for both my

---

2   gnappell.org/bio.htm.

3   The Cobbold Commission was set up to determine whether the people of North Borneo supported the proposal to create the Federation of Malaysia.

parents, as my father was banned from entering Sabah from 1963 until 1986, effectively halting his research among the Rungus for over 20 years.[4]

Understanding, even from afar, that the traditional culture of the Rungus people was being lost due to the rapid modernization of the Kudat peninsula, my father delved into another line of inquiry, the health and social consequences of rapid change. While the theoretical work for this research was conducted while my father was a Senior Research Associate at Brandeis University, the fieldwork that solidified his argument was conducted in 1980–1, while living in a resettlement village among the Bulusu' of what was then East Kalimantan, Indonesia.[5] Additionally, this research period brought into sharp relief the need for urgent anthropological work to be undertaken among the rapidly vanishing cultures of the world, so that their histories and ways of being could be preserved as a resource for future generations.

All of these formative personal and research experiences culminated in 1993 in the creation of the Urgent Anthropology Fellowship Programme. A brain child that was brought into fruition at a meeting with Jonathan Benthall at the American Anthropological Association conference in Washington DC. This process was detailed by my father in Chapter 1 of this volume.

After my father's death we received condolences from around the globe. Perhaps most meaningful, in light of his commitment to indigenous rights and the preservation of culture, were the messages that we received from the peoples of Sabah thanking my parents for their work preserving the Rungus Momogun culture. Of particular value will be the multi volume Cultural Dictionary that was started by my father and mother, and which is now being completed by members of the Sabah Oral Literature Project.[6]

.

---

4   In an interview with Alan Macfarlane in April of 2004 (www.sms.cam.ac.uk/media/1107023), Appell discusses this experience in greater detail.

5   On a personal note, while I was raised as a young child among the Rungus, it was during this field trip, when I was able to conduct my own research on the impact of social change on children's play, that my career as a psychological anthropologist was truly forged (see Appell-Warren, L. 1987. 'Play: the development of kakada' and social change among the Bulusu of East Kalimantan'. In *Meaningful Play, Playful Meaning,* ed. G.A. Fine. Champaign, ILL: Human Kinetics Publishers, Inc.)

6   www.firebirdfellowships.org/sabah-oral-literature-project.html.

Introduction

The anthropology of displaced communities

Robert Layton

This volume brings together papers by six holders of the Royal Anthropological Institute's Urgent Anthropology Fellowships, together with four further contributions. George Appell (Chapter 1), describes the history and rationale of the Urgent Anthropology Fellowships and sets out the programme's objectives: to support ethnographic research on disappearing or threatened cultures and, where appropriate, to assist indigenous peoples in their struggle to control their own destinies. In the concluding chapter (Chapter 10), Appell explains how his own commitment arose from the traumatic experience of living with, and studying, a displaced community of swidden cultivators in Borneo whom the Indonesian government had removed to what Appell characterizes as a 'cultural concentration camp'. While Appell describes the Urgent Anthropology programme as the rebirth of a research paradigm that attaches more importance to ethnography than to theory, it is not a simple return to nineteenth-century 'salvage ethnography', but provides a deeper understanding of the dynamics of social relationships when people are displaced from their home communities. The Urgent Anthropology Fellowships are intended to protect and strengthen communities whose culture and social life are under immediate threat. Displaced communities exemplify such vulnerability. Indeed, they pose fundamental questions about a community's capacity to reproduce its normal social relations and transmit its culture when deprived of economic resources and political agency.

This introduction aims to step back from the case studies and provide an overview of how displaced peoples can recreate and sustain social relationships under precarious conditions. It includes the most extreme situations experienced in Auschwitz concentration camp and the Soviet

Gulag. The introduction draws on studies of refugee camps including those by Abusharaf (Chapter 2) and Sansculotte-Greenidge and Barber (Chapter 3), but also others taken from the growing anthropological literature. Appell's first-hand account of an Indonesian 'cultural concentration camp' in this volume also has parallels in the enforced confinement of Australian Aboriginal communities on government settlements, documented by Bardon and Bardon (2006).

I echo other criticisms of authors who take the Western jet-setting 'nomad' possessed of social and cultural capital as a model for the kind of displacement that is said to be typical of our times. Voluntary labour migrants typically retain social links with their community of origin. While some forced migrants also participate in networks linking them to more fortunate members of their ethnic group, their community of origin may have been destroyed.

Malkki's influential critique of the opposing 'sedentarist' perspective in writing on refugees (Malkki 1992), which implies that fleeing from home reduces refugees to their bare humanity and that they cannot rebuild social relationships in displacement, is also important. The evidence of Primo Levi and Alexander Solzhenitsyn shows that even in a Nazi concentration camp or the Soviet Gulag, tenuous social relationships are constructed. Similar strategies reappear in the less extreme case of refugee camps. Based on his forced displacement from France during the Second World War, Lévi-Strauss speculated that, in a concentration camp, people stripped of their past and their culture might rely on spontaneous, 'non-crystallised' forms of relationship that recreate 'elemental and universal processes' of human social interaction (Lévi-Strauss 1969:42). The case studies below show that displaced people almost always draw on familiar social strategies to rebuild social networks, not spontaneous and inchoate practices.

Anthropology has never adhered to Thomas Hobbes's vision, propounded at the time of the English Civil War in *Philosophical Rudiments*, that humans are naturally anarchic:

> by experience known to all men and denied by none, to wit, that the
> dispositions of men are naturally such that except they be restrained
> through fear of some coercive power, every man will distrust and dread each
> other.
>
> (quoted in Peters 1967:62)

On the contrary, anthropology has developed in the tradition of John Locke (1960, first published 1689) and Adam Ferguson (1995, first published 1767), arguing that humans are intrinsically social, that humans have always been capable of building cooperation and exchange because they recognize that social order is in their long-term self-interest. Before the state assumed responsibility for upholding the law, people owed their safety to 'the warm attachment of their friends, and to the exercise of every talent which could render them respected, feared or beloved' (ibid.:211).

Displacement and social order
Jet-setting mobility
Nigel Rapport and Andrew Dawson argue that the transnational movement of people is the dominant feature of modern social life:

> Exile, emigration, banishment, labour migrancy, tourism, urbanization and counter-urbanization are the central motifs of modern culture, while being rootless, displaced between worlds, living between a lost past and a fluid present, are perhaps the most fitting metaphors for the journeying, modern consciousness.
>
> (Rapport and Dawson 1998:23)

In common with Gupta and Ferguson (1992), Rapport and Dawson question whether there ever existed a state in which human communities were fixed and stable, where people could securely identify one place as 'home'. Their list, however, compresses some very different experiences. Labour migration has increasingly ceased to be a form of exile or banishment, and tourism has little in common with a year in Auschwitz.

Anthony Elliott and John Urry also celebrated the glamour of the Western jet-setting nomad: 'Simone is a British-based academic, originally from Brazil' (Elliott and Urry 2010:1).[1] She passes through airport security barriers in New York, where she will deliver a conference paper and act as a consultant for a private company, checks her BlackBerry mobile phone, calls a friend, worries about the time she's spending away from her family, phones her husband in London and so on. 'Identity in the "rich north" is significantly constituted as, and inscribed in the scripts of, a *mobile life*' (ibid.:3, original emphasis).

Elliott and Urry coin the term 'network capital', which the successful rich jet-setter can accumulate to facilitate their mobile life (ibid.:10–11). These precious but indispensable items are specified as: appropriate documents, visas, money and qualifications to ensure safe travel; colleagues, friends and family living at a distance who can issue invitations; the ability to access reliable computerized information, use text messaging, email, the internet and

---

1   Given that Elliott and Urry state early on in their book that 'the[ir] interviews have been fictionalised, condensed and several voices combined into one' (Elliott and Urry 2010: xi), 'Simone' is probably a composite character.

so on; electronic and 'real' points at which information can be stored including electronic messages, answering services, secretaries and offices; the means to rearrange appointments while on the move; safe and secure meeting places in clubs, hotels or offices; access to cars, trains, ships, aircraft; time and resources to co-ordinate the above seven forms of capital when there is 'system failure' (ibid.:10–11). It seems almost laughably obvious from this list how short of 'capital' refugees are, although some are more lacking than others. Elliott and Urry do concede that refugees, asylum seekers and slaves have mobility thrust upon them (although not, in this case, like Malvolio's imagined greatness), but give them little consideration.[2]

Tim Cresswell criticizes the common assertion in recent social science that culture and the social are no longer tied to places, but have become hybrid. 'In contemporary social thought, words associated with mobility are unremittingly positive ... [mobility] is seen to be progressive, exciting, and contemporary' (Cresswell 2006:25). Deleuze and Guattari's prototypical image of the nomad envisages, according to Cresswell, 'a desert imagined as flat, smooth and curiously isotropic' (that is, imposing no constraints on movement) in which postmodern nomads attempt to free themselves of all roots, bonds and identities, thereby resisting the state (ibid.:49).

Mark Jamieson (Chapter 6) and Emma Gilberthorpe (Chapter 7), on the other hand, document the negative long-term effects of the passage of strangers through their local communities: the ebb and flow of economic opportunity in the market economy, the intervention of multinational companies offering often temporary opportunities, and the arrival of powerful strangers in local communities which then suffer damage to their traditional culture and social life. Gilberthorpe presents contrasting case studies of the impact of open-cast mining and oil extraction in highland Papua New Guinea. Jamieson documents the impact of foreign logging companies, combatants in the US-sponsored Contra War (1979 to 1990) and the gratuitous availability of cocaine packages, abandoned by marine smugglers fleeing customs vessels, in two villages on Nicaragua's Mosquito Coast.

Migration and international networks

Studies of labour migration during the latter half of the twentieth century often underline the strong social links between a migrant community and its community of origin. Velayutham and Wise (2005) describe the hold that South Indian Tamil communities exercise over their members who have migrated to Singapore, demanding they return to marry someone of a suitable

---

2   Urry classes refugees as one of thirteen overlapping 'social practices of travel', and they are given even less consideration (Urry 2000:17).

caste in their natal village, and take care of the needs of their less well-off relatives in South India. A very similar situation among Pakistani immigrants in the UK is presented by Shaw (2000) and Charsley (2006). Charsley finds that culturally distinctive marriage customs are actually strengthened rather than diluted in the migrant community.

In some cases, flight as refugees may also be embedded in wider transnational networks, even when forcibly displaced peoples may have suffered the destruction of their community of origin. Oliver Bakewell (2004) found that Angolan refugees from the civil war who fled to Zambia were joining kin who had moved earlier and were part of a long-term trend of movement from the former kingdom of Mwanta Yavwa in the Democratic Republic of the Congo to Zambia, via Angola. During the first half of twentieth century, people were moving either from Zambia to Angola to avoid paying taxes imposed by the British, or in the other direction to avoid forced labour in Angola. When the repatriation of Angolan refugees from Zambia was being considered between 1995 and 1998, over 20 per cent of those planning to settle in Angola had not lived there before, while almost 20 per cent of former residents had no intention of returning. The late senior chief in the district where Bakewell carried out his research had declared that no one should be referred to as an ex-refugee; they were all his people. (Perhaps labour was scarcer than land in that district?) In fact, Bakewell writes, there is today no practical way of distinguishing a former refugee from anyone else (ibid.:36).

Horst (2006:23, 95) learned that after Somali refugees were moved from the environs of Nairobi to Dadaab, it became difficult to distinguish refugees from local Kenyan Somalis (cf. Hyndman 2000:88, 158). One refugee working in the logistics department estimated that of 45,000 refugees in one camp, 11,000 were local Kenyans. Kwesi Sansculotte-Greenidge and Laura Barber (Chapter 3) found that a Darfuri refugee camp located in the country of a related Chadian ethnic group was also sufficiently well-provisioned that some local Chadians were 'moonlighting' as refugees.

Horst's study of Somali refugees in the Dadaab camps in Kenya is particularly good at documenting the existence of a continuum between voluntary travel and forced migration, and provides a fuller account of features recorded earlier in Dadaab by Hyndman (2000:149). Horst (2006) shows that the Somali are transnational nomads. Traditionally they coped with insecurity by practising mobility, investing in social networks and diversifying investments across different livelihood strategies. One Somali living in the United States with his family told Horst that they treat the border between the United States and Canada as they would treat the Ethiopia–Somalia border: with little regard. The second strategy is to maintain a strong social network whose members provide mutual aid to each other. It was common to find refugees in Dadaab who have relatives in Somalia, Kenya, South Africa, the Middle East, Canada, the United States, Australia or Europe. The third strategy was risk reduction through strategically dispersing investments in family members and activities. Horst estimates at least 10 to 15 per cent of Somali camp residents in Dadaab were receiving remittances, which they often shared with others in the camp. *Taar* are privately owned radio sets that people can use, for a small fee, to contact relatives in Kenyan cities, other parts of Africa and abroad. These radios were used to exchange general information, including news of fighting in Somalia, to influence individual decisions about migration through information on risks and opportunities in other places, to ask someone to return to camp to help a sick relative and to transmit money both into and out of the camp. At one end of the spectrum, Khaliif, a relatively wealthy man, declined resettlement in the United States because, he explained, the camps provide free food, education and medical treatment, and a piece of land on which to build a house without paying rent. He had several relatives living in Western countries who sent him remittances and he owned camels, cows, goats and chickens.

At the other extreme to Khaliif, 10 to 15 per cent of camp residents received nothing, and were often malnourished. Horst quotes the case of women from a minority clan who had lost their only way of life. Many of them were widows, many had been raped. They felt despised and useless in their own community. A Somali aid worker told Horst: 'In reality, you need power, connections or money ... The real vulnerables will always lose out since, by definition, they do not have any of the[se]' (Horst 2006:102). Horst was reminded not to disregard the great insecurity around Dadaab, to be aware that rations are insufficient, health facilities poor and opportunities for work or education few. Hyndman (2000:90) points out further disadvantages suffered by women in Dadaab: they are less likely than men to speak English, they have less access to legitimate employment and fewer opportunities to be involved in consultation or decision-making.

Before his untimely death, Ananda Raja, a former holder of an Urgent Anthropology Fellowship, had promised us a paper on how Burmese refugees in Thailand maintain an international network. In his synopsis he wrote that Karen refugee camps in Thailand are connected by formal institutional networks, informal social networks (some of which extend to villages and towns in Burma), conventional information flows and electronic means of communication. Some Karen refugee self-help organizations, he wrote, are linked through the internet and e-mail to the larger world and to other refugees who have successfully sought asylum in the West.

The importance of information

Horst noted the importance of access to information about the world outside the refugee camp. Lack of reliable information or contact with the outside world is profoundly destabilising. In one of his last publications, Primo Levi recalled that, on their arrival in Auschwitz, guards chillingly told the prisoners that, because no one would believe what any survivors said, they were effectively defeated as soon as they entered the camp (Levi 1989:11–12).

The destructive effect that a lack of information has on refugees' behaviour is exemplified by Wendy James (1997). James and the crew she was helping to make a *Disappearing World* film within a refugee camp sheltering both Uduk and Nuer were suddenly aware of a wave of movement, as a seemingly leaderless body of Uduk men flowed through the camp, armed with makeshift weapons, trying to block Nuer on the two margins from coming together. Initially told by Nuer that some Uduk had killed a Nuer woman, James subsequently established that there had been a river bank scrap between two children, one Uduk and one Nuer. Women on both sides had joined in, then an Uduk man tried to separate them. Nuer men nearby were enraged to see him handling their women. Sticks and spears were thrown. An old woman was stoned by retaliating Uduk, and false rumours of her death flew. 'What seemed like thousands of people, mostly men but also women, were rushing towards the river to attack the Nuer ... We realised all control had gone' (ibid.:118). Two years later, James learned that three Nuer men had been killed by stoning in the second attack.

Like the Nazi guards at Auschwitz, oppressive leaders may actively destabilize shared meanings as a means to disempower their victims. Zoë Crossland (2000) argued that the abduction of the 'disappeared' and their subsequent anonymous burial were indices of the ruling Argentine Junta's power and a denial of the victim's agency: 'since we "disappeared" you, you're nothing' (2000:153). She also quotes a member of the Argentine Junta who denied the self-evident practices of abduction and torture: 'It must be understood there has been no violation of human rights' (ibid.:149). This denial of the plain truth parallels a Bosnian Croat officer's assertion that, after the troops under his command had shelled it for several weeks, the famous medieval bridge in Mostar linking Bosnian Croat and Muslim communities 'probably fell down on its own'.[3] Rana Mitter, in his study of twentieth-century Chinese history, notes that during the Cultural Revolution, words such as 'class', 'bourgeois' and 'humanist' could mean whatever a group or person in control chose them to mean. The Red Guard phase (1966-9) was thus defined

---

3   www.independent.co.uk/news/croats-destroy-mostars-historic-bridge-1503338.
     html (accessed 30 April 2019).

almost entirely according to power relations, not moral norms or shared understandings (Mitter 2004:209).

Forced displacement

Cresswell (2006), like others cited below, attaches particular importance to Liisa Malkki's dissection of the political dimension of refugee status from a sedentarist perspective. Referring to Cirtautas (1957), Malkki's concern is that the supposed loss of roots, bonds and identities among refugees makes uprootedness seem like a pathology (Malkki 1992:32). 'Our sedentarist assumptions about attachment to place lead us to define displacement not as a fact about sociopolitical context, but rather as an inner, pathological condition of the displaced' (ibid.:33). Malkki (33n) also cites Hannah Arendt (1973:294, 300) on Second World War refugees in Europe: 'the abstract nakedness of being nothing but human was their greatest danger'. Malkki identifies a misleading sedentarist metaphor: culture is rooted in the soil, so people who are 'uprooted' leave their culture behind them. Her own fieldwork among Hutu refugees who had fled Burundi to settle in Kigoma township in western Tanzania revealed them to be resourcefully manipulating multiple identities derived or borrowed from the township during their quest for assimilation. Many were unsure about whether they would ever return to Burundi; they had created lives that were located in the present circumstances of Kigoma. Identity, Malkki concludes, is always mobile and processual. In the penultimate chapter of this volume, Jean and John Comaroff provide an amusing account of how, seen from the perspective of the South African host community, invasive plants provide a figure of speech through which to express resistance to incoming, displaced peoples. Cresswell argues that neither the followers of the sedentarist school, nor those extolling modern nomadism as a form of freedom, are particularly aware of the ideological nature of the meanings they ascribe to mobility. 'Politics, power and ideology are not parts of their lexicon' (Cresswell 2006:55).

Malkki's conclusion that refugees do not leave their culture behind, but continue to rely on it to make sense of their experience, is supported by Sandra Dudley (2012) in her study of Karen refugees in Thailand, and by Laura Hammond's study of resettled Ethiopian refugees (Hammond 2004). Hammond concludes that refugees never completely lose their agency and do not arrive at their resettlement location stripped of their culture and identity. Yet uprootedness is not necessarily an empty metaphor; flight may be hard for peasants whose subsistence, community networks and rituals are closely tied to their home villages. Burundians were reluctant to return to Angola (Bakewell 2004) because they were afraid their village land would already have reverted to bush, while the first Ethiopians to return from a refugee camp in

Sudan were those who still had land in the Ethiopian highlands, and they went because it was time to plant their seeds (Hammond 2004).

Prison camps: society degree zero?

Liisa Malkki challenges the claim that the refugee represents humanity 'at our most basic and naked level', stripped of agency, culture, place and history (Malkki 1995:12). Nonetheless, fleeing refugees and concentration camp inmates provide opportunities, however unwelcome, to investigate social interaction at its rawest and apparently most elementary level. Cindy Horst (2006:24, 60) comments that while refugees do retain agency, it can only be exercised within a social network. Deprived of a network of social connections, the exercise of agency must at best be severely limited. One Somali refugee told Horst that, while fleeing, she simply wondered every day whether she would be alive that night; she was too worried to sit and eat, so would just drink milk or water then move on. The Hutu refugees with whom Malkki worked also experienced life during their flight through the forest from Burundi as chaotic formlessness, a total suspension of the social displaced by the sheer will for bodily survival. It was only after those fleeing Burundi arrived in Tanzania and met up with other refugees that they were able to restore some clarity to their lives.

In a recent sequel to her earlier ethnographies of the Uduk, Wendy James (2007) follows their transformation from a coherent, emplaced community into refugees brought about by the civil war in Southern Sudan. James describes the tragic physical destruction of the society she had studied and documented for many years. Her study is surely unique in its wealth of detail, as told verbatim to James by people with whom she had previously worked, when she caught up with them in refugee camps and other displaced locations. James provides many vivid details of personal suffering, excruciating loss, death from starvation and firearms. The overall effect is an unrivalled sense of the chaos of war, although closing chapters describe the revival of dances and the use of song to comment on inept leadership and to recall dangers escaped.

After service in the French Army, Claude Lévi-Strauss fled France as a refugee in 1941 (Johnson 2003:8). In his 1955/1973 memoir of travel and anthropological research, he gives a moving account of the voyage among a motley collection of passengers escaping the Nazi advance into France:

> I did not begin to understand the situation until the day we went on board
> between two rows of helmeted *gardes mobiles* with sten guns in their hands
> ... preventing all contact between the passengers and their relatives or

friends who had come to say goodbye, and interrupting leave-takings with
jostlings and insults.

(Lévi-Strauss 1973:24)

Many of the passengers on the voyage were severely affected by the
spitefulness and stupidity they encountered among the crew, who believed
that, as refugees, they had been stripped of their social identity. Lévi-Strauss
made his way from the ship's destination in Puerto Rico to the United States,
where he taught at the New School for Social Research in New York, and
spent many hours in library research. One of the fruits of this period was
The Elementary Structures of Kinship, first published in 1949. Presumably
reflecting on his experiences during the Second World War, in that work Lévi-
Strauss characterizes communities under bombardment and in concentration
camps, in the quotation supplied above, as 'non-crystallised forms of social
life ... arising spontaneously out of accidental circumstances' (Lévi-Strauss
1969:42). Speculating on whether we could ever observe the spontaneous
emergence of social relations he cites the meeting of two strangers seated at
the same table in a French café, where contact is made when each offers the
other a glass of wine from the small carafe that comes with the meal. The two
carafes have in fact been filled from the same barrel, but the exchange of like
for like, he argues, creates a social bond comparable to the exchange of sisters
in 'archaic' societies. Despite being aware this is a French custom, Lévi-Strauss
characterizes it as 'an example, rare in our society ... of the formation of a
group for which ... no ready-made formula of integration exists' (ibid.:59).

In the years following publication of that book, two outstanding accounts
of life in forced labour camps became available: a participant's account of life
in Auschwitz by Primo Levi (1979) and a fictionalized account of life in a Soviet
prison camp by Aleksandr Solzhenitsyn (1963). There are striking parallels
between the two. Of the four major types of social transaction (reciprocity,
patronage and market exchange for use value or for profit), the reciprocity
anticipated by Lévi-Strauss is only marginally achieved. The overwhelmingly
unequal relationship between captors and prisoners has the consequence that
accessing even the meanest forms of patronage from superiors is foremost
among prisoners' goals, with clandestine market exchange coming second.
These accounts capture the social costs of forced displacement at its most
extreme.

Primo Levi, a captured partisan, was deported from Italy early in 1944
and sent to Buna-Monowitz, a sub-camp of Auschwitz. The first Russian
patrol arrived to liberate the camp on 27 January 1945, at just about the same
time Solzhenitsyn was arrested, not to be released until Stalin's death in 1953.
Solzhenitsyn's book is based on his personal experiences of life in a labour

camp for long-term political prisoners in northern Kazakhstan. For both Levi and Solzhenitsyn, imprisonment is indefinite; no one knows when, or if, they will ever be released. Both are engaged in forced labour, Levi helping to build a chemicals factory, Shukov (Solzhenitsyn's *alter ego*) a power station. The prisoners in both camps have been stripped of any previous rank. All are attempting to survive on a meagre diet of soup and bread whose intrinsic character leads to convergent strategies: in both camps, prisoners try to avoid arriving at the head of the meal queue, since the richest soup is at the bottom of the pan. Bread becomes a medium of exchange. Small possessions such as one's spoon, with which to eat the soup, are highly prized and carefully guarded against theft.

Above all, the prisoners in Auschwitz strove not to be reduced to the condition of *muselmann*, so bereft of agency that they could no longer remember, observe or express themselves (Agamben 2002:33–4), a state in which, as one former *muselmann* recalled, he had wandered through the camp like a stray dog (ibid.:170). During his philosophical reflections on Auschwitz, Agamben is particularly taken by Primo Levi's observation that only the *muselmänner* who went to the gas chambers fully experienced Auschwitz; the survivors were only partial witnesses.[4] It is, however, the social strategies to which the survivors resorted that I want to highlight and, to these, Primo Levi was both witness and participant.

Rapport and Dawson (1998) concede that communities that have been forcibly displaced may search out their own people and customs to offer lifebelts against disempowerment. This is confirmed by Levi and Solzhenitsyn. In both camps, prisoners from the same ethnic community stuck together. There was also a more indefinable sense of mutual forbearance. In Buna-Monowitz some fellowship develops among members of the same dormitory block, 'tacit pacts of non-aggression with neighbours; of understanding and accepting the customs and laws of a single Kommando [work team]' (Levi 1979:62). Solzhenitsyn describes how, when a missing prisoner is found at the end of the day's labour, some of those kept waiting in the cold shout insults at him, but others hold their tongues because they see he is about to be hit with the guard's rifle butt. Shukov engages in a tangled series of transactions involving reciprocity and barter with team mates, managing to filch an extra bowl of soup for the two Estonians in his team by confusing the cook. In return he begs some tobacco from the Estonians. Shukov then buys a small portion of tobacco from the Latvian team member with money he has earned making slippers from rags and repairing torn jackets, enabling him to return what

---

4   Agamben is here citing an untranslated Italian publication by Levi (Agamben 2002:120).

he owes the Estonians. Hyndman (2000:108) records the somewhat similar strategy of a woman refugee in Dadaab, who fetches water and sells it to other households. She uses the money to buy firewood that had been collected in bulk by the owner of a donkey cart, and divides the wood into smaller portions to sell in the local market where cigarettes, spices, tea, 'candies', camel's milk and so forth received as food aid are also available.

Although Levi establishes one or two friendships, the stresses tending to undermine friendship are far higher in Buna-Monowitz even than in the Gulag. Every few months there is a 'selection', where the prisoners who have been in the camp the longest have to demonstrate their fitness; the less fit are weeded out and sent to the gas chambers to make room for newcomers. The average life expectancy for an unresourceful prisoner who could find no way to ameliorate their condition was three months. Levi (1979:392) estimates that during the harshest periods the death rate in Soviet camps was around 30 per cent, whereas in the German camps between 90 and 98 per cent died. In general, Levi concludes, people are willing to establish friendships with the strong, the adaptable and the astute because they hope later to gain some benefit, but not with the sickly, who have no useful contacts and are doomed soon to die. Levi's best friend Alberto shows, among all the Italians, the best survival instincts, and they trust each other. Levi and Alberto meet up each day on the return march from the factory and share scraps of information.

The starvation diet of soup and bread drives prisoners in both camps to attach themselves to superiors in search of the smallest benefits. Any prisoner in Shukov's camp whom the cook recruits to help prepare and serve the gruel gets an extra portion, which means there is less for everyone else. In Buna-Monowitz extra portions of soup are allocated to each dormitory hut, to be distributed at the discretion of the Kapo, the man in charge of the block. He gives some to his friends and protégés, then rewards the hut-sweepers, night-guards, lice-controllers and other 'prominents and functionaries', keeping some back to pay for goods smuggled in from the factory. In the Soviet camp, receipt of food parcels confers status. No Jewish prisoner in Buna-Monowitz receives parcels, but German criminals, political prisoners and Allied prisoners of war in the camp receive better treatment. They and the German civilian workers become potential patrons who can supply food and ragged clothing. People boasted of their civilian 'protectors'. 'If one offers a position of privilege to a few individuals in a state of slavery, exacting in exchange the betrayal of a natural solidarity with their comrades, there will certainly be someone who will accept' (ibid.:97). Such conditions are not conducive to Lévi-Straussian reciprocity.

One of the most powerful institutions that prisoners in both camps bring with them from previous experience is market exchange. In Shukov's camp, trading is limited (see above), but the Greek Jewish traders from Salonika in Buna-Monowitz have established a regular marketplace. Some prisoners sell spare shirts they acquired by pretending their own was stolen while they washed. Others are expert at kitchen theft, and bring vegetables to trade. Soup has a stable price, but the supply of vegetables is unpredictable and prices vary. Third-rate tobacco is also sold and used to buy bread from civilians. The prisoner acquires an extra portion of bread in camp, trades it for tobacco on the market, then exchanges the tobacco for more bread from a civilian worker. The prisoner eats the surplus and puts the remaining bread ration back on the camp's market.

Perhaps the closest that social relations in either camp come to the spontaneous emergence of social relations where, in Lévi-Strauss's terms, no 'ready-made formula' for social interaction exists are isolated instances of Nash equilibria, as described by Nasar (1998). In a Nash Equilibrium, even where there is no umpire to enforce an agreement, social relations spontaneously reach an equilibrium point, 'a situation in which no player could improve his or her position by choosing an alternative available strategy' (Nasar 1998:97). The escort of guards on the way back to Shukov's camp each evening, for example, order some of the prisoners to drop the scraps of wood they have scavenged for firewood, but never all of the wood, because the guards know that if they did so the prisoners wouldn't even bother to scavenge and the guards would receive no firewood either. The guards at Buna-Monowitz are violently opposed to prisoners trading their gold fillings for goods obtained from civilians in the factory, because they know they will get hold of the gold from the teeth of prisoners sent to the gas chambers. But there is a shortage of tools and equipment in the camp, and prisoners who can steal these things from the factory they are constructing can readily trade them for the extra portions of soup handed out by the camp guards.

Tools of oppression

Appell's case study of the Indonesian 'cultural concentration camp' in Borneo (Chapter 10) reveals some striking parallels with the tools of oppression experienced by Levi and Solzhenitsyn, including: no appeal to a higher authority in cases of abuse; the requisition of labour; poor nutrition; contempt for the inmates' culture; arbitrary rules; the deprivation of subsistence resources; the deprivation of information. Similar cases can be found in Australia (e.g. Bardon and Bardon 2006; Pushman and Walley 2006; Rosser 1978). In 1970, the central Australian settlement at Papunya had 1,400 residents; this presented a huge challenge to social order among people who, ten to twenty years previously, had been living in bands of around thirty people dispersed across the Central Australian desert, occasionally meeting up with 200 to 300 others for major ceremonies but unprepared for close contact with traditional enemies, permanent camps and a chronic shortage of bush food within walking distance. The Aboriginal people were obliged to get permission from the white superintendent to travel to other settlements or cattle ranches. Geoff Bardon sensed it was 'a death camp in all but name' (Bardon and Bardon 2006:131).

The school Bardon joined as an art teacher had 150 pupils. Its aim was to assimilate Aboriginal children to Euro-Australian culture. Hunger was a frequent problem, and the free lunches the school provided were the main feature drawing children to lessons. To promote a sense of self-respect based on Aboriginal culture, Bardon asked some senior men to paint traditional murals on the school wall. The murals were completed thanks to the goodwill of Bardon's Aboriginal teaching assistant, Obed Raggett, and the support of the headmaster. The artists were amazed that any European would show an interest in their work, but were motivated to complete the murals by the money they earned, which would help them buy a vehicle to give them greater mobility and escape from the camp. In September 1971, Bardon took fifty paintings created after the murals into Alice Springs to sell. The money earned gave the artists and their families independence from government handouts for days, perhaps even weeks.

The response of the Northern Territory administrators was swift. When Bardon returned from holiday in late January 1972, the sympathetic school principal had left and the settlement superintendent had been replaced. The new superintendent told Bardon, 'They're Government Aborigines, therefore they're Government paintings' (ibid.:37). When Bardon brought a long-awaited cheque for $800 in payment for numerous works, the new superintendent announced in front of the artists that he was deducting $775 to pay for the materials supplied, leaving $25 for the artists! Bardon was forced to leave at the end of July 1972. Obed Raggett was forbidden from working as a translator, and the government welfare office in Alice Springs put pressure on the school to destroy the murals, deeming them to be graffiti. A small ray of hope was that the man Bardon had nominated as his successor, Peter Fannin, had been appointed and seemed to have established a working relation with the artists. Happily, many artists were soon able to escape to a small camp on their traditional territory, and the subsequent success of the Papunya art movement has been documented by Fred Myers (2002).

Thanuja Mummidi (Chapter 5) notes Cernea's list of the nine risks of impoverishment caused by displacement: landlessness, joblessness, homelessness, marginalization, food insecurity, increased morbidity, loss of access to common property resources, community disarticulation and education. Although uniquely voluntary (among our case studies), those in Mummidi's study who were resettled did suffer impoverishment, poorer nutrition and enforced dependency, in their case due to induced dependence on food handouts and a loss of diversity in the diet. As in Appell's case study (Chapter 10), those resettled encountered a total disregard and disrespect for their culture among those who hoped to 'develop' them.

The testimonies of Levi and Solzhenitsyn concerning the threats displaced communities can face in the struggle to perpetuate their society and culture are paralleled by other case studies in this volume. Rogaia Abusharaf (Chapter 2) describes how displacement deprived southern Sudanese women living in a shanty town near Khartoum of shelter, access to food, affective networks and physical protection. The displaced women experienced northern Sudanese contempt for their culture; northerners despise southerners and call them 'slaves' or 'servants'. Kwesi Sansculotte-Greenidge and Laura Barber (Chapter 3), in their study of refugee camps in Chad and Ethiopia, similarly document the effect on refugees deprived of country, community, prestige and property. Traditional leaders are weakened if there is no income that they can tax. Refugees are compelled to seek protection, but are denied access to livelihood or economic opportunity. Roxanne Hakim (Chapter 4) shows that the loss of access to natural resources, land rights and self-sufficiency suffered by Adivasi hill villages displaced by the Sardar Sarovar (Narmada) Dam made economic change inevitable. Relocation to Hindu villages on the plains caused rapid change in house structure, dress, language and economy as people sought to adapt to the host society. Abusharaf (Chapter 2) focuses on two radical adaptations undertaken by Southern Sudanese refugee women to their host culture, the adoption of female circumcision and the smoke bath (*dukhan*).

The construction of social relationships among refugees
Contrary to Lévi-Strauss's claim, 'Non-crystallised forms of social life' do not arise 'spontaneously out of accidental circumstances'. Refugees may, however, still struggle to bring familiar social strategies to the task of coping with displacement. Hammond highlights the difficulties faced by resettled Ethiopians when people do not share common personal histories: 'The rules of proper or reasonable behaviour and interaction were thrown into question: some were still valid, some needed to be renegotiated ... [and] still others had lost their utility or meaning' (Hammond 2004:11). Horst (2006:14, 16) acknowledges that while refugees are not reduced to their raw humanity, they do tend to be stripped of their multiplex identities, such as clan membership, place of origin and history, thus restricting their movements and economic initiatives. Refugees 'must act to rebuild social networks, economic structures,

and patterns of political expression and representation, often in adverse circumstances' (Hammond 2004:208).

Three familiar types of social interaction have been documented among recent studies of refugees who attempt to rebuild a community. First, the exchange of goods as tokens of a continuing relationship, as in the practice of reciprocity explored by Marcel Mauss (and subsequently Lévi-Strauss), though patron–client relationships may also develop. Second, the exchange of goods for their use value (Adam Smith's brewer, baker and butcher). Third, the exchange of goods for a profit (Marx's mercantile exchange). I will explore each of these in turn.

Tokens of continuing relationships

The successful exchange of goods as tokens of continuing relationships depends on the development of trust,[5] and is probably most easily achieved when one has existing relatives and friends in a refugee camp whose well-being is as uncertain as one's own. Horst (2006:24), citing de Waal's study of famine in Darfur (de Waal 1989), points out that the threat to a way of life may be more damaging than the threat of starvation. Many of the resettled Somali refugees with whom Hammond lived had been in the same group initially escorted from Ethiopia to Sudan by the Tigrayan People's Liberation Front and, in Sudan, they had lived together in Safawa camp. Ananda Rajah (2002) noted that Karen identity is primarily based on affiliation to the home village. Many of the Karen refugees who fled from Burma to Thailand following the collapse of the headquarters of the Karen National Union (KNU) and Karen National Liberation Army (KNLA) after a major offensive by the Burmese armed forces, came directly from their destroyed villages (Dudley 2012). Members of one village travelled together, only leaving those too old or sick to make the journey. Others hid in the jungle and later came to join relatives in the camp.

Of former Ethiopian refugees who had been resettled far from their original homes, Hammond writes: 'Sharing ... was considered one of the most basic principles of community cohesiveness ... Inability to share signified an absolute failure to participate in the life of the community' (Hammond 2004:70). Earlier she states, 'Community cohesion was generated through the daily exchanges of goods, favours, and knowledge; borrowing was considered the raw material that neighbours and kin used to weave their lives together' (ibid.:15). Members of the community are those who 'share certain responsibilities for each other, who owe and are owed certain debts to others, but who for the most part refuse to act on these debts' (ibid.:23).

---

5   See Axelrod (1990) on the iterated Prisoner's Dilemma.

Some social networks among returnees had already been built before they left Sudanese refugee camps. Cash and food were more available in Safawa, the second, more permanent, camp to which refugees were sent, strengthening relationships with kin and neighbours, and allowing contributions to savings and burial associations to be renewed. Gaim Kibreab (2004) found that while they were refugees in Sudan, displaced Eritreans actually expanded their social networks and developed new skills. Between 1989 and 1998, nearly 180,000 refugees returned from Sudan to Eritrea, but they settled in border towns, not in their original home communities; the networks and friendships they had built while they were refugees were more important than those they had left behind two to three decades earlier. The towns were revitalized by their presence.

While they are less tied to a particular place than peasants, even traditional nomads do not move across a desert that is 'flat, smooth and curiously isotropic' (Cresswell 2006:49). Pastoral politics is based on coalitions of kin. In Somalia, access to permanent water sources is controlled by the more powerful clans, to which smaller clans attach themselves for protection. Larger groups have an advantage in disputes because their strength discourages smaller groups from taking vengeance, and each member has to contribute less when compensation for murder is paid (Schlee 2002). Horst (2006) notes that a person's safety depends more on the strength and goodwill of his clansmen than on his wealth, so loyalty is more important than personal gain: information, goods and services are channelled through the clan. Access to information provides security and reduces risk. Clan members help each other in herding and in planting and harvesting crops. The transfer of resources reduces localized risk where some people temporarily have abundant resources and others do not (cf. Layton 2005). Clansmen who have businesses help those who do not. When Somalis fled the civil war they headed toward the strongholds and traditional areas of their clans, sometimes across national borders. The significance of clan identity therefore increased and members of the elite, who had not previously taken clans seriously, had to become conscious of which clan they belonged to: 'Everybody was looking for their own clan, their own family' (Horst 2006:58). A similar phenomenon occurred during the break-up of Yugoslavia, when city dwellers had to rediscover their identity as Serbs, Croats and Bosnians (see Layton 2006:132–3). In Dadaab, cooperation between friends and neighbours was based on proximity. People worked on these social relationships more than intra-clan relations because they are not 'natural', in the way that kinship is, and continuing trust was protected from betrayal by the sanctions of gossip and social exclusion. In Izzbba, the Sudanese camp studied by Abusharaf (Chapter 2), 'Neighbours in the host community step up to fill the role as fictive kin, both ready and willing to enter into a new chain of exchanges and conversations.

Where access to resources is unequal, however, social networks can create patron–client relationships. Concentration camps are deeply embedded in grossly unequal power relations within a hostile, dominant society. People are forced to labour for their captors. Their lack of control over subsistence production profoundly undermines friendship and cooperation, tending to split the community into individuals who compete with, and are willing to betray, one another in the quest for the most demeaning attachment to patrons with resources to spare. A clandestine market draws people into ruthless calculations of profit and loss in the exchange of the smallest items. They have minimal agency in the shaping of social relationships. In Solzhenitsyn's autobiographical novel, Shukov's team were able to choose their team leader, a man valued for his ability to protect them from greater oppression, but in Buna-Monowitz, Levi's team could only choose their youngest member as its messenger-clerk, who earned their respect because he kept his promises, was gentle and friendly, and befriended the less privileged. Almost all the skills and status people previously possessed were erased in the concentration camp, although a few skills such as story-telling and metalworking proved useful.

Many of these traits also characterized the Rwandan refugee camps studied by Pottier (2002). Until they were removed, 'troublesome' community leaders diverted food away from poor refugees. As two widows explained to Pottier: 'There was no justice. The rations widows received were small, we got pushed aside and often received nothing at all. Young people snatched food away from us' (ibid.:136). The professionalism and skills of many refugees went unnoticed, and they were rendered dumb and dependant. Refugees' analytical skills in managing water, fuel, food aid and health were not recognized. One Rwandan staff member commented, 'UNHCR knows how to turn intellectuals into beggars' (ibid.:143). Many knew their former homes had been occupied by others, and the loss of farms removed the power older refugee men had once possessed to exercise control over junior relatives. Sansculotte-Greenidge and Barber (Chapter 3) contrast the position of elders in two other refugee camps. Traditional procedures for settling disputes were formally recognized by UNHCR and followed by the Eritrean refugees in Ethiopia documented by Barber, who found them the most effective means to achieve true forgiveness, but they were not recognized by CARE, the NGO managing Mile Darfuri refugee camp in Chad. Here a dual system for resolving disputes emerged, with refugees preferring to rely on traditional procedures, of which the authorities were apparently unaware, for minor disputes, and only using the CARE-sponsored courts to resolve persistent problems.

Horst notes that relief aid, which entails no reciprocity, 'unmistakably determines an unequal power relationship between giver and receiver' (Horst 2006:72), a point made forcibly by Alex de Waal in his study of famine relief in Darfur (de Waal 1989). Simon Turner found that in a camp for Burundian refugees in Tanzania, men's status had declined, and women were describing UNHCR as 'a better husband' (Turner 2004:94). It was important to be on good terms with an NGO employee who could ask favours in return, in this way establishing a patron–client relationship. Abusharaf (Chapter 2) describes the unequal power relationships between the southern Sudanese women joining a refugee camp and the northern Sudanese who were already resident there.

Market exchange for the use value of goods

Market exchange, primarily for use value, of items as small as single cigarettes or teabags, is probably the easiest mode of exchange to construct in a refugee camp, as the Greek Jewish traders in Buna-Monowitz demonstrated (see above). In the Karen refugee camp studied by Dudley (2012), cultivating small patches of vegetables and gathering edible wild plants enabled a local economy in which goods and services were exchanged. This gave refugees a sense of limited control over the new environment and raised self-esteem. Somali women in Dadaab operated circulating credit systems that enabled them to set up bread-baking or samosa-making businesses, or businesses for the 'less well-off' selling single teabags or cigarettes (Horst 2006:85; cf. Hyndman 2000:109). While they were refugees in Sudan, the Ethiopians studied by Hammond (2004) gradually overcame their helplessness and dependency to become ingenious entrepreneurs. Everyone depended on cash income – from farm labour, trading between refugee camps and/or towns, or from small businesses set up inside the camps – to supplement their food ration. Women were, however, especially vulnerable to violence because their main potential sources of income – brewing alcohol, selling cigarettes and prostitution – were all illegal. In the Burundian refugee camp studied by Turner (2004) there were cigarette sellers, hairdressers, brothels, bars and businesses brewing maize beer.

Trade primarily for profit

Trade primarily for profit is harder to establish. It requires financial capital and may need licences. While in the Sudanese refugee camp, the Ethiopians studied by Hammond (2000) had opened teahouses and restaurants to serve truck drivers, health and relief workers, and government officials. But trade between camps and town was illegal; Hammond cites the case of a man sent to prison for driving to Port Sudan to buy kerosene and clothes to resell at a higher price in the camp. The Eritrean refugees studied by Kibreab (2004) were more successful, and during the late 1980s Eritrean refugees dominated cross-border trade between Sudan and Eritrea. On a more modest scale, some of the young men among Turner's Burundian refugees in Tanzania had started small businesses buying extra rations of oil and maize and reselling them to Tanzanians or investing in a bicycle and transporting people between the main road and the refugee camp (Turner 2004). Horst (2016) reports that before 1991, Somali refugees were controlled by the Kenyan government and integration with the local population was allowed to develop; refugees had a right to education, employment and freedom of movement. Unfortunately refugees in Mombasa started businesses but evaded paying taxes, while those who could afford to rent flats in Nairobi pushed rents up beyond the reach of poorer local Kenyans, who were forced to move to shanty towns (Hyndman 2000:161). Resentment among the local population caused the government to close many camps and move refugees to the remote locations of Dadaab and Kakuma, where UNHCR took away the refugees' right of movement.

Mitigating the effects of displacement

The studies reviewed in this introduction demonstrate how remarkable is the human capacity to rebuild social relationship among displaced peoples. From the perspective of the RAI's Urgent Anthropology programme, the above case studies identify three factors that can make important contributions to the survival of a displaced people's way of life: rights to land, the ability to retain a coherent community through exchange and the negotiation of shared values, and the degree of similarity between the cultures of the displaced and their hosts.

The case of Mishamo, documented by Malkki (1995), contrasts diametrically with the case described by Appell (Chapter 10). The Tanzanian government had sent these Burundian refugees to establish a planned, physically isolated refugee camp, Mishamo, while the other refugees Malkki studied had moved individually to an established township, Kigoma, where they dispersed among non-refugee neighbourhoods. Far from stripping the displaced community of the means to self-sufficiency, the Tanzanian government gave the refugees in Mishamo land and allowed them self-determination. They constructed their own wells, roads, schools and dispensaries, and registered their villages as cooperatives on the Tanzanian principle of Ujamaa. Their hard work boosted the agricultural output of the region. The community constructed an intersubjective history of themselves as a Burundian 'nation in exile', waiting to return.

In her contribution, Noriko Sato (Chapter 9) investigates how a Syrian Christian community of former refugees from Turkey was not only able to construct an agreed narrative of their displacement, but to revise it in response to changed political circumstances after the Ba'ath Party's rise to power. (How the Christian community is being affected by the current civil war in Syria cannot be investigated at present.)

The value of rights to land is underlined in several of the case studies in this volume. In the case discussed by Rogaia Abusharaf (Chapter 2), a recently introduced form of land tenure had enabled camp residents to escape their self-perception as displaced people and to become owners and residents. In the Indian case described by Thanuja Mummidi (Chapter 5), the Konda Reddis' original forest habitat was evidently left undisturbed and neither logged nor flooded. They did not lose access to their traditional resources and were able to choose whether to stay or resettle.

The hill dwelling Vasava Bhils of Makhadkhada, an isolated village on the banks of the River Narmada in the Satpura Hills of Gujarat, India, were less fortunate. They were displaced by the controversial Sardar Sarovar (Narmada) Dam Project and relocated in a plains village. Roxanne Hakim (Chapter 4) found that, while the Vasava Bhils' desire to be accepted by their new hosts (who look down on hill people) resulted in some changes to the culture of the Adivasi, their core philosophy was not affected. The differences between the religious rituals of the displaced community and their hosts were less radical than in the Sudanese case described by Abusharaf. Not all hill communities were displaced by the construction of the dam. Once they had achieved economic security, the displaced villagers moved to reinforce their links with fellow hill communities that had not been flooded, and strengthen their continuing culture. The displaced Adivasi were able to retain all but the territorially based aspects of their religion, despite outwardly conforming to their Hindu hosts, and after some time erected their own pantheon of sacred stones in their new community.

References

Agamben, G. 2002. *Remnants of Auschwitz: Witness and Archive* (trans. David Heller). New York: Zone Books.

Arendt, H. 1973. *The Origins of Totalitarianism.* New York: Harcourt Brace.

Axelrod, R. 1990 [1984]. *The Evolution of Co-operation.* New York: Basic Books.

Bakewell, O. 2004. 'Repatriation: Angolan refugees or migrating villagers?' In P. Essed, G. Frerks and J. Schrijvers (eds), *Refugees and the Transformation of Societies: Agency, Policies, Ethics and Politics*, pp. 31–41. Oxford: Berghahn.

Bardon, G. and Bardon, J. 2006. *A Place Made after the Story: The Beginnings of the Western Desert Painting Movement.* Aldershot: Lund Humphries.

Charsley, K. 2006. 'Risk and ritual: the protection of British Pakistani women in transnational marriage'. *Journal of Ethnic and Migration Studies* 32:1169–78.

Cirtautas, C. 1957. *The Refugee: A Psychological Study*. Boston: Meador.

Cresswell, T. 2006. *On the Move: Mobility in the Modern Western World*. London: Routledge.

Crossland, Z. 2000. 'Buried lives: forensic archaeology and Argentina's disappeared.' *Archaeological Dialogues* 7(2):146–59.

De Waal, A. 1989. *Famine that Kills: Darfur, Sudan*. Oxford: Clarendon Press.

Dudley, S. 2012. *Materialising Exile: Material Culture and Embodied Experience among Karenni Refugees in Thailand*. Oxford: Berghahn.

Elliott, A. and Urry, J. 2010. *Mobile Lives*. Abingdon: Routledge.

Ferguson, A. 1995 [1767]. *An Essay on the History of Civil Society*. Cambridge: Cambridge University Press.

Gupta, A. and Ferguson, J. 1992. 'Beyond "culture": space, identity, and the politics of difference.' *Cultural Anthropology* 7:6–22.

Hammond, L. 2004. *This Place Will Become Home: Refugee Repatriation to Ethiopia*. Ithaca, NY: Cornell University Press.

Horst, C. 2006. *Transnational Nomads: How Somalis Cope with Refugee Life in the Dadaab Camps of Kenya*. Oxford: Berghahn.

Hyndman, J. 2000. *Managing Displacement: Refugees and the Politics of Humanitarianism*. Minneapolis: University of Minnesota Press.

James, W. 1997 'The names of fear: memory, history, and the ethnography of feeling among Uduk refugees.' *Journal of the Royal Anthropological Institute* 3:115–31.

——— 2007. *War and Survival in Sudan's Frontierlands: Voices from the Blue Nile*. Oxford: Oxford University Press.

Johnson, C. 2003. *Claude Lévi-Strauss: The Formative Years*. Cambridge University Press.

Kibreab, G. 2004. 'Refugeehood, loss and social change: Eritrean refugees and returnees.' In P. Essed, G. Frerks and J. Schrijvers (eds), *Refugees and the Transformation of Societies: Agency, Policies, Ethics and Politics*, pp. 19–30. Oxford: Berghahn.

Layton, R. 2005. 'Are hunter-gatherer immediate return strategies adaptive?' In T. Widlok and W. Tadesse (eds), *Property and Equality*, Vol. 1: *Ritualization, Sharing, Egalitarianism*, pp. 130–50. New York: Berghahn.

——— 2006. *Order and Anarchy: Civil Society, Social Disorder and War*. Cambridge: Cambridge University Press.

Levi, P. 1979 [1958, 1963]. *If This Is a Man – The Truce*, trans. R. Feldman. Harmondsworth: Penguin.

——— 1989. *The Drowned and the Saved*, trans. R. Rosenthal. New York: Random House.

Lévi-Strauss, C. 1969 [1949]. *The Elementary Structures of Kinship*, trans. J.H. Bell and J.R. von Sturmer. London: Eyre and Spottiswoode.

——— 1973 [1955]. *Tristes Tropiques*, trans. J. and D. Weightman. London: Jonathan Cape. [French edition]

Locke, J. 1960 [1689]. *Two Treatises of Government*. Cambridge: Cambridge University Press.

Malkki, L. 1992. 'National geographic: the rooting of peoples and the territorialization of national identity among scholars and refugees'. *Cultural Anthropology* 7:24–44.

——— 1995. *Purity and Exile: Violence, Memory, and National Cosmology among Hutu Refugees in Tanzania*. Chicago: University of Chicago Press.

Mitter, R. 2004. *A Bitter Revolution: China's Struggle with the Modern World*. Oxford: Oxford University Press.

Myers, F. 2002. *Painting Culture: The Making of an Aboriginal High Art*. Durham, NC: Duke University Press.

Nasar, S. 1998. *A Beautiful Mind*. London: Faber.

Peters, R. 1967. *Hobbes*. Harmondsworth: Penguin.

Pottier, J. 2002. *Re-Imagining Rwanda: Conflict, Survival and Disinformation in the Late Twentieth Century*. Cambridge: Cambridge University Press.

Pushman, T. and Walley, R.S. 2006. 'Koorah coolingah (children long ago)'. Berndt Museum of Anthropology Occasional Paper No.8. Perth: Berndt Museum of Anthropology, University of Western Australia.

Rajah, A. 2002. 'A "nation of intent" in Burma: Karen ethno-nationalism, nationalism and narrations of nation'. *Pacific Review* 15:517–37.

Rapport, N. and Dawson, A. 1998. 'Home and movement: a polemic'. In N. Rapport and A. Dawson (eds), *Migrants of Identity: Perceptions of Home in a World of Movement*, pp. 19–38. Oxford: Berg.

Rosser, B. 1978. *This is Palm Island*. Canberra: Australian Institute of Aboriginal and Torres Straits Islander Studies Press.

Schlee, G. 2002. 'Regularity in chaos: the politics of difference in the recent history of Somalia'. In G. Schlee (ed.), *Imagined Differences: Hatred and the Construction of Identity*, pp. 251–80. Münster: LIT.

Shaw, A. 2000. *Kinship and Continuity: Pakistani Families in Britain*. Amsterdam: Harwood.

Solzhenitsyn, A. 1963. *One Day in the Life of Ivan Denisovich*, trans. R. Palmer. Harmondsworth: Penguin.

Turner, S. 2004. 'New Opportunities: angry young men in a Tanzanian refugee camp'. In P. Essed, G. Frerks and J. Schrijvers (eds) *Refugees and the transformation of societies: agency, policies, ethics and politics*, pp. 94-105. Oxford: Berghahn.

Urry, J. 2000. *Sociology beyond Societies: Mobilities for the Twenty-First Century*. London: Routledge.

Velayutham, S., and Wise, A. 2005. 'Moral economies of a translocal village: obligation and shame among South Asian transnational migrants'. *Global Networks* 5:27–47.

1

The RAI's Urgent Anthropology Fellowships and the Anthropologists' Fund for Urgent Anthropological Research

George N. Appell

I have no hesitation in characterising the corpus of descriptive ethnography which we have produced as by far the greatest achievement in anthropology, the crowning glory of our discipline.
George Peter Murdock (1972:17)

The origin of the Urgent Anthropology Fellowship programme

At the 1993 meetings of the American Anthropological Association in Washington, DC, I met with Jonathan Benthall, the then director of the Royal Anthropological Institute (RAI). I discussed with him a vision I had of developing a programme for basic ethnographic research on disappearing cultures and languages. This programme would contribute to anthropological knowledge and theory as well as provide indigenous peoples with the results of such research. With this knowledge they would be better prepared in their struggle to control their own destinies. By then I had raised a small amount of funds to initiate such a programme.

Benthall, as representative of the RAI, was the last of a series of people from various organizations that I had approached over a number of years with this vision. But it was Benthall who saw the importance of it for the future of anthropology. And it was he who developed an unusually innovative programme to bring this vision to fruition. Under Jonathan Benthall's direction, the RAI would establish a programme of Fellowships in Urgent Anthropology that would be awarded annually with each lasting for a period of eighteen months.

The fund's objective

I prepared the mission statement for the fellowship programme to formalize my vision, and this was accepted by the RAI Council with minor changes, as follows:

> The objective of the Fellowships is to support basic ethnographic research on disappearing or threatened cultures and languages that will make a fundamental contribution to anthropological knowledge and serve, where appropriate, as an aid to indigenous peoples in their struggle to control their own destinies. As basic ethnographic research has proven to be of material aid and help to indigenous peoples, grantees are encouraged, where appropriate, to:
>
> a) Report to the people concerned relevant records made in the course of the study of their culture and history, so as to help them make use of valued aspects of these in the construction of their futures;
>
> b) Foster respect, where this has been eroded, for their culture and language and their preservation, including the development of local interest in collecting oral histories and traditions and the incorporation of these in the educational system;
>
> c) Collect data on the traditional patterns of land use and rights and make them available for the people;
>
> d) Facilitate the study of local medical practices and their incorporation into modern health-delivery systems; and
>
> e) Report violations of human rights to pertinent human rights organizations.
>
> f) It is expected and required that scientific publication will result from this research.

Implementation

It was Jonathan Benthall's creative design for the organization of the programme in Urgent Anthropology Fellowships that has made it grow and become so successful. The RAI would administer the scheme, and to do so they established a Committee on Urgent Anthropology. The RAI would also advertise the fellowships and participate in the selection of fellows. Applicants were required either to have a doctoral qualification in anthropology or its equivalent, or be nearing completion of doctoral research.

The actual housing of fellows would be undertaken by universities who would compete to host the programme. The university selected would host the fellowships for three to five years, and then another university would have the opportunity to host the programme. When they were not in the field doing research, the programme's fellows were expected to reside for the main part at the host university and contribute actively to the research activities of the host department of anthropology. The department of anthropology would supervise the fellows' research and the writing up of the results of their research.

Funding of the fellowships would come from two sources. The host university would contribute one-third of the cost of the fellowships. The other two-thirds of the cost would be met by the Anthropologists' Fund for Urgent Anthropological Research, which I established in the United States. Finally, fellowships were to be and are awarded without discrimination of ethnic or national origin or residence.

The inaugural Fellowship in Urgent Anthropology was awarded in 1995 to Dr Roxanne P. Hakim for research among the Vasavas of Gujarat, India.[1] The scheme has grown very successfully and productively over the course of the last sixteen years. The importance of the fellowships and their success in terms of intellectual productivity owes much to the organizational skills and vision of Jonathan Benthall!

The Anthropologists' Fund for Urgent Anthropological Research

On my part, I founded the Anthropologists' Fund for Urgent Anthropological Research (AFUAR) in December 1993, for the purpose of raising funds to support the fellowships. To forward the aims of this programme and to get its ideas accepted, I asked a group of influential anthropologists to be intellectual sponsors of this effort (see Appendix 2).

The fund

The AFUAR continues to seek contributions with the goal of raising an endowment to support at least two fellowships per year on the income generated from the fund. The monies contributed to the fund are held in an American bank account. Following the selection of the next Fellow in Urgent Anthropology by the committee of the RAI, in cooperation with the host university, funds are transferred to the RAI.

Jonathan Benthall early on established the policy that all monies contributed to the fund and the work of the RAI are to be spent solely on research. Both the AFUAR and the RAI make no charge for administrative services.

The host universities

The first host university was Goldsmiths College, part of the University of London, which is the largest centre for anthropological research in the

---

1   For a list of subsequent fellows, see Appendix 1.

United Kingdom. This inaugural five-year programme of fellowships, which was extended for a sixth year, was established by the RAI in association with Goldsmiths' anthropology department, which agreed to maintain their interest and involvement in the programme and give advice where appropriate. In 2001, the RAI entered into an agreement with the University of Durham to continue the programme of fellowships, and hosted the programme until 2006. It is testimony to the importance that Durham set on the programme that in financially very strained times they had found the funds to cover their contribution over the six-year period. The next host for the fellowship programme was the University of Kent at Canterbury, for the period 2007 to 2010. After this, Goldsmiths College once again hosted the Fellowships, starting in 2011 with two Fellowships of 18 months each over a three-year period. From 2013 to 2020, the British Museum hosted the Fellowships. The 2014–17 cycle focused specifically on threatened Nile Valley communities in northern Sudan. The 2018–20 cycle will have a special focus on the Arctic.

Directors of the RAI

In 2000, Jonathan Benthall retired as director of the RAI. Hilary Callan, selected as the new director, competently took over the oversight of the scheme and ably advanced its goals. In 2010, Hilary Callan stepped down as director. The new director, Dr David Shankland, has been wholeheartedly behind this programme and has suggested innovations to make it more valuable such as a establishing a regular RAI seminar on urgent anthropology.

The decline of basic ethnography and the need for the RAI Fellowships

The RAI programme of Urgent Anthropology Fellowships is in essence a paradigm shift, or perhaps better, a paradigm rebirth, for the profession of anthropology. To understand the significance of this, we have to briefly review trends in the profession of anthropology during the last half of the twentieth century.

One of the foundational pillars of anthropology has been the concern to record the varieties of the world's cultures before they disappeared under successive waves of modernization. This is one of the reasons anthropologists went out to Native American reservations in the early days of anthropology (see Gruber 1970). But this work was not only significant for its contributions to knowledge, it was also significant for the very peoples themselves. In the 1950s, those of us in the anthropology graduate school at Harvard were the first to be regaled with the story of how members of the Hopi Pueblo went to the library in Gallup, New Mexico, to read early accounts by anthropologists of Hopi life. However, we quickly found such interest in basic ethnography had begun to fade against the growing interest in anthropological theory. Furthermore, funding for research eventually became largely invested in projects that would test theories. The exemplar of this trend was Cora Dubois's announcement to us graduate students that we had better read Edmund Leach's account of highland Burma (Leach 1954) as this was indicative of a shift in anthropological inquiry towards theoretical issues. This new trend was found not only in American anthropology but also in British anthropology. Raymond Firth wrote in the introduction to Leach's book:

> Some of us, for example, have not hesitated to tell our students in private
> that ethnographic facts may be irrelevant – that it does not matter so much
> if they get the facts wrong so long as they can argue the theories logically.
> But few of us would be prepared to say in print, as Dr Leach has done, that
> he is usually bored by the facts which his anthropological colleagues present.
>
> (Firth 1954:vii)

The trend reached its zenith when the incoming head of the anthropology division of the US National Science Foundation in 1974 wrote that applications dealing with a theoretical issue would be given preference.

The loss of basic ethnography as one of the foundational pillars of anthropology has had its consequences, one of which has been the increasing growth of fads and fashions in anthropology. Saltzman (1988) has listed the number of these that he has experienced during his career. In 1992, I argued that the emphasis on fads and fashions in anthropological inquiry was the result of the loss of our centring ethos of basic ethnography. What has happened to this ethos? Why is salvage ethnography no longer one of our concerns? And is not the loss of this the cause of our identity crisis (Appell 1992)?

Field research in North Borneo

To return to reviewing graduate studies in the late 1950s: I was faced with a dilemma. I wanted to do research for my doctoral dissertation in a region in South-East Asia that was anthropologically unknown territory. I was therefore hard put to frame a theoretical problem to investigate. My dilemma was resolved in 1959 when I was granted a research fellowship in the Department of Anthropology and Sociology at the Institute of Advanced Studies of the Australian National University. There, under the leadership of Professor J.A. Barnes, the focus was on basic ethnographic accounts of social systems, not on problem-based research. I went to what was then called the Crown

Colony of North Borneo (now Sabah, Malaysia) to conduct research on an indigenous people as there had been no anthropological research done there. I first explored various regions of North Borneo to locate a research site. I finally discovered that the Rungus, a people of the Kudat Peninsula, were a very interesting group to get to know. My wife and I are still working with our friends there after more than fifty years, and are gathering interesting and rich data. The Rungus socio-cultural system provided important ethnographic data that has made major contributions to the understanding of cognatic societies, property relationships, land tenure and oral literature (Appell 1976, 1985a, 1985b). In North Borneo I also found that there were around 100 ethnic groups whose socio-cultural systems were unknown. Today they have all been modernized, losing their traditional socio-cultural systems. Of these ethnic groups, only four or five have had good ethnographic studies made of their cultures before they were lost. This experience was one of the significant factors that led to my concern over developing a programme for urgent ethnographic research.

An ethical issue

Before we leave the problems arising from a focus on theory, there is one issue, an ethical one, which needs to be addressed. In 1991 I raised the point that, too often, problem- or theory-oriented research is conducted to resolve an issue in our own society and at the expense of indigenous peoples:

> Is it fair, is it right, does it represent justice, for those in western societies to go out and solve their intellectual and social problems on the cultural backs of indigenous peoples? In other words, aren't we being unethical in attempting to resolve our own societal problems through the study of them in other societies? This is not to argue that we should not do research; but it is to argue that when it is driven by our concerns and leaves the needs of the indigenous people out of focus, it is unethical. We should do total ethnography, the study of the whole society first, and then if it contributes to solving our own problems, well and good. But first, we must provide the local people with a full statement of their traditional ways, their customary ways, which they can use either now or later for their own benefit. They have to be able to see their social system and cultural system as an 'object' to use, to modify, just as those who are in power and prey on the local peoples do. And to have it captured in ethnography enables them to deal with the modern world more successfully if they have to give it up, for then they have not lost it. In other words, in the west we have historical societies and associations to preserve the record of our progress. Why should not these also be made available for indigenous peoples who do not have the

resources to do so themselves? We as anthropologists have an obligation to provide the materials for these through our research, and this will help fulfill the functions that historical societies and other types of cultural societies provide to others, functions which are critical for enabling the members of any societies to adapt successfully to the stresses of social change.

(Sutlive and Appell 1991:xxxiv)

This ethical issue is raised in response to a tendency in the discipline of anthropology to treat the 'other' as an object, which dehumanizes them (Appell 1991).

The initial call to develop a fund

In 1973 I made a formal call for the development of an urgent anthropological research programme, quoting Lévi-Straus:

I do not view the recording of the sociocultural systems of nonliterate peoples before they disappear to be trivial or without relevance, as some have argued, nor does Lévi-Strauss (1966). This is necessary, he states, in order to enlarge 'our narrow-minded humanism to make it include each and every expression of human nature, thereby, perhaps, ensuring to mankind a more harmonious future' (1966:6) ... [We] need to devote a greater amount of our resources to the study of these societies ... I believe, however, it is also the anthropologist's duty, as Lévi-Strauss (1966) has pointed out, to help the members of the society being studied to appreciate their own sociocultural traditions and develop methods of recording and understanding them.

(Appell 1973:20)

But there was no response.

At this point it is useful to go back to review a trend in the last half of the twentieth century other than the focus on theory. There was an interest among certain anthropologists in undertaking action to alleviate the plight of indigenous peoples around the world while eschewing ethnographic research and anthropological knowledge and experience in this effort. The life-ways of indigenous peoples were being destroyed by deforestation, dams, mines, plantations and crude modernization attempts. In some instances there were outright directed attempts to destroy cultures, a form of ethnocide.[2] To deal with the problem of helping indigenous peoples, some anthropologist took the strange position that anthropological theory, experience and understanding had nothing to contribute to that work. This was the explicit philosophy of

---

2   See Appell (Chapter 11) for an example.

a group of anthropologists in the United States who formed an organization to help indigenous peoples. I was invited to join the board of directors. I was surprised when the president proclaimed at one meeting that there was nothing in applied anthropology that was of any use to their efforts. At the same time, they were sponsoring a programme to provide anthropologists in schools in South Africa, so as to aid the local teachers of a group of hunters and gatherers. I mentioned quietly to those going out on the programme that they might learn from accounts of what had happened in the schools for the Indians of the Great Plains. I was ignored. Years later I found out that those in the programme were surprised that the children in the schools were being beaten when they came back from trance dances. I also had attempted to get the organization to support a basic ethnographic programme similar to the one I proposed to Jonathan Benthall. I was told that anthropology was not the solution but the problem, and I was fired from the board. Later on I heard that they had attempted to introduce economic development in various ethnic groups. In doing so the anthropologists interfered with the distributive justice of the society involved. As a result some individuals gained economic and social advantage over others, which caused social conflict. Anthropologists should never contribute to increasing conflict in a society (see Appell 2002, n.d.). I found it disquieting to discover how the history of the anthropological experience was ignored and devalued, while intervention was based on materialist Western values, the very values that have contributed to the plight and destruction of indigenous societies (Appell 1991, 2002). I found the same problem in the deliberations of the Commission on Human Rights of the American Anthropological Association (AAA), of which I was a member. Apparently when taking action, anthropologists tend to ignore their anthropological theory and experience.

Shortly thereafter I helped form another organization for the benefit of indigenous peoples. Again I ran into the same attitude that held ethnographic work to be useless and a waste of time. The executive director from our sister organization, who sat on our board, maintained he could determine what an ethnic group needed in a visit of two days. I was a bit astounded since even after two and a half years among the Rungus I could not tell them what they really needed; I wanted them to tell me. So I resigned.

For the next fifteen years I approached various foundations and organizations under the umbrella of the AAA with my proposal for an urgent anthropology programme, but my argument fell on deaf ears. Apparently those in power did not, and many still do not, understand the implications of the anthropological project. As a last hope to get a programme established for urgent anthropology that would also help indigenous peoples, I turned to the RAI, of which I had been a member for years. This resulted in the historic meeting with Jonathan Benthall in June 1994.

The value of the Urgent Anthropology Fellowship programme that arose from this meeting was attested to in a two-day seminar at the University of Kent at Canterbury in September 2010. The seminar, 'New Directions for Urgent Anthropology Research', was to review the fifteen years of research fellowships funded by the Anthropologists' Fund for Urgent Anthropological Research. Its objectives were to:

- assess the impacts of past research designed to investigate and preserve endangered cultural, bio-cultural and linguistic diversity;
- understand the contemporary contexts of struggles of indigenous peoples worldwide;
- debate the future role of anthropological research, knowledge and public advocacy in maintaining cultural and biological diversity.

The participants in this seminar left with great enthusiasm for the Urgent Anthropology programme, claiming that this was the most exciting and exhilarating meeting they have ever attended, and one of great relevance to the discipline of anthropology. Papers by many of the contributors to the seminar are published here.

APPENDIX 1
Urgent Anthropology Fellows

2018   Dr Susan Crate, 'Engaging longitudinal ethnography in circumpolar Russia to track unprecedented change, facilitate community collaborative research and bolster adaptive response into the future'

2018   Dr Sveta Yamin-Pasternak, 'Yupik, Chukchi, and Inupiaq communities on the Russian and Alaskan sides of the Bering Strait'

2016   Dr Enrico Ille, 'Date palm production and socio-economic changes along the Nile in northern Sudan (Abri, Dongola, Dar al-Manasir)'

2014   Dr Karin Willemse, 'The Abri area of northern Sudan'

2012   Dr Margarita Huayhua, 'The Indian as a problem in the Andes'

2010   Dr Jan Peter Laurens Loovers, 'Tracing trails with Teetl'it Gwich'in: poetics, well-being, memory and land in circumpolar Canada'

2009   Dr Simron Singh, 'Anthropological and ethnological research and documentation among the inhabitants of the Nicobar Islands, India'

2008   Dr Rahile Dawut, 'Ugyur pilgrimage rites in Xinjiang'

2008   Dr Thomas Thornton, 'The effects of rapid climate change on indigenous Northern coastal peoples, with particular reference to marine food resources and indigenous knowledge'

2007   Dr Dario Novellino, 'Enabling the "indigenous voice": beyond technocratic solutions to forest conservation on Palawan Island (the Philippines)'

2006   Dr Thanuja Mummidi, 'The Konda Reddis: perspectives on their social organisation and shifting cultivation overlooked by developmental intervention'

2005   Dr Mark Jamieson, 'Language and identity among the Sumu people of the Rio Siquia, eastern Nicaragua'

2005   Dr Tatiana Bulgakova, 'Bringing traditional Nanay knowledge from the archive to the school'

2004   Dr Emma Gilberthorpe, 'Living with oil: the impact of resource development in Papau New Guinea'

2003   Dr Rogaia Abusharaf, 'The impact of Arabization and Islamization on identity and self-hood among the Southern Sudan's indigenous peoples'

2002   Dr Ananda Rajah, 'Karen refugees in Thailand'

2001   Dr Noriko Sato, 'Syrian Orthodox Christians'

2000–3 Professor Alan Macfarlane and Dr Mark Turin, 'Digital processing of anthropological information'. A website, Digital Himalaya, was produced as part of this project.

2000   Dr Christopher Duncan, 'The Halmahera of Indonesia'

1999   Professor Veronica Strang, 'Aboriginality in North Queensland'

1999   Dr Bartholomew Dean, 'Urarina in the Peruvian Amazon'

1998   Dr Cai Hua produced a video *Daba/Na Shaman* on the revival of religion among the Na of south-west China.

1996   Dr Stuart Kirsch, 'Resisting the mind: the Yonggom and the world system'

1995   Dr Roxanne P. Hakim, 'The resettlement experiences of a Vasava Bhil community affected by the Sardar Saroval (Narmada) Dam Project in western India'

Appendix 2
List of sponsors

David F. Aberle† (University of British Columbia)

K. Alexander Adelaar (University of Melbourne)

Nathan Altshuler† (College of William and Mary)

George N. Appell†, founding sponsor (Brandeis University)

Laura W.R. Appell†, founding sponsor (McGill University)

Diane Austin-Broos (University of Sydney)

Joan Bamberger (Wellesley College)

Jonathan C.M. Benthall (Royal Anthropological Institute)

Brent Berlin (University of Georgia)

Megan Biesele (Rice University)

Robert Blust (University of Hawaii)

John H. Bodley (Washington State University)

Erika Bourguignon† (Ohio State University)

Donald E. Brown (University of California, Santa Barbara)

Thomas Buckley† (University of Massachusetts, Boston)

Pat Caplan (Goldsmiths College)

Janet F. Carsten (University of Edinburgh)

Michael M. Cernea (World Bank)

Norman A. Chance (University of Connecticut)

Benjamin Colby (University of California, Irvine)

Harold C. Conklin (Yale University)

William Davenport† (University of Pennsylvania)

John Davis† (All Souls College, Oxford)

Robert K. Dentan (State University of New York, Buffalo)

Amity A. Doolittle (Yale University)

Michael R. Dove (Yale University)

Richard Allen Drake (Borneo Research Council)

Brian Durrans (British Museum)

Timothy Earle (Northwestern University)

James F. Eder, Jr. (Arizona State University)

R.F. Ellen (University of Kent at Canterbury)

Sir Raymond Firth† (London School of Economics and Political Science)

James J. Fox (Australian National University)

Charles Frantz† (State University of New York, Buffalo)

Thomas M. Fraser, Jr.† (New Hampshire)

J. Derek Freeman† (Australian National University)

Robert Gardner† (Harvard University)

Rosemary Gianno (Keene State College)

Peter R. Goethals† (Hawaii)

Walter R. Goldschmidt† (University of California, Los Angeles)

Anthony Good (University of Edinburgh)

Felicitas D. Goodman† (Denison University)

J.R. Goody† (University of Cambridge)

Robert J. Gordon (University of Vermont)

P. Bion Griffin (University of Hawaii, Honolulu)

Stephen F. Gudeman (University of Minnesota)

Marie-Françoise Guedon (University of Ottawa)

Alfred Harris† (University of Rochester)

Olivia Harris† (Goldsmiths College)

Eric Hirsch (Brunel University)

Robert K. Hitchcock (University of Nebraska)

Anna Hohenwart-Gerlachstein† (IUAES-Commission on Urgent Anthropological Research)

W.W. Howells† (Harvard University)

Dell Hymes† (University of Virginia)

Nitish Jha (Consultative Group on International Agricultural Research)

Cornelia Ann Kammerer (Brandeis College)

William Kelly (Yale University)

Victor T. King (University of Hull)

A. Thomas Kirsch† (Cornell University)

Stuart Kirsch (University of Michigan, Ann Arbor)

Claude Lévi-Strauss† (Collège de France)

E. Douglas Lewis (University of Melbourne)

Celia Lowe (University of Washington)

Alan MacFarlane (University of Cambridge)

T.N. Madan (University of Delhi)

Luisa Maffi (Terralingua)

Robert A. Manners† (Brandeis University)

Charity A. McNabb (Firebird Foundation for Anthropological Research)

Torben Monberg† (Fredensborg, Denmark)

Brian Morris (Goldsmiths College)

C. Patrick Morris† (University of Washington)

Shuichi Nagata† (University of Toronto)

Rodney Needham† (All Souls College, Oxford)

Ida Nicolaisen (University of Copenhagen)

Stephen Nugent† (Goldsmiths College)

Eugene Ogan† (University of Hawaii)

Kazunori Oshima (Doshisha University)

Robert Paine† (Memorial University of
   Newfoundland)

Richard J. Parmentier† (Brandeis
   University)

Stephen L. Pastner† (University of
   Michigan, Ann Arbor)

James L. Peacock (University of North
   Carolina, Chapel Hill)

Anton Ploeg (Nijmegen University)

Laura Rival (University of Oxford)

Paul B. Roscoe (University of Maine,
   Orono)

Benson Saler (Brandeis University)

Clifford Sather (University of Helsinki)

Bernard J.L. Sellato (University of
   Provence)

Parker Shipton (Boston University)

Daniela F. Sieff (Real World Pictures)

Masri Singarimbun† (Gadjah Mada
   University)

Melford E. Spiro† (University of California,
   San Diego)

Leslie E. Sponsel (University of Hawaii,
   Honolulu)

Vinson H. Sutlive, Jr. (College of William
   and Mary)

R.L. Tapper (School of Oriental and
   African Studies)

Mark Turin (University of Cambridge)

Motomitsu Uchibori (Hitotsubashi
   University)

Evon Z. Vogt† (Harvard University)

Reed Wadley† (University of Missouri)

Laura P. Appell Warren (St Mark's School)

Peter Wogan (Willamette University)

References

Appell, G.N. 1973. 'Basic issues in the dilemmas and ethical conflicts in
        anthropological inquiry'. Module 19. New York: MSS Modular Publications.

——— 1976. 'The Rungus: social structure in a cognatic society and its symbolism'.
        In G.N. Appell (ed.), *The Societies of Borneo: Explorations in the
        Theory of Cognatic Social Structure*, pp. 66–86. Washington: American
        Anthropological Association.

——— 1985a. 'Integration of the periphery to the center: processes and consequences'.
        In G.N. Appell (ed.), *Modernization and the Emergence of a Landless
        Peasantry: Essays on the Integration of Peripheries to Socioeconomic Centers*,
        pp. 3–49Williamsburg, VA: Studies in Third World Societies Publications.

——— 1985b. 'Land tenure and development among the Rungus of Sabah, Malaysia'.
        In G.N. Appell (ed.), *Modernization and the Emergence of a Landless
        Peasantry: Essays on the Integration of Peripheries to Socioeconomic
        Centers*, pp. 115–55. Williamsburg, VA: Studies in Third World Societies
        Publications.

——— 1991. 'Dehumanization in fact and theory: processes of modernization and the
        social sciences'. In J.A. Lent (ed.), *Social Science Models and Their Impact
        on the Third World*, pp. 23–44. Williamsburg, VA: Studies in Third World
        Societies Publications.

——— 1992. 'Scholars, true believers, and the identity crisis in American
        anthropology'. *Reviews in Anthropology* 21:193–202.

——— 2002. 'Our vision of human rights is too small! Anthropological perspectives on fundamental human rights'. In S.M. Nurul Alam (ed.), *Contemporary Anthropology: Theory and Practice*, pp. 419–47. Dhaka: Dhaka University Press.

——— n.d. 'The moral grounds of anthropological inquiry: towards an anthropology of ethics and an ethics grounded in anthropological theory'. Unpublished m.s.

Firth, R. 1954. 'Foreword'. In E.R. Leach, *Political Systems of Highland Burma: A Study of Kachin Social Structure*, pp. v–viii. Cambridge, MA: Harvard University Press.

Gruber, J.W. 1970. 'Ethnographic salvage and the shaping of anthropology'. *American Anthropologist* 72:1289–99.

Leach, E.R. 1954. *Political Systems of Highland Burma: A Study of Kachin Social Structure*. Cambridge, MA: Harvard University Press.

Lévi-Strauss, C. 1966. 'The disappearance of man'. *New York Review* 28:6–8.

Murdock, G.P. 1972. 'Anthropology's mythology'. *Proceedings of the Royal Anthropological Institute of Great Britain and Ireland 1972*, pp. 17–24.

Saltzman, P.C. 1988. 'Fads and fashions in anthropology'. *Anthropology Newsletter* 29(5):1, 32.

Sutlive, V.H., and Appell, G.N. 1991. 'Introduction'. In V.H. Sutlive (ed.), *Female and Male in Borneo: Contributions and Challenges to Gender Studies*, pp. xi–xlvi. Williamsburg, VA: Borneo Research Council.

2

Reckoning urgency

Making do in a Sudanese war-displaced community

ROGAIA MUSTAFA ABUSHARAF

The shifting sands of Sudan's politics

The ethnography for this chapter, conducted before the secession of South Sudan in 2011, is intended to provide the ultimate source on how Sudan's displaced women viewed themselves and their lives in the context of a conflict-ridden society. Drawing from testimonials and biographies of forced migration, I aimed to bring the plight of the women to international attention. I also hoped that documenting the tremendous impact of political upheaval on women as gendered, classed, raced, and embodied beings would elucidate the gender-specific way in which women suffer before, during, and after massive violence (Abusharaf 2009). Widely considered to be at the forefront of complex emergencies, research on the broader problem of forced migration as concept and experience needs to be positioned within the context of 'the environments, which an individual inhabits before, during, and after situations and interactions with others' (Rapport and Overing 2000:332). Based on previous publications (Abusharaf 1998, 1999, 2003, 2004), this work lays out the critical intersections of social, economic, political, historical and cultural processes and provided the context necessary to increase awareness of the persistent vulnerability of individuals and communities experiencing the aftermath of war.

Overall, we know precious little about the mechanisms that Sudanese citizens employ to cope with political violence. Therefore, my interest in the manifold meanings and metaphors of displacement and forced migratory currents was shaped largely by a need to fill glaring gaps in the anthropological research on the issue and on the urgency it signifies. In the years following decolonization, the concept of urgency in anthropology did not figure prominently either at abstract levels or in diverse fieldwork situations. Anthropologists produced a significant body of literature on a wide array of cultural phenomena (such as law, gender, moral order, codes of conduct, land, kinship, magic, religion, proselytization, the economy and ritual symbolism). But, in general, they did little research on the impact of colonization or the postcolonial politics responsible for recreating the hierarchies of dominance that caused internal displacement, rural–urban migration and crossings across national frontiers. Urgent anthropology is committed to heightening human creativity and agency. Therefore, it provides an invaluable frame for understanding the complex existential conditions of present-day Sudan, especially the subjective formulations of the experiences of southern Sudanese internally displaced women. This article will explore the implications of cultural loss and the corresponding renegotiation of identity and self that this entails.

The social and political lay of the land

The Sudan, which was Africa's largest country in area (1 million square kilometres) before the secession of the south of the country, is a territory of cultural, historical and strategic importance, as well as an incubator of major theories in socio-cultural anthropological knowledge. A large number of anthropologists were attracted to the unique amalgam of diverse ethnicities and their various languages. The Sudan was also looked upon as a bridge connecting Africa and the Middle East. Its location deeply influenced its history, culture and politics in the colonial period (1898 to 1956) and continued to shape political ideology well after independence in 1956.

During the colonial era, adhering to prevalent pseudoscientific notions of race, the British attempted to control their subjects by exploiting ethnic differences (Abusharaf 2013). One of the ways they did so was by halting freedom of movement between northern and southern Sudan. Conceptually, insight on this can be gleaned from Nicholas Thomas's analysis of colonial governance:

> Colonial discourse theory can homogenize colonizing actors, as it
> arguably effaces the agency of the colonized. In reaction to this elision of
> subjectivity an analysis could privilege the agency of colonial actors such as
> missionaries and administrators; but it might end up resembling a great deal
> of conventional colonial history and fail to deal with the texted character
> of these agents and histories, and the discursively complex nature of their
> endeavors.
>
> (Thomas 1994:105)

The consequences of the British closed-door policy on ethnicity, nationalism, constitutionalism and minorities were devastating. New 'frontiers of violence' arose and were later solidified by postcolonial northern governments. While some educated elites from the south found opportunities for upward mobility and economic well-being, their potential contribution to nation-building after independence was utterly disregarded. In addition, perpetuation of colonial policies of unequal development led to new divisions and also reinforced old ones. This, in turn, created new indices of exclusion and inclusion and margin and centre via new vocabularies that were not translated in the language of inclusivity. Sudanese independence came to embody a momentous rite of passage packed with ambiguity.

Exacerbating the prevailing uncertainty about the political future of inclusion and diversity in the country at independence was the question of Sharia law's role in the Sudan, which surfaced initially but was not adopted before 1983. Given the Sudanese secular tradition, conservative politicians were unable to impose their will on the Sudanese people. But that situation radically shifted when the military dictator, Jaafar Nimeiri, who seized power in a 1969 coup, refashioned himself as an Imam in 1983 and established an Islamist government. This resulted in violence aimed at opponents and disadvantaged populations across the country. In a society with marked ethnic diversity and religious affiliations, the wholesale enactment of Sharia law – or the September Laws, as they came to be known – threw the country back into a long round of civil war from 1983 to 2005. Resistance to the government's pursuits of Arabism and Islamism by both non-Muslims and secular Muslims was seen as a sign of disconnect between state and society. Vehemently opposed to the regeneration of opposing socio-political transcripts and cultural models, the Southern Sudanese Peoples Liberation Army, and its political wing, the Southern Sudanese Peoples Liberation Movement, responded to the call to arms with enthusiasm. The fighting grew fiercer with the coming to power of Omer Al-Bashir in a coup-d'état in 1989, and laws shaped by ideological models became even more crystallized in flogging, amputating and executing others of different political stripes and religious faiths. These practices represented the crux of what Al-Bashir labelled the 'civilizational project'. Translated by him as holy war, Al-Bashir continued to embark on wiping out the poor in southern Sudan. Within this context, the lack of empathy for the south displayed by successive governments of northern Sudan became indisputable. The pervasive political violence in the country was meted out at Southerners with utmost rigor. The accompanying economic, social and symbolic violence that accompanied their exclusion was devastating.

Southern people's sense of grievance and ineffable suffering became incontestably real (Abusharaf 2013). As they continued to be subject to the state's violations and atrocities, widespread competition over scarce resources and systematic marginalization compounded ethnic differences. Marginalities, subalternities and stratifications inherent in colonial epistemology reappeared, newly veneered, under the notion of sovereignty. This reality led Francis Deng astutely to point out that the 'Sudan is a country at war with itself' (Deng 2006:155). The president infringed upon numerous conventions, including the UN's International Covenant on Civil and Political Rights and other provisions of equality and fairness such as those enshrined in Article 22 of the Universal Declaration of Human Rights. For southerners, who had suffered from both burdensome colonial inheritances as well as unscrupulous postcolonial governance, the question of what it meant to be marginal became concretized in lived experiences. Unspeakable violence committed at the hands of regimes whose lust for power and property reigned supreme persists with terrible tenacity today.

Such was the fate of an overwhelming majority of Sudanese citizens in general, and southerners in particular, who were forced to bear the brunt of the longest running war in the African continent, one that disenfranchised, desolated and devastated millions and sent them both across the border to neighbouring African countries and to crowded squatter settlements and camps in Khartoum. When they voted overwhelmingly to secede in 2011, southerners saw it as the only means to end their marginality.

Losing ground

It is within this historical context that internally displaced women found themselves in camps and shantytowns in Muslim Arabized northern Sudan, where they continued to face violence and repression. They also confronted crimes against their cultural rights in their various expressions. It is true enough that culture as a concept cannot be reduced or reified, as individuals belonging to a specific background may or may not conform to an absolute cultural frame upon which consensus is built. However, it is important to stress that inability to engage in revered traditions created an enormous void in the life of the displaced. This was compounded by systematic exclusions in the economic, political and civil realms. According to a UNICEF report, the overwhelming majority of displaced women and children suffered from economic exploitation, abduction, malnutrition and lack of water resources, substandard sanitation and hygiene, and lack of access to health care and education (UNICEF 2001).

Several questions were raised in the course of my research. These included: How is loss to be understood in the southern Sudanese milieu? How did displaced women adapt when confronted with a complex urban dilemma, one that required a different set of skills to survive? The question of loss is operationalized through a series of inquiries among those who participated in this study and whose statements showed that the most obvious casualty of war was loss of cultural rights. But I contend that southern Sudanese women have acted in response to their challenges in ways that are exceptionally complex (see Abusharaf 2009). During my research I made no attempt to homogenize either Arab hosts or African newcomers, and took into consideration the infinitesimal number of details that resist easy generalities. I also realized that any discussion requires a consideration of networks, memory and location, factors that Preston (1997) sees as crucial to the understanding of political and cultural identities. Finally, I approached this research in the terms employed by Eisenbruch (1991), who, in his analysis of South Asian refugees in New Zealand, interrogated and transcended the essentialism implied in the diagnosis of post-traumatic stress disorder that typifies research paradigms on the mental life of refugee populations.

The women came from ethnically, linguistically and religiously different communities from southern Sudan itself: the Acholi, Anyuak, Azande, Bor, Didinga, Dinka, Baka, Bari, Berta, Bongo, Kakwa, Karamojo, Koma, Kwkwu, Lango, Lotuka, Lotuho, Luwo, Madi, Mangbetu, Moru, Mundu, Murle, Nuer, Schilluk, Sere, Turkana, and Uduk. In Izzbba, the squatter settlement, or *el-sakkan el-ashawi*, in which I did my research, the women said they came from the five main regions and countries of the south: southern Kordofan, southern Blue Nile, Upper Nile, Bahr El Gazal and Equatoria (see also Loveless 1999). Thus, Arab Muslim, non-Arab and non-Muslim peoples of many ethnicities confronted each other's cultures and languages, giving the squatter settlement a distinct, if grim, personality. The important point is that given their circumstances, the women's ideas about self, gender and community were – and still are – constantly being renegotiated, in part because of the extended period of time they had lived in Khartoum – some since as far back as 1983. Contact with a mix of various other ethnic, religious and linguistic communities, as well as the process of forging new communities, networks of associations, exchanges and mutual attachments, has intensified this renegotiation.

In this process of negotiating life in an urban space, the women embarked on yet another journey of life in the margins. On the one hand, Khartoum was a location where decisions about war and peace were made. On the other, as one social worker commented, it was 'urban hell'. In this regard, I concur with Bryan Roberts's emphasis on individual subjectivity in understanding the political economy of urban life (Roberts 1975). Fundamental to his analysis is the agency of individuals in navigating difficult predicaments in urban locations. He argues:

> This is our chance to bring the individual back into our analysis as someone who is not simply the puppet of forces beyond his or her control, but as a force contributing to shaping the course of events.
>
> (ibid.:136)

My research made clear that prolonged residence in the squatter settlement influenced the strategies the women employed, a phenomenon that is intimately linked to the question of a minority population's access to cultural rights. Lorube, a southern Sudanese refugee, regularly interacts with northerners. She lives with them and has learned about their food, crafts, marriage, witchcraft and sorcery, and she is prepared to embrace some of their practices. Lorube was circumcised when she converted to Islam. However, she resents the fact that northerners despise southerners and call them 'slaves' and 'servants'. If we were to assess the meaning of cultural rights in southern Sudanese cosmology, we would be confronted with an impressive abundance of cultural expressions and rules that govern every aspect of one's existence. The fact that the very foundation of village society had been blasted to bits meant that whatever notions and significance people attached to their practices were also shattered.

Loss can be understood not only from the testimonies of the residents themselves, but also from the rich ethnographic work that was carried out by pioneering British anthropologists and district commissioners, who captured the richness of the peoples and cultures of southern Sudan in *Sudan Notes and Records*. The volumes they produced included divergent forms of ethnographic knowledge on the marked diversity of southern Sudan. Among many other 'traditional structures', these include classifications of age, clan classifications and childbirth rituals. The southern Sudanese practised cultural rites of passage that modified the body, such as facial scarification, branding and teeth removal, and enacted kinship rules, including those governing betrothal and marriage, following laws and rules regulating inheritance and property ownership, compensation for injury, the distribution of resources, totems and magic. Also documented are oath-taking, rainmaking and sacrifice, initiation and burial, acknowledgement of supreme beings and guardian spirits, and the transmission of stories told around the evening fire.[1]

---

1   For extensive discussions of these practices, see *Sudan Notes and Records*, published since 1918.

The losses incurred in the involuntary abandonment of the aforementioned rites of passage were captured in hundreds of accounts collected in this project. I have detailed these experiences elsewhere (Abusharaf 2005), but, in brief, the women described the loss of traditional rituals such as brewing beer, which not only provides income but also had ceremonial significance in birth, marriage and death practices. They also talked about being forced to cover their bodies, for instance, and they repeatedly said they felt anxiety about losing their 'consciousness of being'. The women, in short, feared as well as grieved the loss of their cultural rights.

References to preferring death to life were common. I interpreted this to mean that the state had metaphorically pronounced them dead. In other words, death was the definitive allegory, discursively framed in power politics that denied victims their fundamental rights to dignity and freedom from domination (Abusharaf 2013). The women's experiences illustrate that as war destroys family forms and kinship systems, concepts of self, identity and belonging take on complex new meanings.

The implications of migration on the formation of one's identity, particularly gender identity, are crucial, and should be situated within particular histories. I agree with Valentine Daniel that a 'semiotic perspective on the self, on life, and on being human is unavoidably historic and incorrigibly trinary' (Daniel 1996:189).[2] Displaced women begin to see change as an innovative way to create 'permanence in transience', or what Aihwa Ong (quoting James Clifford) describes as 'dwelling in traveling' (Ong 1995:350). As I suggest, prolonged residence in shantytowns and camps as well as the sheer reality of Sudan's civil war have generated new symbolic meanings of space that, in turn, have created affective relationships of interdependence and sustenance between people. Finding shelter, wherever it may be, is a more immediate concern for displaced people than the need to live among relatives. It is also important to note that the kinship 'vacuum' that results from displacement does not go unfilled. Neighbours in host communities step up to fill roles as fictive kin, both ready and willing to enter into a new chain of exchanges and conversations. Despite the importance of these new relationships, a sense of cultural loss remains and serves as a powerful force that contributes to the reshaping of ideas and values. Indeed, this interpretation sheds light on the existential nature of identity, which, as suggested below, is an interactive process, sensitive to changing circumstances. Or, as Erchak said, the self, 'as a specific and experiential concept, is always on the move' (Erchak 1992:3).

---

2   These issues have also been poignantly examined in the works of Bariagaber (1999), Deng and Cohen (1998), Hackett (1996), Morawska (2000) and others.

Consequently, the particular milieu of displaced women's lives necessitates the invention of new selves, selves that must be micromanaged and be in sync with the realities of their new surroundings. As Bateson lucidly points out:

> just as change stimulates us to look for more abstract constancies, so the
> individual effort to compose a life, framed by birth and death and carefully
> pieced together from disparate elements, becomes a statement on the unity
> of living. These works of art, still incomplete, are parables in process, the
> living metaphors with which we describe the world.
>
> (Bateson 1989:18)

It is also important to point out that because women face gruelling abuse as sexed bodies – victims of sexual violence and torture before, during, and after both flight and arrival in new communities (see Eastmond 1993; Habib 1995; Hackett 1996; Indra 1998) – a feminist ethnography seems fitting for a textured, multilayered analysis of their experiences. This is because it identifies them both as women facing the challenges of crafting new selves and as displaced persons dealing with formidable obstacles in a new venue. Feminist ethnography helps to promote an understanding of 'how gender has become an ordering category of anthropological analysis' (Visweswaran 1997:592), and for this reason, it should not be viewed as a reductive way of reporting women's problems. Indeed, since 'womanhood is a partial identity' (Abu Lughod 1990:25), a 'privileged relationship between a feminist ethnographer and the oppressed people she may study is not automatically rooted in her womanhood' (Harrison 1997:89). Feminist ethnography in no way excludes the recognition that women are raced, classed and gendered subjects. According to Abu Lughod:

> feminism and ethnography are practices that could shake up the paradigm
> of anthropology itself by showing that we are always part of what we study
> and we always stand in definite relations to it.
>
> (Abu Lughod 1990:25–26)

In this respect, differences in women's experiences can be viewed as assets rather than as liabilities. As Miriam Cooke points out in her study of the war in Lebanon:

> in this world of shifting standards, I borrow meaning from these women. I
> build my story on foundations they have laid. My hope for myself and for
> all embarked on this venture, this cultural crossing, is that a recognition
> of our own strangeness will not serve to silence, but will rather allow for

the proliferation of multiple stories each of which will contribute to the
flourishing of shared understandings based on mutual respect.

(Cooke 1996:12)

In the Sudan, reporting women's stories is particularly necessary because
women themselves long to talk. Beverly Bell points out that in a similar
situation, Haitian women wanted to recount painful stories 'both for catharsis
from the horror and for relief from a lengthy enforced silence' (Bell 2001:xi).
The experiences of war-displaced women in Izzbba bear striking resemblance
to the scenario that Bell has articulated. A compelling analysis of women's
concerns should be situated within broader intersections of ethnicity and
gender, that is, anthropologically minded feminism and a feminist-minded
anthropology; practices in which our intellectual and political agendas do not
necessarily collide, but instead go hand in hand. (Bourgeois 1997).

Therefore, with a feminist anthropology in mind, in the renegotiation
of identity and self, displaced southern women began to look up to their
neighbours who adhered to heretofore unknown practices such as female
circumcision, practices that continued to be contested in activist circles in
Khartoum. Although female circumcision is deeply entrenched in the north,
where 91 per cent of the population practise it, it is not practised in the south
(Anon. 1995).[3] Thus, in the lines that follow, the focus is on the ritualized
genital surgery known as female circumcision as well as other less extreme
types of body modification and adornment, which were also common.

Female circumcision among displaced women

The question of why southern Sudanese women started to adopt the practice
of female circumcision following their arrival in Khartoum is particularly
difficult to answer, but it provides one of the most salient examples of identity
transformation and points sharply to the contingency and the versatility of
displaced women. This adoption also exemplifies a horizontal transmission of
tradition, that is, not from one generation to offspring, but across ethnic groups.
A number of situations that arose in a forced migratory context necessitated
the adoption of this controversial ritual simply to feel they belong. As a
practical activity associated with gendered rituals, female circumcision enabled
many women to take on a new sense of social personhood. As abhorrent as
many people believe the practice to be, historically it has been a source of
joyous celebration and elaborate festivities in northern Sudanese communities.
People justify their support for it by arguing that it preserves virginity, enhances
femininity and increases the purity and cleanliness of the body.

---

3   I have discussed these wide-ranging rituals elsewhere (Abusharaf 2009).

But historically there has also been apprehension over the possible acceptance of the ritual by southern women. For example, in 1938, the British governor of Kordofan addressed his concern about female circumcision in south-west Kordofan. The Dinka in the tribal and Arab areas did not practise it; the mixed Arab-Dinka, however, did. The governor instructed the chief of the area to prevent its spread.[4] Then, in 1946, the British outlawed the practice. Part of the reason it has persisted is because attitudes towards sexuality and reproduction are at the heart of Sudanese cultural and religious beliefs. Discussing sexuality is extremely curtailed by cultural taboos. To a great extent, this interdiction is intimately linked to how Sudanese society views sexuality in the first place, as an ominous threat that, if left unchecked, endangers one's purity and morality. Social and physical regulation, therefore, is aggressively pursued. The factors influencing the adoption of female circumcision are linked to questions about strategy, voluntary choice versus coercion, the need for security and the perceived requirement to adhere to a new culture.

Sources of documentation

In addition to authoritative testimonies of the women I interviewed, NGOs and community activists have also documented the increasing incidence of female circumcision. During my visit to the Sudan in 1996, considerable concern was developing over its spread. According to one social worker from a local NGO, 'While we're trying very hard to curb the practice among people who practised it for thousands of years, now we have started to receive news about its spread among southerners who didn't know about it before'. A report by the United Nations stated that traditional practices including the most extreme form of female genital mutilation – infibulation, or pharaonic circumcision – are common among displaced people (United Nations 2000:59). Arnna Abdel Rahman, who heads the Sudanese National Committee for Traditional Harmful Practices Affecting the Health of Women and Children (SNCTP), proposed developing of a sensitization campaign for the displaced. It was urgent, she said, because illiteracy and ignorance in the camps was contributing to a perception among southerners that female circumcision is an 'urban fashion' and a 'religious requirement' (Rahman 1995:2).

One of the most compelling sources of documentation of the practice has been the SNCTP's effort to promote alternative employment for midwives who derive large incomes from the practice. The president of the organization

---

4   D.M.H. Evans Administrative Papers 1937. G/ / S #787. File no. 710/6/ 1-49. February 6, 1939. Appendix IV of the 1937 Report on Sudan. G/ /S 701 Unofficial Correspondence, SAD.

said that southern midwives who learned how to perform the operations from their northern counterparts could also work as agents for change, so the organization started a shop that would employ midwives as vendors. This strategy, also adopted by the UN Inter-Africa programme, has been one of the most effective tools in the fight against the problem. In 2002, I accompanied SNCTP social workers to Wad El-Bashir, one of the largest camps in Omdurman. The workers planned the visit to inquire about the progress of the shop. Ten southern Sudanese midwives were present at the time. Though they expressed frustration with working in the shop, they ended the meeting by reiterating their commitment to its success. There is no doubt that the inclusion of southern midwives in both these programmes can play a role in either the proliferation or the obliteration of this unyielding tradition.

News reports have also covered the issue. Andrew Hammond wrote that while war encouraged the spread of female circumcision, peace could give a much-needed boost to combat it (Hammond 2002). Hammond cited Samira Amin, a founding member of the Sudanese Network for Eradicating Female Circumcision, who stated that:

> a 2001 survey of street children who live in the capital's displaced
> communities showed 67 percent of them had undergone what medical
> textbooks call genital infibulation. These are people from the Dinka tribes in
> the south, the Nuba Mountains, and the Felata in the west, who did not do
> this before. It is a transmitted trend.
>
> (ibid.)

Dr Constantine Jervase, a surgeon from Bahr Elghazal quoted by Hammond, said that southerners are 'copying' the practice from Arabs. He stated that potentially they are adopting this for assistance or to 'please their masters'. Regardless of their motive, he unequivocally stated that something needed to be done to stop its spread (citied in ibid.). The governing question in the context of displacement and forced migration is this: Does this adoption reflect an attempt by displaced women to reduce the distance between themselves and their hosts?

What values, whose values?

In his study of revitalization in Trinidad, Morton Klass tackles the exasperating intricacies involved in changing values and ideologies by asking such critical questions as:

How are values expressed? Can we ever be sure the same value is present,
even when two people make the same choice in different situations? Is it
possible that one and the same value may be expressed by different choices
in varying circumstances?

(Klass 1991:10)

In the cultural theory that supports the continuation of female
circumcision, substantial weight is placed on notions of purity and defilement.
Purity, heretofore, has had numerous connotations, including morality,
uprightness, decorum and wholesomeness, all virtues to cherish and behold.
Girls are taught that these desirable qualities can best be achieved through
circumcision. Consequently, they are also taught that external genitalia are
potential sources of *najasa*, pollution and defilement, considered repulsive
states to be avoided at all costs. As a statement of both physical and moral
impurity, the concept of *najasa* extends to diverse situations. For instance,
women are implored by religion to perform ritual purification, known as *ghusl*
(bathing), after menstruation, intercourse, birth and other activities deemed
polluting, or *najis*. For these women, becoming pure and clean not only helps
establish their social personhood, but also differentiates them from other
women who do not practise circumcision and are therefore impure. In several
communities, circumcision is important because it gives voice to gender and
collective ethnic identity, serving to define the border between themselves
as pure (*taharat*) and others as polluted (*nijsat*) women. The lesson about
circumcision as purity cannot be isolated from religious instruction as a
whole. Although there is no established link between religion and genital
cutting (as least for females) in many communities, circumcision is believed
to be a part of religion.

Southern women interviewed for my research described Muslim husbands,
and in some cases Christian husbands, insisting on and often forcing them to
be circumcised. These women also talked about the discrimination they felt,
as if they were in a 'different society', as one woman said. They wanted to fit
in; they did not want to be 'impure'. A Christian nurse from Juba, for instance,
told me her story during a visit to the Carton camp, where she had been
employed at the health centre for two years. She had first-hand knowledge
of female genital mutilation: her southern Christian husband, who lived in an
Arabic-speaking Muslim town, coerced her into undergoing the procedure.
Her husband had good relations with the local Arab men, which influenced
his thinking. 'Men talk to each other about it', she said. 'This is how he found
out and insisted that I get the operation, and went so far as to tell the midwife
who delivered my child to cut and sew'.

The preceding narrative presents an anomaly. In a migratory context, the husband's adoption of the idea that female circumcision is essential to womanhood and femininity cannot be isolated from broader understandings of ways in which newcomers attempt to integrate into host communities. However, as noted earlier, embracing rituals does not always reflect identical values and moralities, as evidenced in Max Gluckman argued long ago. He notes that, although it is important to establish common explanations for ritual phenomena, 'it is essential to grasp that there are fundamental differences between them and also between modes of interpreting them' (Gluckman 1997:40). Therefore, acquiescence to new norms and belief systems can be seen as one part of a series of adjustments that women make to overcome their sense of cultural loss and marginalization.

Given the complexity of female circumcision practices among the displaced, certain issues should be addressed. First, the majority of displaced women adopt this practice as adults – it is only occasionally performed on young girls. When I asked Sayda, a shantytown resident about the practice, she responded:

> Personally, I'm not supportive of circumcision, but my older sister is. She decided to undergo the ritual and asked a midwife to circumcise her. When I asked her why, she kept telling me *sakit sakit* ('for no reason'). But I know there are reasons. She wants to be like other women who she hangs out with. Girls, however, are not circumcised unless they have *doodaya* ('vaginal itching').

Since the practice in the north is performed on young girls of six to nine years old, its adoption by adult displaced women is a major departure.

Second, the fact that several women said they underwent circumcision after marrying Muslim men also raises significant questions regarding the values and justification of the practice, since the most significant rationale for the practice is intermarriage. Regardless, it is reasonable to suggest that in a forced migratory context the adoption of the practice is a strategic move by the displaced to find a place in the host society and reduce the distance between themselves and their hosts. Several grassroots workers told me that the overwhelming majority of displaced women started to see the practice as an urban innovation. However, whether this practice is an outcome of an 'urbanization of consciousness' or not is a question that requires further investigation.

Dukhan as metaphor

Other rituals that displaced women adopted, such as the smoke bath (*dukhan*), also provide examples of the transformation of self. By all accounts, *dukhan* is a beautification ritual among women in northern provinces, usually performed after sunset. After large numbers of southern displaced women settled in northern camps, they became acquainted with *dukhan* as they had with henna and other forms of body adornment. *Dukhan* is only practised by those who are married or about to get married. Associated with sensuality and eroticism, it is believed to boost sexual gratification.

As part of the ritual, a series of steps must be followed carefully before one bathes in smoke. First, a blend of scented sandalwoods is placed inside a hole. A *birish* rug, woven from palm branches, is then placed over the hole. To start bathing, a woman strips naked. Her body is then thoroughly rubbed with *karka*-scented oil made from animal fat, orange peel and clove essence. The woman sits on the rug, allowing the rising smoke to fumigate her body. Women rarely perform *dukhan* alone. Usually, they rely on the help of female kin, neighbours and friends to add wood as needed or to provide water to compensate for the massive amount of sweat released while bathing, which can last for an hour or more. A body scrub known as *dilka* is then used to clean the body and to reveal glistening skin. A warm shower concludes the process. Although women insist on the benefits of *dukhan* for health reasons, such as curing body aches, its links to sexuality cannot be glossed over. *Dukhan* is frequently regarded as an invitation to engage in sex. In a society where expression of sexual desire is condemned, as discussed earlier, the explanation of the ritual as an incitement to have sex is by no means unreasonable. To participate in the *dukhan* ritual is to engage in a cult of femininity in which clear rules about the construction of ideal womanhood are followed with astonishing passion.

Displaced women who adopted the practice of *dukhan* have not been spared the harsh censure of southern men. Theodore, a 47-year-old social worker, expressed his astonishment at the ritual by saying:

> I don't know why these women are doing *dukhan*. As men, we hear that
> the *dukhan* is performed when a woman is too wide and that *dukhan* helps
> tighten her. The southern women here are mostly single or widowed. What
> do they need it for?'

Notwithstanding this view, the women I talked to provide a more textured and nuanced reason for adopting *dukhan*. As Rebecca, a 37-year-old Dinka explains, 'When you go by your neighbour's place to see her and you find her digging a hole, you too dig a hole to bathe in it'. What Rebecca alludes to is that active participation in social practices provides a means through which people can gain understanding as individuals while simultaneously learning how to become a member of a community. It is a response to a situation in which compensation is sought for lost networks and idioms that gave meaning to social existence before displacement. This, of course, does not imply that all southern displaced women have adopted *dukhan*. Instead, it shows how women respond to new situations and contexts with dynamism and creativity. Rites and rituals such as *dukhan* cannot be isolated from the larger context of social action. Rather, it is within the context of displaced women's responses that one can appreciate the symbolic and practical aspects of the adoption of *dukhan*, a ritual that seems to play a useful role in community understanding and reconciliation as women construct bridges across ethnic boundaries and create new identities.

Conclusion

Despite the importance of these new relationships, a sense of cultural loss still remains and serves as a powerful contribution to reshaping ideas and values. The fact that displaced women find an inner rhythm and equilibrium in the face of extreme difficulties provides compelling evidence of human tenacity and resilience. This chapter has attempted to draw on the strengths of an element of urgent anthropology to unravel the experiences of displaced women, both in their forced migration from southern Sudan and in their responses to life in northern Khartoum. Drawing on literature that examines the effects of forced migration on cultural transformation, I have proposed that gendered rituals have enabled women to refashion their lives in the new surroundings as they struggle to create a sense of centeredness and direction.

Without resorting to the positivism of cause and effect arguments, it becomes apparent that the inability of women to carry on cultural traditions in refugee settlements led to subsequent renegotiations and evaluations. This point was made with crystal clarity in the loss of cultural rights: the right to brew alcohol, wear traditional dress, perform ethnic dances and perform marriage, birth, and death rituals in the same way they were celebrated at home. Women had to assume new roles as they struggled to create a space for themselves in the host community's established order. Recently, the population of Izzbba was given some sense of ownership when a new land tenure plan shifted the perceptions people had of themselves from *naziheen* (displaced) to owners and residents.

Whether it is circumcision, or any newly introduced ritual, engaging in these acts can only be appreciated in the context of the public presentation of self. This presentation enables a sense of neighbourliness and sociality, and it also celebrates belonging, rather than promoting distance from other members of the community. Women find themselves in circumstances that require them to elbow their way in to a new multicultural scene, one in which they are prompted to put together new concepts of self and community. These narratives portray a great challenge to essentialist concepts of self and identity as these discursively constructed aspects of personhood become contingent upon the everyday and existential realities surrounding displaced women. If 'identity is the way in which we more or less self-consciously locate ourselves in our social world' (Preston 1997:43), one might even conclude that these rituals are a brilliant masquerade, done to 'get by' in a new cultural environment. The experiences of displaced women, recounted in this article, not only mirror their inner strength and adeptness, but also act as 'groping footsteps' toward peace-making and conflict resolution in the war-torn country.

As this study was conducted before secession, it is important to note that from the recent achievement of independence by the Republic of South Sudan means that the future of these interviewees hangs in the balance. The road home is fraught with difficulty and the task of repatriation most staggering. The stories of these women's lives continue to be one of unrelenting liminality. Conversely, war as an act of aggression and dominance obliterated the basic entitlements held by people and their communities: shelter, access to food, social networks and protection. In the light of these extraordinary situations, they attempted to find a footing in a location fraught with paradoxes.

Acknowledgements

I am grateful to the RAI Urgent Anthropology Fund and Durham University for their support. This chapter is part of a larger project, and segments have appeared in my book *Transforming Displaced Women: Politics and the Body in a Squatter Settlement* (2009). Other parts were also appeared in an essay in *Anthropology and Humanism*. Permission to republish these passages is gratefully acknowledged.

References

Abu Lughod, L. 1990. 'Can there be a feminist ethnography?', *Women and Performance* 5(1):7–27.

Abusharaf, R. 1998. 'Unmasking tradition: a Sudanese anthropologist confronts female circumcision and its terrible tenacity', *The Sciences* 38(2):22–8.

——— 1999. 'Virtuous cuts: female genital excision in an African ontology', *Differences: Journal of Feminist Cultural Studies* 12(1):112–40.

——— 2003. 'When war affects decisions: an interview with Lory Hough', *John F. Kennedy School of Government Bulletin* 15 (spring).

——— 2004. 'Life in Khartoum: probing forced migration and cultural change among war displaced women', *Rosemary Rogers Working Paper* 30. Cambridge, MA: MIT Center for International Studies.

——— 2005. 'Smoke Bath', *Anthropology and Humanism* 30(1):1–21.

——— 2009. *Transforming Displaced Women in Sudan: Politics and the Body in a Squatter Settlement*. Chicago: University of Chicago Press.

——— 2013. 'Seeds of succession', *Transition: An International Review* 110:73–89.

Anon. 1995. *Sudan Demographics and Health Survey*. Baltimore: Institute for Resource Development/Macro International.

Bariagaber, A. 1999. 'States, international organizations, and the refugee: reflections on the complexity of managing the refugee crisis in the Horn of Africa', *Journal of Modem African Studies* 37(4):591–619.

Bateson, M.C. 1989. *Composing a Life*. Berkeley, CA: Grove Atlantic.

Battaglia, D. 2000. 'Towards an ethics of the open subject: writing culture in good conscience'. In H. Moore (ed.), *Anthropological Theory Today*, pp. 114–51. Cambridge: Polity Press.

Bell, B. 2001. *Walking on Fire: Haitian Women's Stories of Survival and Resistance*. Ithaca, NY: Cornell University Press.

Bhabha, H.K. 1994. *The Location of Culture*. London: Routledge.

Cooke, M. 1996. *Women and the War Story*. Berkeley: University of California Press.

Bourgois, P. 1997. 'Confronting the ethics of ethnography: lessons from fieldwork in Central America'. In F. Harrison (ed.), *Decolonizing Anthropology*. pp. 111–27. Washington, DC: American Anthropological Association.

Daniel, E.V. 1996. *Charred Lullabies: Chapters in the Anthropology of Violence*. Princeton: Princeton University Press.

Deng, F.M. 2006. 'Sudan: a nation in turbulent search of itself', *Annals of the American Academy of Political and Social Science* 603(1):155–62.

Deng, F., and Cohen, R. 1998. *Masses in Flight: The Global Crisis of the Internally Displaced*. Washington: Brookings Institution.

Eastmond, M. 1993. 'Reconstructing life: Chilean women and the dilemmas of exile'. In G. Bujis (ed.), *Migrant Women: Crossing Boundaries and Changing Identities*, pp. 35–55. Oxford: Berg.

Eisenbruch, M. 1991. 'From post-traumatic stress disorder to cultural bereavement: diagnosis of Southeast Asian refugees', *Social Science and Medicine* 3:673–80.

Erchak, G.M. 1992. *The Anthropology of Self and Behavior*. Rutgers University Press, N.J.

Gluckman, M. 1997 [1947]. 'Ritual'. In A. Lehmann (ed.), *Magic, Witchcraft, and Religion*, pp. 40–4. Mountain View, CA Mayfield.

Habib, A. 1995. 'Effects of displacement on Southern women's health and food habits', *Ahfad Journal* 12(2):30–52.

Hackett, B. 1996. *Pray God and Keep Walking: Stories of Women Refugees*. London: McFarland.

Hammond, A. 2002. 'Sudan peace may help end female circumcision'. *Reuters* (21 August): freerepublic.com/focus/news/737051/posts (accessed 17 October 2018).

Harrison, F. 1997. 'Ethnography as politics'. In F. Harrison (ed.), *Decolonizing Anthropology*, pp. 88–110. Washington: American Anthropological Association.

Indra, D. (ed.). 1998. *Engendering Forced Migration*. New York: Berghahn.

Klass, M. 1991. *Singing with Sai Baba: The Politics of Revitalization in Trinidad*. Prospect Heights, IL: Waveland Press.

Loveless, J. 1999. 'Displaced populations in Khartoum'. Report. Save the Children Denmark/Channel Research. Copenhagen.

Morawska, E. 2000. 'Intended and unintended consequences of forced migrations', *International Migration Review* 34(4):1049–87.

Ong, A. 1995. 'Border work: feminist ethnography and the dissemination of literacy'. In R. Behar and D.A. Gordon (eds), *Women Writing Culture*, pp. 350–73. Berkeley: University of California Press.

Preston, P.W. 1997. *Political/Cultural Identity: Citizens and Nations in a Global Era*. London: Sage.

Rahman, A.A. 1995. 'Research proposal for training midwives in displaced camps'. Khartoum: Sudanese National Committee for Traditional Harmful Practices Affecting the Health of Women and Children (SNCTP).

Rapport, N. and Overing, J. 2000. *Social and Cultural Anthropology: The Key Concepts*. London: Routledge.

Thomas, N. 1994. *Colonialism's Culture*. Princeton, NJ: Princeton University Press.

Visweswaran, K. 1997. 'Histories of feminist ethnography', *Annual Review of Anthropology* 26:591–621.

3

Case studies in asocial reproduction

Displacement, leadership and conflict resolution among refugees in the Horn of Africa and the Sudan

Kwesi Sansculotte-Greenidge
and Laura Barber

This chapter examines the effect of displacement and humanitarian intervention on traditional systems of leadership and conflict resolution among Darfuri BeRà or Zaghawa refugees in eastern Chad and Eritrean Kunama and Tigrinya refugees in northern Ethiopia. Initially, it will examine traditional systems of leadership, prior to displacement. These pre-displacement systems will then be contrasted with new administrative structures in the refugee camps and host countries in order to expose the deeper impacts of long-term displacement and interaction with the 'humanitarian sector' on traditional systems of leadership regionally. Systems of conflict resolution between refugees and the host communities as practised in the camps will also be analysed to provide a detailed assessment not only of change but also continuity in the social systems of displaced peoples. The chapter concludes that the resilience of traditional systems among displaced peoples is closely related to the perceived and actual strength of traditional institutions. This strength is determined by two distinct, but closely related factors: the nature of newer institutions established by humanitarian actors, and the manner in which the displaced arrived in their new homes, the refugee camps.

There is a considerable body of literature on conflict resolution and peace accords between states, or states and their constituent regions, or even states and their subjects (e.g. Becker and Mitchell 1991; Burton 1990; de Silva and Samarasinghe 1993; Woodhouse and Ramsbotham 2000). However, there is comparatively little written on communal conflict resolution. This chapter will help to bridge this gap, by focusing on communal conflict resolution among refugees in the Horn of Africa and the Sahel.

The chapter examines the impacts of long-term displacement on traditional systems of leadership and conflict resolution among refugees in the Horn of Africa. It will highlight some of the challenges brought about by humanitarian intervention in the leadership and conflict resolution institutions of displaced peoples by comparing the experience of refugees from four communities, displaced by two very different conflicts in two very different states. It will explore continuity in traditional systems of leadership and conflict resolution among Darfuri BeRà or Zaghawa refugee inhabitants of two camps in eastern Chad and Eritrean Kunama and Tigrinya refugees in northern Ethiopia.

In the vast majority of cases, the movement of refugees and internally displaced peoples is a complex and chaotic affair. The events prior to, during and after their flight leave them scarred both emotionally and physically. In addition to mental trauma, refugees suffer from the very real loss of country, community, family, prestige and property. Social bonds and familial relations are often torn asunder, frequently leading to a decline in the moral authority of traditional leaders. As a result, displacement can become the focus for far-reaching social and cultural change and upheaval. Any study of displacement is thus inherently a study of societies in change and cultural adaptation. This chapter will focus on two such cases of forced migration and the process of adaptation and change they have imposed on peoples in the greater Horn of Africa.

While some scholars argue that the actual distinction between forms of migration in Africa are problematic, due to a blurring of the lines between political and economic reasons for movement (Misago and Landau 2005), our case studies provide no such ambiguity. For the purpose of this chapter the term 'refugee' is used in a narrower sense, wherein it refers to individuals or groups of people who have been compelled to cross international borders to seek protection, but not livelihoods or economic opportunities. Official responses to displacement, by both the international humanitarian community (donors, UN agencies and implementing partners) and national governments, have long been informed by a combination of political priorities and rights-based imperatives. Where the two are mutually reinforcing, official responses to displacement can be rapid, well-resourced and effective (ibid.). When rights and political priorities conflict, humanitarian principles are often compromised.

Our case studies, Darfuri refugees in Chad and Eritrean refugees in Ethiopia, exemplify protracted refugee situations. As highlighted by Loescher *et al.* (2008), such situations are not only caused by instability, but in many cases generate instability themselves by destroying traditional leadership structures and social bonds, politicizing and militarizing refugees and in some cases host populations. Loescher *et al.* argue that protracted refugee situations are not inevitable, but caused by political inaction (ibid.:26). These situations usually endure because of problems in the country of origin and restrictions on the rights of refugees in host countries and communities. In spite of this, the far-reaching impacts of long-term displacement on traditional institutions are only now being explored. Furthermore, unresolved refugee situations are often a source of tension for host countries and the home countries of refugees, as is the case with Burmese refugees in Thailand, Burundian refugees in Tanzania and Darfuri refugees in Chad.

In Africa, displacement was previously characterized by high levels of host-community support for efforts to assist internally displaced persons and refugees. This support was often justified through anti-colonial (or anti-apartheid) solidarity, or in other cases ethnic ties (Misago and Landau 2005). During the early independence era, the international community provided, through the United Nations High Commissioner for Refugees (UNHCR) and international NGOs, what seemed like a limitless amount of assistance. These bodies were also actively involved in finding durable solutions to displacement with a particular emphasis on the local integration of refugee populations.

This all changed with the end of the Cold War. Brought on by geopolitical changes beginning in the early 1990s, the international community's engagement with refugees has primarily had a dual focus: first, to provide assistance to recently displaced populations in a timely manner by delivering humanitarian assistance to refugees and war-affected populations; and second, to focus on repatriation. While international support for such emergency situations is commendable, it is somewhat limited given that over two-thirds of refugees in the world today are not living under emergency conditions, but instead trapped in protracted refugee situations (Loescher *et al.* 2008:26).

The combination of economic stagnation and increased democratic competition brought by the end of the Cold War meant that policy and practice were characterized by a retreat from the fundamental principles of asylum and international refugee law and Nation States' abrogation of their responsibilities for protection. Rather than welcoming refugees, states increasingly introduced restrictive measures to stem the flow of immigrants and refugees and remove refugee populations from their territories. A key part of this process has been the drive by African states to place the rights or interests of states and host populations, couched in notions of citizenship, over refugee rights.

The lack of both an international and continental approach to dealing with refugee populations, and the complex security history that caused their displacement, has meant that programmes of assistance, designed to be temporary measures, are increasingly becoming semi-permanent features of the continent's humanitarian landscape. In the Horn of Africa in particular, humanitarian assistance policies are shaped less by the changing nature of conflict or the needs of the displaced than by the interests of the region's states and international donors. Brought on by the contraction of state resources, and a relative decline in international support since the end of the Cold War, restrictive asylum policies have been enforced in the Horn of Africa.

There are numerous cases in which host communities continue to show solidarity with refugees and provide assistance even when governments and international actors are absent (for example, Sri Lankan Tamils in southern India, Mozambicans living along South Africa's eastern borderlands and Guatemalan refugees in Belize). There are even more, usually less publicized, cases of host communities organizing to exclude 'outsiders' and 'foreigners' from livelihoods and even the most basic necessities of survival. Indeed, a tendency towards exclusionary, if not outright xenophobic, practices has become one of the hallmarks of contemporary responses to displacement. From riots in South Africa to the expulsion of Arabs in Niger, refugees and migrants have become political scapegoats across Africa. As a result, a study on how refugee leadership reacts to change, both in situations when refugees are either welcomed and deemed unwelcome, is both timely and of immense use to academics and policymakers alike.

Shimelba refugee camp, Tigray, northern Ethiopia
Background
Shimelba refugee camp was established in 2000 and has hosted a large population of Eritrean refugees. They were initially settled in a location called Waalanhibi in the Tigray region of northern Ethiopia, some 1,200 kilometres north of Addis Ababa. As that location was too close to the border with Eritrea, the camp was relocated to Shimelba in June 2004.The Shimelba camp is located about 45 kilometres south of the Eritrean border in a semi-arid and rocky landscape dotted with trees and shrubs. At the time of LB's 2008 fieldwork, about 14,300 Eritrean refugees lived in the camp. The Kunama make up about 30 per cent of the camp population; the rest are Tigrinya (UNHCR 2008). Shimelba camp hosts refugees who fled Eritrea during the border conflict of 1998 to 2000, as well as Eritreans that continue to escape their homeland to avoid mandatory national service and the worsening economic situation in the country.

It is predominantly male Tigrinya youths from Eritrea who have continued to enter Shimelba refugee camp since the war ended in 2000. Many of these refugees are students from the University of Asmara, which closed in 2005. University students have frequently been targets of forced conscription by the Eritrean government, and Ethiopia has been willing to offer these students asylum in its refugee camps. Most came to Ethiopia by themselves and do not

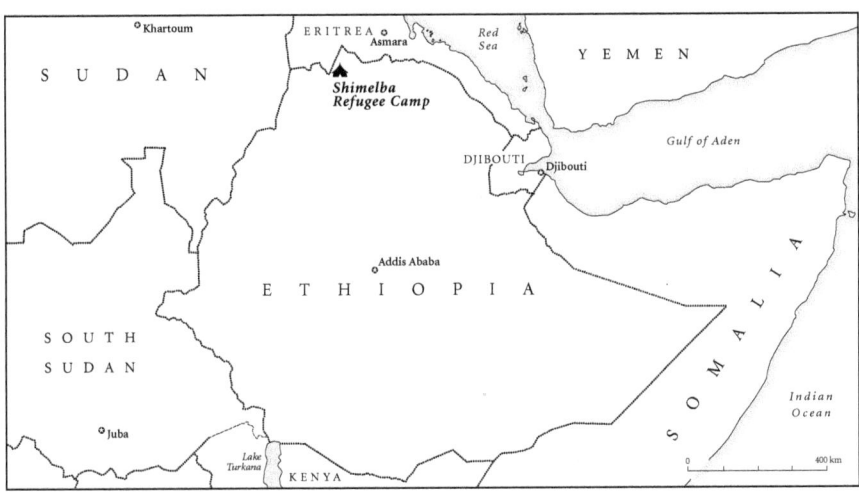

Figure 3.1   Map of Ethiopia and Eritrea showing the location of Shimelba refugee camp.

have any family support networks in the camp, which refugees normally use as a coping mechanism (UNFPA 2007:4).

For the majority of Eritrean refugees, the possibilities of either repatriation or resettlement are extremely unlikely, and the Ethiopian government currently upholds a policy to prevent the integration of Eritrean refugees into Ethiopian society. As the prospect of long-term displacement is increasingly becoming a reality for many Eritrean refugees, the resilience of traditional leadership structures is essential to provide a sense of identity and strengthening unity among those who are displaced.

There are two primary leadership systems used to resolve conflicts occurring both within the camp and between the refugees and the host community: first, the structures and institutions established by the government; and second, traditional mechanisms involving the intervention of indigenous elders and religious leaders. The section will examine the impact that modern refugee camp structures and the circumstances specific to the experience of displacement have had upon the traditional leadership systems of both the Kunama and Tigrinya ethnic groups in Shimelba refugee camp.[1]

---

1   The analysis in this section is based upon data collected during research conducted by Barber for ZOA Refugee Care in Shimelba refugee camp, northern Ethiopia, May 2008.

Kunama and Tigrinya traditional systems

The Kunama are descended from Nilo-Saharan people of the Nile Valley who settled in the extremely fertile western lowlands of the Gash Barka region in Eritrea. Kunama people are settled agro-pastoralists who share a common language, but are divided into four clans – the Kara, Suwaa, Serma and Gumma – of which there are several sub-clan divisions (Ranard 2007). Despite diversity across clans, the Kunama have historically been bound together by their rich cultural heritage and traditional customs (England 2008).

Kunama social structure is organized according to ancient practices, with traditional elders playing key leadership roles within the community. The customary laws that guide conflict resolution processes are not officially recorded in a text due to high levels of illiteracy but have endured through generations as elders have passed on the laws orally to their successors.[2] The *langa mana*, or 'mediators', are a group of three widely respected elders selected by each Kunama village who deal specifically with conflict resolution. Local elders and traditional village courts have been able to maintain legitimacy and authority within the social structure because they are founded upon Kunama customary laws that all members of society have historically respected and abided by. It is predominantly the elders, or *langa mana*, of each Kunama village who adjudicate local issues and cases of domestic conflict within the village. Within the Kunama leadership structure there are also judges or mediators called the *sanga nena*. There is only one *sanga nena* at any time, traditionally belonging to the Suwaa clan. This is a hereditary rather than appointed position, and the person specifically hears more serious crimes such as homicide. Under customary law, the perpetrator's payment of a penalty (decided by the *sanga nena*) followed by a traditional reconciliation ceremony involving the families of both sides, is designed to restore justice and bring about forgiveness. Thus, traditional leaders among the Kunama are entrusted with the role of relationship building, of which the end goal is sustainable peace within the community.

The Tigrinya ('speakers of the Tigray language') people are the largest ethnic group in Eritrea, comprising approximately 50 per cent of the total population. They inhabit the densely settled central highlands (*kebessa*) of the country, particularly the districts of Hamasien, Seraye and Akkele-Guzai. The Tigrinya are distinguished primarily because of their language and Orthodox Christian culture, which the majority of the group practise, with the exception of the Djiberti, who are Muslim.

---

2   Kunama customary law document provided by Zoa Refugee Care, Ethiopia, May
     2008.

In contrast to the Kunama, the large Tigrinya ethnic group is not bound together as tightly by traditional structures. However, this is not to suggest that traditional actors have become irrelevant within the group. The Tigrinya people in Eritrea continue to uphold respect and trust in traditional institutions and leadership, which remain firmly in place. Due to the pervasiveness of Orthodox Christianity within Tigrinya culture, religious leaders in particular are relied upon to provide guidance and to mediate when conflict arises within the group. The process of conflict resolution initiated by a group of traditional elders involves a negotiation and mediation process that seeks to achieve forgiveness for the perpetrator and thus integrate him/her back into the community. Within Tigrinya law the issuing of a penalty is crucial to successfully attaining justice and therefore 'true forgiveness' in the resolution of conflicts (see Favali and Pateman 2003).

Modern structures established in Shimelba camp

Since fleeing Eritrea, both groups and their traditional leadership systems have come into contact with the modern structures set up in Shimelba camp. Established by the Ethiopian Administration for Refugee and Returnee Affairs (ARRA), both groups have a central refugee committee, which is in place to address the major issues facing refugees in the camp. The central committees have three levels at which issues can be addressed: the block level, the zonal level and the central committee level. At each level, refugees are elected as representatives by their group for their respective central committee. On occasion, the central committees of the groups may come together to deal with an issue that affects all groups in the camp, such as the distribution of non-food items (for example clothes and plastic sheets).

ARRA is responsible for physical and legal protection within the camp. With regards to responding to conflict, ARRA works closely with the Ethiopian Central Refugee Committee structure to address serious issues facing refugees. For example, in circumstances of conflict with a member of the local community, refugees may go to their block/village leaders to discuss a problem, who would then refer the case to ARRA and the Central Refugee Committee, who would work together in responding to the problem. The police based in the camp will investigate cases of violent conflict that have involved physical injury, including gender-based violence, rape and theft.

There are fundamental differences in approach to conflict resolution between these modern structures and the traditional processes as practised by the Kunama and Tigrinya in Eritrea. The modern leadership structures operating in the camp are situated within the framework of international legal norms and requirements, and thus follow processes which are essentially punitive in nature. The attainment of justice through punishment is perceived as an end in itself. Whilst justice is certainly imperative within traditional conflict resolution processes, it is perceived by elders and mediators to be only part of an overall process of reconciliation through forgiveness and relationship building between two conflicting parties.

The continuation of traditional systems in Shimelba refugee camp

The Kunama in particular have adapted the new administrative structures constructed by ARRA and UNHCR to incorporate traditional mechanisms inherent to Kunama social structures and customary law. For example, the Kunama have established a village system resembling that of Kunama society in Eritrea, and have replaced the modern block leaders with three 'village leaders' in each of the Kunama zones of the camp. The fact that Kunama *langa mana*s can also be elected as village leaders suggests that traditional actors have penetrated the newer structures. As a consequence, Kunama elders can help to mediate in conflicts within modern structures.

This kind of integration is also apparent within the Tigrinya structures but to a much lesser extent. The Tigrinya utilize block leaders of the UNHCR system at the local level to address issues, and thus have not integrated traditional mechanisms to the extent of the Kunama. However, traditional leaders among the Tigrinya continue to be integral within the Tigrinya community. Whilst religious leaders continue to play a significant role in addressing issues facing the Orthodox Christian and Muslim Tigrinya, it is primarily the elders' association that responds to conflict within the Tigrinya community as a whole. The Tigrinya elders' association has seventy members who represent all the Tigrinya in the camp. There are ten elders who deal specifically with negotiations, and two of these are also religious leaders.

When there is a problem, a fairly standard procedure is followed. Usually the victim or her/his relatives will go to the house of an elder to report a conflict. Utilizing the same processes for conflict resolution in Eritrea, a group of three or four elders will come together to mediate the conflict. They will discuss the issue together and then make a decision with regards to who is in the wrong and decide on a penalty to be paid to the victim. However, Tigrinya elders readily admit that respect for the penalty process, so inherent to traditional law, has decreased among the current generation of Tigrinya youth. Since youths account for such a large proportion of Tigrinya in the camp, it is apparent that this punishment mechanism is consequently used less frequently in Shimelba camp.

While one Tigrinya youth professed that he did not feel comfortable discussing issues with Tigrinya elders, the majority of Tigrinya youth claimed that, in contrast to the modern structures established in the camp, the elders' procedural structure is the shortest, most effective way of reaching true reconciliation. They also suggested that religious leaders were the most significant actors should a conflict involve refugees of the same religion.

Among the Kunama, domestic intra-group issues are very rarely dealt with through the block and central committee system, as most issues within the group can be solved at the community level by the *langa mana* or the *sanga nena*. It is only in extremely serious cases, such as those involving the local community or with other ethnic groups in the camp, that the Central Refugee Committee might be involved in conflict mediation. Even in a specific Kunama case referred to ARRA or the police by the *sanga nena*, traditional actors would continue to be involved in the mediation process as they would continue to assist the relatives on both sides to settle problems between the families in a peaceful manner.

It is apparent therefore that the central role of the *sanga nena* in the process of conflict resolution – that of rebuilding peaceful relations between two conflicting parties – retains importance within the refugee camp environment. In accordance with Kunama customary law, there continues to be a fixed penalty for both male and female victims of homicide: four bundles of white clothes, spears and knives for a male victim and household utensils for a female victim. Traditional reconciliation ceremonies also continue to be conducted by the *sanga nena* within the camp. For instance, after a penalty has been paid by a perpetrator's relatives, a forgiveness ceremony takes place in order to rebuild relations between both families. It was stated by members of the Kunama that this procedure continues to be successful at bringing about forgiveness and forging strong relations between two conflicting families in the camp.

It is also apparent that the traditional *langa mana* elders retain considerable respect and importance within the camp context as they continue to be primary actors in mediation processes at the community level. If a land dispute between Kunama neighbours arises, for example, it is reported to the mediators, with the assistance of witnesses, and the *langa mana* will decide who owns the land, and a penalty must be paid by the encroacher. As in Eritrea, the penalty under Kunama customary law may also depend upon the crime. For example, in the case of the theft of a goat, the penalty will be four goats, and the penalty to be paid for a stolen cow will be two cows. In a case of conflict involving a Kunama and the local community over grazing land, for example, the mediators may gather with the elders of the local community to seek a peaceful resolution.

It is further evident that there are significant differences between the two main refugee groups in terms of commitment to and reliance upon traditional leaders for resolving conflict within the camp. For example, it was clear that the Kunama tend to approach occupants of traditional roles prior to turning to modern institutions in the camp. The Kunama continue to be guided by their customary law rather than incorporating externally imposed international laws, whereas although the Tigrinya youth maintain confidence in traditional elders and religious leaders to respond to domestic issues in the first instance, they are less reliant upon traditional mechanisms for serious cases of conflict. The majority of those interviewed claimed that they would approach their block leaders or ARRA under such circumstances.

Am Nabak and Mile refugee camps, Wadi Fira, eastern Chad
Background
The civil war in Darfur, pitting the local Fur against the Sudanese government and the government-backed Janjaweed militia, began in 2003. Darfuri refugees began to seek sanctuary in Chad the same year. At the time of Sansculotte-Greenidge's fieldwork during 2005-6, a high level of violence was continuing. The humanitarian crises in Darfur and eastern Chad grabbed international headlines. However, this attention was not translated into action. Estimates of the human cost of this manmade disaster up to 2008 vary from 150,000 to 300,000 casualties. In addition to this, over 270,000 Darfuri had fled to Chad, while another 2.5 million were internally displaced.[3] What began as a rebellion in February 2003 evolved into what the UN described as the 'worst humanitarian crisis in the world today', when the Khartoum regime and allied militias (the Janjaweed) launched scorched-earth tactics. In the Chadian regions of Wadi Fira and Ouaddai, 270,000 Darfuri refugees have found sanctuary in twelve refugee camps, while another 20,000 to 30,000 try to survive along the border between Darfur and Chad with little or no assistance from the outside world. It is among the Darfuri refuges in Chad, and more specifically those in the camps of Mile and Am Nabak,that the research reported here was undertaken.

In many respects, the site of a refugee camp is of paramount importance in predicting the nature and indeed the severity of a whole host of problems that a camp and its population will encounter. Most of the refugees in Chad crossed the border from Darfur when their villages were attacked. Once in Chad, most refugees congregated a few kilometres from the border in makeshift 'spontaneous camps', where they remained for almost a year, until the first proper refugee camps were constructed. As a result, the Chadian camps are well planned and well managed compared to larger camps in Darfur, southern Sudan and Ethiopia. The exception is Am Nabak, which was still considered a 'spontaneous camp' or 'transit site'. The primary concern

---

3   Figures based on UNHCR estimates, June 2008.

in the selection of sites for permanent camps is the location of underground aquifers.

The camps of Mile and Am Nabak work excellently as comparative case studies due to their similarities: both are run by the NGO CARE; both are predominantly inhabited by BeRà; both have similar administrative structures.

The two camps also exhibit numerous differences: Mile is surrounded by the Tama ethnic group (a different group to that of the refugees) on whose territory the camp is located; Am Nabak is surrounded by the Kobe tribal section of the BeRà ethnic group (a group to which the refugees are closely related); Mile is an established camp, whereas Am Nabak is classified as a transit camp; the population of Mile is dominated by the Galla section of the BeRà; the population of Am Nabak is dominated by the Kobe and Kapka sections of the BeRà. It is these differences that make the two camps an ideal comparison in terms not only of basic administrative structures but also with regard to the role of traditional leaders in the camps.

Am Nabak was established in May 2004. Since the Darfuri rebels took to calling themselves Tora Bora – after the hills in southern Afghanistan where Osama Bin Laden was thought to be hiding in early 2004 – the camp has been known by the CARE staff who work there as Kandahar. Its inhabitants maintain contact with Darfuri rebels in the mountains to the west of the camp. A large number of BeRà rebels – both Darfuri and Chadian – use the camp as a rest spot and logistical hub. However, the camp came into existence some time before this as a spontaneous transit camp.

In most aspects, Am Nabak is very different from Mile and the other camps. Firstly, since the area of Am Nabak contained no underground aquifers, water to supply the camp's needs had to brought in from Gureada, some 43 kilometres away. As a result, the UNHCR and the implementing partners are constantly planning to move the camp to a better location, farther north. This move is opposed by both the refugees and the host community. Further, because the camp is not seen as a full-blown refugee camp like Mile, the budget allocated to it by UNHCR is much smaller, and there are no permanent structures, only tents. Due to security problems on the road between Am Nabak and the field office in Gureada, the management of the camps was moved from Gureada to Iriba (capital of the Dar Kobe) in 2006.

Mile refugee camp was opened on 6 May 2004 after the drawing up of a memorandum of understanding between the NGO CARE, the government of Chad and the UNHCR. The community service programme was initiated on 1 June 2004. In late 2006, when our research was undertaken, the camp had a population of 13,419. The camp is located in the region of Wadi Fira, in the department of Gureada, in the sub-prefecture of Gureada/Lima and the canton of Koursige, which has some thirty-one villages. The camp site was

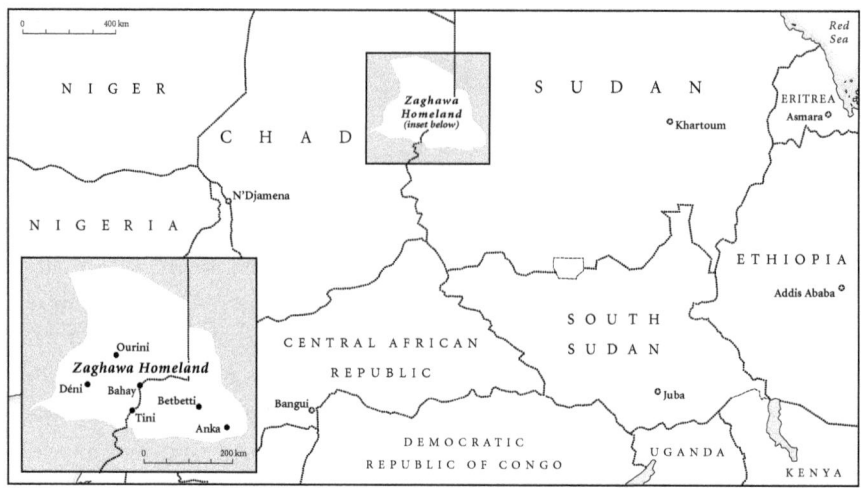

Figure 3.2   The Zaghawa homeland.

selected by the UNHCR simply because of the underground aquifer, which was located some 2 kilometres from the village of Mile. Mile is located some 22 kilometres north-west of Gureada. The entire department of Gureada is home to the Tama ethnic group, making Mile a Darfuri enclave in the heart of Tama territory.

The majority of the camp's residents belong to the BeRà ethnic group, more common known as the Zaghawa. They are followed in number by members of the Tama and Fur ethnic groups. While the Fur are also refugees from Darfur, the Tama are actually Chadian citizens of Tama origin moonlighting as Darfuri refugees to gain access to UNHCR food aid and social programmes. They are, nonetheless, counted as refugees and live, more or less permanently, in the camp alongside more genuinely displaced persons.

Traditional leadership in Chad and Darfur

Like the Eritrean refugees in Ethiopia, the inhabitants of Mile have two systems available to them for the resolution of conflicts: first, the structures and institutions established by the UNHCR; and second, a traditional mechanism, known in Darfur as *uddiya*, which involves the intervention of elders known as *ajaweed* (sing *ajwadi*). However, it is here that the similarity between the two camps ends. Whereas in the Eritrean case a designated social and political space was created for traditional leaders, no so such space was created in Mile. Thus, the traditional system has had to run in parallel to, and in most cases unbeknownst to, the official camp structures.

The BeRà are divided into seventeen regional groupings, each headed by a paramount ruler. These rulers are known by a host of different names depending on the historical origin of the position and ruling family. Thus, Dar Kobe, with its capital in Hiri-Ba (known in Arabic as Iriba), the Bediyat and the Kapka of Tundebey all have sultans (Arabic for 'authority'). Dar Galla on the other hand is ruled by a *shartai* (a corruption of the Daju term *chorte*, which has the double meaning of 'drum' and 'chief'), while Dar Tuer, Unai, Sueni, Furnung and Anka all have *malik*s (Arabic for 'king') and Dar Ila Diggin is ruled by a *bazi* (derived from the Arabic rendering of the Turkish term *pasha*, *basha*). Below the level of regional groupings are tribes, known as Be A Ah.

In Darfur, the *mandub* occupies a position below the level of paramount ruler. The *mandub* is best described as the agent of the paramount ruler, with extensive powers and jurisdiction over several tribes. He is followed by the *omda*, a term introduced to Darfur by the Turkish overlords of Egypt and Sudan. Each Be A Ah or tribe is headed by an *omda*, the *airr ke*.

Be, or 'branches', are not headed by a particular leader since they may be present in more than one area. Villages or groups of villages are, rather, headed by a *sheikh*, who is elected from among the inhabitants of a village. In many instances this vote simply serves to confirm an already established line of succession, in which a son takes over from his father. In other cases however, there are heated contests between two or more candidates for the post of *sheikh*.

All *sheikh*s follow similar rules in relation to taxation. A *sheikh* keeps a register of taxable persons in his village, and once or twice a year he collects taxes, in the form of currency or produce. *Sheikhs* are entitled to keep 20 per cent of this revenue as their own, and the rest must be given to his superior, the *omda* in Dar Zaghawa. The *omda* receives taxes from all his subordinate *sheikh*s. Before passing this up to his own superior he will be allowed to keep 10 per cent for himself. The rest is then passed on to the *shartai*, in the case of Dar Galla, or the sultan in the case of Dar Kobe and so on. At this, the highest level of the system, the paramount rulers can take 5 per cent of the tax revenue as their own and the rest is passed on to a government official, usually the *mahafis* (provincial head) or *wali* (state governor) in Darfur. In Chad this system of leadership is known as *ndhim al-hilla*, or the village system, while in Darfur it is known as *idara ahalia*, or native administration.

In eastern Chad, the Tama live south of the BeRà. Sedentary farmers, the Tama are the traditional rivals of the BeRà, with whom they compete for pasture, farmland and more recently political power. It should be noted that, due to a long history of civil strife, the system of tax collection by *sheikhs* is almost non-existent in Chad. In some areas there has been no real taxation via *Ndhim al-Hilla* for at least forty years. However, another key role of the *sheikh* is in dealing with land claims and divorce proceedings. They are in a sense the first port of call in the village when there is a dispute of any kind,

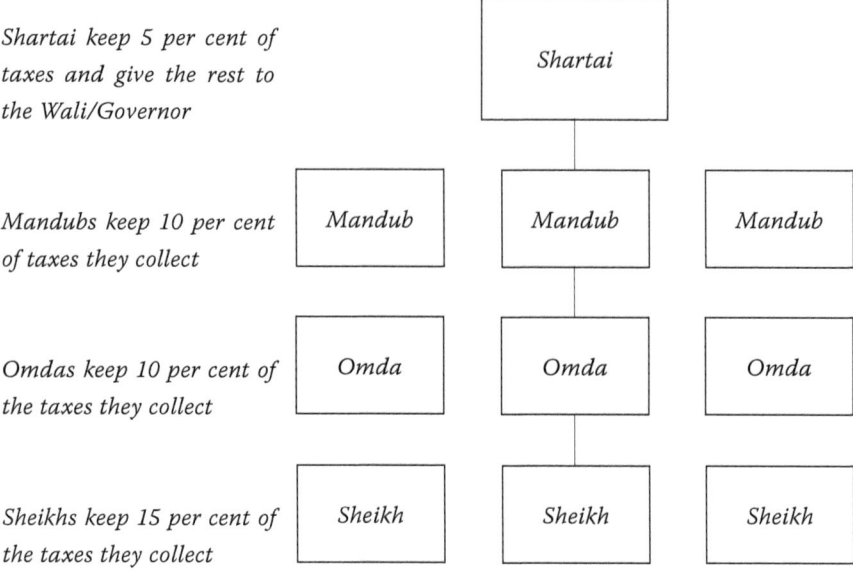

Shartai keep 5 per cent of taxes and give the rest to the Wali/Governor

Mandubs keep 10 per cent of taxes they collect

Omdas keep 10 per cent of the taxes they collect

Sheikhs keep 15 per cent of the taxes they collect

Figure 3.3   Traditional authority structure in Darfur and neighbouring Chad.

and they are custodians of customary law and key figures in conflict resolution and mediation. In Darfur and among Darfuri refugees, mediation is known as *Juddiya*.

For *Juddiya* (traditional dispute resolution) to take place, the *ajawid* must be accepted by all conflicting parties. This acceptance is based on their reputation as being wise and knowledgeable about tradition. Traditionally, *Juddiya* ends when a settlement of some sort is reached; this settlement need not be all encompassing, but should re-establish some sort of harmony through the payment of compensation. To achieve this, the rhetorical skills of the *ajawid* – appealing to the wisdom of the parties and to their honour – are important, but the process is also political because pressure is put on the parties to agree.

In Darfur, *ajawid* are, by traditional practice, elderly people who are versed in communal customs and customary laws. They are not, however, neutral in the Western sense of the term. Their practice is to exert pressure on the party resisting a settlement until they accept the recommendations the *ajawid* has decided on (Mohamed and Badri 2005). In this way *ajawid* act as facilitators, mediators and arbitrators, depending on what is needed. According to Ali Ali-Dinar, a scholar who is himself from the lineage of the sultans of the Fur, the *ajawid* form part of a system for the regulation of group land rights and ethnic boundaries (Ali-Dinar 2004a, 2004b, 2004c).

Modern structures established in Am Nabak and Mile refugee camps

Mile refugee camp is managed by CARE Canada on behalf of the UNHCR. The CARE administration consists of forty-five staff members based in Gureada (37 kilometres away), who make trips to the camp every weekday from mid-morning to mid-afternoon, if the security situation allows. Mile's administration is based on a template used by the UNHCR in nearly all refugee and internally displaced people camps. Thus, Mile is divided into ten zones, each with five blocks of approximately eighty tents or 350 inhabitants. Mile is a trilingual camp, with Arabic and BeRà Ah being used by the refugees and French being the preferred language of the camp staff. As a result, the names associated with the camp are often duplicated in French and Arabic. Thus, each zone is headed by a *chef de zone* or *sheikh al-zone*; and each block by a *chef de block* or *sheikh al-harr.*

Each *chef de zone* is selected from among the various *chefs de block*. The camp also has a *comité principal* or *majlis al-sheyuk*, which has sixteen members: ten *chefs de zone* or *sheikhs al-zone*, and six others, three of whom are women. Though tasked with the management of the camp, they simply rubber-stamp decisions already take by either the Chadian state's refugee agency, the Commission Nationale d'Accueil et de Réinsertion des Réfugiés (CNAR), CARE or the UNHCR.

Most of Mile's inhabitants, who are from at least fifty different villages in Darfur, arrived chaotically over a long period of time. As a result, many do not know if their *omda* or *sheikh* is present in the camp. Each of these numerous villages may have had a *sheikh* of their own, but the inclusion of close to fifty traditional leaders in the management of the camp is not feasible.

Like Mile, Am Nabak is divided into ten zones, each with four blocks. However, superimposed on this block system are four clusters, which represent the home villages of the refugees. The refugees of Am Nabak, unlike their counterparts in Mile, are from the Kobe regional grouping of the BeRà. Kobe territory is located mainly in Chad, but it does extend into Darfur, where there are only a handful of Kobe villages, the largest being Tine. Links across the porous border are strong among the Kobe, and as a result when the Darfur conflict began the inhabitants of the border villages of Tine, Girgira, Habila and Tundebay were invited to ride out the conflict with their kin and neighbours in Am Nabak.

The fact that many Darfuri Kobe had very close kin in Am Nabak, and that annual migration routes brought the herders of Am Nabak to the Wadi Sheadi in Darfur, meant many of the inhabitants of Am Nabak knew the refugees personally, and thus were willing to have them take up residence in their village. The refugees arrived with their *Sheikhs* and *Omdas*, and as a result there are interesting differences between the camps, both in terms of the CARE administration in the camp and the role of traditional leaders.

The continuation of traditional systems in Am Nabak and Mile refugee camps

An interesting feature of Am Nabak is that Tine, Habilah, Tundebey and Girgira represent the four main Kobe and Kapka population centres in Darfur. When their satellites are included they represent the entire Kobe and Kapka population of Darfur, roughly half of whom now reside in Am Nabak refugee camp. Also present in the camp are the endogenous rulers of these four villages. Thus, the brother of the current sultan of Tine (heir to the sultanate), along with the sultan of Tundebey, Hassan Bargo, the *Sheikh* of Habilah and the *Amir* of Girgira, Abdul Malik Bahar, and a number of their subordinates are all present.

The forced displacement of entire villages and their leadership has had an interesting impact on the leadership structure of not only the refugees but also their Chadian Kobe hosts. It has strengthened links between certain Darfuri BeRà and Chadian members of the same ethnic community. The Kobe and Kapka endogenous leaders of Am Nabak have been able to form very close links with the royal family of Hiri-Ba (Iriba). Though they will never admit it, they have in some ways become attached to the sultan of Hiri-Ba as his clients. The sultan now acts as an arbitrator when the four leaders cannot come to an agreement, much to the dismay of high ranking Darfuri leaders. The sultan also acts as a mediator when there are problems between refugees and locals, a rarity in Am Nabak, but a serious problem in other refugee camps such as Mile, Iridimi and Bahai. Thus, the process of adaptation to outside political forces continues.

In Mile, however, the *sheikh*s who are present are given few roles in the CARE-run administration. The *mahkama*, or court, is the one exception. The *mahkama* forms the basis of the legal system of the camp. The court itself grew out of the CARE-created *Comité des Sages/Majlis al-Ugala'a* (Council of the Wise). This committee is organized by zone, with each zone having a three-member committee. Each committee then selects one member to represent them on the camp-wide *majlis al-ugala'a*.

The CARE-created *Majlis al-Ugala'a* was mired in problems from the very beginning. Many of the *sheyuk al zonat* (*chefs de zone*) put themselves up for positions on the *majlis* though few had legal or customary law experience; others simply placed their close friends on the court. Soon the committee began to seek the help of the 'old [traditional] *Sheikhs*', many of whom had decades of customary legal experience. It was at this time that Yousuff Terayo

Nour, an expert in Islamic jurisprudence and the head of the Kornoi law court (prior to the conflict), was also invited to sit on the committee.

After an initially shaky alliance between the *Mahkama* and *Ugala'a*, two separate entities emerged. The *Majlis al-Ugalla* was used almost exclusively for intra-zonal problems and disputes. Meanwhile, the *Mahkama* became the legal system of the camp, in the same way that a *Mahkama* or court is the legal system of a village or group of villages in Darfur. Here cases are dealt with by the *sheikh*s, with fines and blood-money rulings being handed out, in a similar fashion to the *sanga nena* of the Kunama, one of the Eritrean case studies discussed above.

It appears that the refugees prefer to have their problems dealt with by an *Omda* or *Sheikh* from their section of the BeRà ethnic group. If this is not possible, they will approach a *Sheikh* with whom they are familiar. There is a long-established tradition among the Darfuri BeRà of having a *Sheikh*, or more frequently an *Omda*, from one's section travel to one's area of residence to deal with communal problems. It would appear that even long-term displacement has not stopped this tradition.

A picture of dual systems of administration and two avenues for conflict resolution thus emerges. At many points there appear to be two complementary systems of administration. There is a well-defined, well-oiled UNHCR/CARE administration present in the camps. But there is also a well-defined, though not so well-oiled, shadow administration.

In this way all refugees have a choice between the UNHCR/CARE established *Sheikh*s, whom they call *Nasara Sheikh*s or 'white-people sheikhs', and the *Sheikh*s from Darfur known as 'old' *Sheikh*s. Small domestic cases are handled by individual *Sheikh*s from either administrative system. Most refugees, however, seem to have a preference for larger or more persistent problems to be dealt with by the *Mahkama*, the CARE-established court.

Conclusion: examining the resilience of traditional systems

Around the world, millions of refugees struggle to eke out a living in squalid camps and urban communities in some of the most insecure and poverty-ridden parts of the world. For most of these individuals, displacement is looking more like a lifelong affair. In fact, the vast majority of the world's current refugees have been in exile for close to a decade, rather than the past norm of a few years (Loescher *et al.* 2008). Such situations continue to constitute a growing challenge for the international refugee protection regime and the international community as the long-term impacts of these displacements are little understood. States, it can be argued, create refugees by failing to protect (or by persecuting) their citizens; however, the international community perpetuates these situations by not taking adequate steps to deter such actions or to protect refugees' right of return when they occur.

The displacement of people as a result of war, insecurity and persecution has become one of the hallmarks of the Horn of Africa. While official responses to such involuntary movements remain significant, changing policy priorities and declining state capacity mean a growing number of people seek assistance and protection outside official mechanisms. As the primary responses to displacement shift from disaster management to the social sphere, the actions and attitudes of host populations and refugees have become increasingly important, while the significance of internationally enshrined rights and humanitarian principles has declined.

Currently, a widening gap has been developing between the needs of displaced people and official responses. It is somewhat ironic that this gap has developed at precisely the same time that conflicts have become more complex in the region. The result is that displaced communities are forced to come up with their own solutions to the problems confronting them. In the majority of cases of displacement in the Horn, a dual approach has been adopted, with displaced peoples utilizing assistance from external actors to supplement their own strategies for survival. One such example is conflict resolution among Darfuri and Eritrean refugees.

The resilience of each group's traditional system of dispute resolution in the environment of displacement can be understood firstly as a result of the continued effectiveness of traditional mechanisms in practice, and secondly on how their strength is perceived by their respective communities. Traditional forms of leadership evidently have most use and greatest effectiveness in resolving conflicts between members of the same ethnic group within a camp. Many refugees claimed that this effectiveness is attributable to the fact that such traditional systems are grounded in the cultural norms and values of their society, which provides the basis upon which traditional leaders are able to assist in rebuilding broken relationships between members of their communities. The bottom-up approach of traditional systems to conflict resolution also instigates participatory practices which give communities a sense of ownership over the resolution process that is fundamental to the building of sustainable peace.

In many parts of the continent, where the presence, capacity and impact of the state's governing institutions and actors is low, endogenous leadership institutions form the only legitimate authority. Although a significant proportion of endogenous African institutions were destroyed by the colonial enterprise, the surviving institutions were remoulded and adapted to suit the needs of the colonial and later postcolonial authorities. Thus, they continue to exist and participate in public affairs at local, regional and state levels, either separately or as members of administrations, parliaments or governments. As governments have tried to respond to demands for services with limited resources, they have come to rely upon endogenous authorities as a resource for communicating with and mobilizing populations (de Sousa Santos 2006; Englebert 2002; Oomen 2002:63; West and Kloeck-Jenson 1999).

Endogenous leaders may also be valued because they provide a sense of continuity and stability in an era of great change. Williams suggests that they can serve as intermediaries to 'ensure that change occurs in an orderly and familiar way' (Williams 2004:121). Yet at the same time, chiefs have also displayed impressive flexibility, adapting to meet the needs of the day in an effort to preserve or enhance their position within local communities.

Traditional mediation in Africa is characterized by the implicit involvement of the whole society in reconciliation. The wider community itself becomes the repository within which conflict resolution was performed and knowledge of practices stored, with mediators (usually male elders) representing the norms and values of the society, especially on moral issues. Ali Mazrui (1994:41–2) argues that the involvement of respected elders in conflict resolution is the defining feature of mediation on the African continent. Such elders are expected to advocate a settlement that would accord with commonly accepted principles of justice in terms of custom, virtue and fairness, and reflect community judgement about appropriate behaviour. Thus, to break or renege on a settlement was to defy the moral order of the society, not just the mediators. Mazuri's ideas are based on a number of assumptions and prerequisites that are often contested, even in the most stable societies.

As Jannie Malan points out:

> A typical immediate goal is to reach an agreement which includes more
> than merely solving the problem or rectifying the injustice. What is
> specifically aimed at in the search for durable peace is genuine reconciliation
> and, where necessary, restitution and rehabilitation.
>
> (Malan 1997:24)

This search for a durable peace means that the key focus of traditional mediation was the reconciling of protagonists with each other, rather than on establishing right and wrong. Thus, punishment was not aimed at retaliation, but rather at restoring equilibrium, usually through the mechanisms of restitution, apology and reconciliation. There was emphasis on justice and fairness, rather than crime and punishment.

Whilst it is clear that, as yet, traditional systems are most successful when resolving intra-ethnic conflicts, traditional mechanisms also have the potential to be a powerful relationship-building tool across communities. The reason for this is that traditional elders are largely respected by the majority of people from all ethnic groups, and certain traditional beliefs and methods transcend ethnic divides, namely where they are concerned with fostering a restitution of the status quo to achieve true reconciliation. Thus, traditional mechanisms hold the capacity to build solidarity and inter-cultural understanding between ethnic groups within a camp and the host community.

Traditional forms of conflict mediation and resolution, like traditional systems of administration, have proved to be remarkably durable. In spite of their shortcomings, traditional courts have a major advantage in comparison to state courts since their processes are substantially informal and less intimidating, with the people who utilize these courts being more at ease in an environment that is not forbidding. Keesing describes the process of settling cases out of court as 'informal litigation', which underlines the need to look for more subtle legal processes side by side with more formal legal systems (Keesing 1981:322). This is true of the *Ajawid* and *Langa Mana*, who preside over traditional courts and are generally charismatic and familiar with the people that use these courts, and are revered to an extent that judges are not. The role of the members of the *Mahkama*, established by the aid agency, is not to hand out harsh punishments that deter Mile's residents from transgressing the law, as would be the case in a Western court. Rather, it is the role of the court members to act as representatives, facilitators, mediators and arbitrators where necessary.

The continued resilience of traditional leadership systems within the refugee camps analysed here is also dependent upon each community's perceptions of these systems. It is evident that the reliance of youth upon them is largely rooted in the strength of the socialization processes within their respective communities. For example, in the Kunama community, where the role and importance of traditional leaders is emphasized from an early age, reliance and trust in traditional leaders is also high, despite the refugee context. The same can be said of the Darfuri refugees who continue to seek out their old *sheikh*s, who are seen as repositories of knowledge and able to bring about real social cohesion through conflict resolution. The fact that traditional mechanisms are less integrated into Tigrinya structures is attributable to a decline in their prominence prior to displacement. Many Tigrinya youths, who make up the majority of the Tigrinya inhabiting Shimelba camp, had already become detached from their traditional cultural roots in Eritrea, having moved to Asmara in search of a modern education.

The perceived strength of traditional systems among displaced people within Shimelba, Am Nabak and Mile refugee camps can also be attributed to the apparent weaknesses of the newer institutions established in the camp. In overlooking the traditional values and cultural norms which are inherent in social relations both within and between the BeRà, Kunama and Tigrinya, newer mechanisms for conflict resolution overlook the breakdown of relationships, which ultimately leads to violent conflict. Thus, the capacity of these modern institutions is limited to short-term conflict resolution because they do not seek to rebuild the relationships that are required to achieve long-term sustainable peace. There is an apparent absence of respect and trust in the newer structures amongst the majority of refugees interviewed.

Despite having sustained their relevance it was observed during our research that traditional leadership positions are considerably challenged and compromised within the camp environment. Many refugees throughout the camps implied that non-traditional actors can be the most appropriate to respond to conflicts specific to the camp environment, such as the distribution of food rations and pass permits. Although the majority of refugees interviewed in both Chad and Ethiopia feel that traditional leaders are the most respected forms of authority, they stressed that ending resource-based conflicts requires a solution at higher levels than that of grassroots-level conflict resolution.

Traditional conflict resolution processes can also become compromised within the displacement context. For example, although the elders in the camps and communities frequently convene to resolve conflicts, the refugees recognize that the host community will not accept the punishment and compensation levels that the refugee elders request. Therefore punishment tends to be biased to take account of the sensibilities of host communities, and the refugees, in order to maintain peace, accept less harsh penalties and less generous compensation levels than those deemed fair under traditional law or host state law.

It is evident that the situation of displacement experienced by refugees in both Chad and Ethiopia continues to have a significant impact upon how the relevance of traditional leadership systems is perceived by their communities. In turn, the resilience of traditional mechanisms in the long term is dependent upon if and how they adapt to respond to conflicts specific to the displacement context.

Acknowledgements

Sansculotte-Greenidge's research in Ethiopia was undertaken in 2008, while research in Chad was conducted between 2005 and 2006. The authors would like to express their deep gratitude to those who made this work possible: the Royal Anthropological Institute, the Emslie Horniman Anthropological Scholarship Fund, the Durham University Graduate School, CARE Chad, the UN University of Peace (UPEACE) in Addis Ababa and ZOA Refugee Care. In addition, thanks also go out to those who helped with their advice and critiques. Finally, this work is dedicated to Shirley Case, a CARE Chad staff member and friend who was killed in Afghanistan on 13 August 2008 while working for the IRC.

References

Ali-Dinar, A.B. 2004a. 'Between Naivasha and Abéché: the systematic destruction of Darfur': www.sudanarchive.net/cgi-bin/sudan?a=pdfandd=Dslpd342anddl=1 (accessed 1 October 2007).

——— 2004b. 'Fostering inclusion? Analysis of the IGAD negotiations'. Unpublished paper: fletcher.tufts.edu/sudanconference2004/outcomes/AliDinar%20 Thurs.pdf (accessed 1 October 2007).

——— 2004c. 'Why Khartoum wants a war in Darfur', *Sudan Tribune* (30 July): www.sudantribune.com/article.php3?id_article=4330 (accessed 1 October 2007).

Becker, E. and Mitchell, C. 1991. 'Chronology of conflict resolution initiatives in Sudan'. Fairfax, VA: Institute for Conflict Analysis and Resolution, George Mason University.

Burton, J. 1990. *Conflict: Resolution and Prevention*. Basingstoke: Macmillan.

De Silva, K., and Samarasinghe, S. (eds). 1993. *Peace Accords and Ethnic Conflict*. London: Pinter Publishing.

De Sousa Santos, B. 2006. 'The heterogeneous state and legal pluralism in Mozambique', *Law and Society Review* 40(1):39–76.

England, K.M. 2008. The cultural adjustment and mental health of African refugees in the United States: the case of the Kunama from Eritrea'. Thesis. Boston: Boston College: dissertations.bc.edu/ashonors/200649 (accessed 12 July 2008).

Englebert, P. 2002. 'Born-again Buganda or the limits of traditional resurgence in Africa', *Journal of Modern African Studies* 40(3):345–68.

Favali, L. and Pateman, R. 2003. *Blood, Land and Sex: Legal and Political Pluralism in Eritrea*. Indiana: Indiana University Press.

Keesing, R.M. 1981. *Cultural Anthropology: A Contemporary Perspective*. New York: Holt, Rinehart and Winston.

Loescher, G., Milner, J., Newman, E. and Troeller, G. (eds). 2008. *Protracted Refugee Situations: Political, Human Rights and Security Implications*. Tokyo: United Nations University Press.

Malan, J. 1997. *Conflict Resolution: Wisdom from Africa*. Durban: ACCORD.

Mazrui, A. 1994. 'Africa: in search of self-pacification', *Africa Affairs* 93:39–42.

Misago, J.P. and Landau, L. 2005. 'Responses to displacement in Africa: the irrelevance of best practice', *Conflict Trends* 3:4–8.

Mohamed, A.A. and Badri, B.Y. 2005. *Inter-Communal Conflict in Sudan: Causes, Resolution Mechanisms and Transformation. A Case Study of the Darfur Region*. Omdurman/The Hague. Afhad University for Women/Novib.

Oomen, B. 2002. '"Walking in the middle of the road": people's perspectives on the legitimacy of traditional leadership in Sekhukhune, South Africa'. Paper presented at the seminar 'Popular perspectives on traditional authority in South Africa', African Studies Centre, Leiden, 17 January.

Ranard, D.A. 2007. 'The Kunama'. Cultural Reorientation Resource Center Refugee Backgrounder No. 3: www.culturalorientation.net/.../ CAL+Backgrounder+03+-+The+Kunama+FINAL.pdf (accessed 18 October 2018).

UNFPA 2007. *Gender Based Violence Report: 2007*: www.unfpa.org (accessed 9 May 2019).

UNHCR 2008. *Briefing Kit: Eritrean Refugee Camp.* Provided by UNHCR Shire Sub-Office, 13 May, 2008.

West, H.G. and Kloeck-Jenson, S. 1999. 'Betwixt and between: traditional authority and democratic decentralization in post-war Mozambique', *African Affairs* 98(393):455–84.

Williams, J.M. 2004. 'Leading from behind: democratic consolidation and the chieftaincy in South Africa', *Journal of Modern African Studies* 42(1):113–36.

Woodhouse, T. and Ramsbotham, O. (eds). 2000. *Peacekeeping and Conflict Resolution.* London: Frank Cass Publishing.

4

Changing patterns of religion and ritual in a Vasava Bhil community impacted by involuntary resettlement

ROXANNE HAKIM

The Vasava Bhils of Makhadkhada, an isolated village on the banks of the River Narmada in the Satpura Hills of Gujarat, India, were displaced by the controversial Sardar Sarovar (Narmada) Dam Project (Baviskar 1995a, 1995b). Through long-term fieldwork both prior to and following displacement, my research aims to document and understand the impact that resettlement has had on the community's economy, religion and social relations. In 1994, the six hamlets of Makhadkhada were resettled in the populated plains of south Gujarat, a distance of about 90 kilometres from Makhadkhada. Within just a year of resettlement there was significant influence by the plains communities. The house and village structure of the Vasavas had changed, along with dress, language, economy and social behaviour (see also Hakim 1996, 1997).

The analysis focuses on changes in ritual and religion, and their impact on constructions of Vasava identity as defined within the community, as well as by non-Vasavas.

Religion as a marker of 'self' and 'other'

Hill Vasavas emphasize their self-identity and the distinction between themselves and plains communities in terms of their distinctive and self-sufficient production patterns. However, plains communities highlight consumption patterns (food, dress) and religious behaviour when differentiating themselves and stating their 'superiority' over hill tribes like the Vasavas (Hakim 2000a, 2000b, 2000c). Changes in production patterns following resettlement in the plains are eroding the self-sufficiency of the hill Vasavas. Plains agriculture requires a mix of food and cash crops, a good knowledge of market prices and the ability to handle middlemen. Obligatory kin-based labour networks have broken down and the dependence on natural resources is no longer possible. As a result, the resettled community's newly emerging production patterns increasingly resemble those of other plains communities and can no longer serve as a distinctive marker of Vasava identity.

The absorption of some aspects of plains religion and ritual is recognized as important to gain the trust of host communities. However, the Vasavas do not see this as undermining their identity as hill Vasavas; an identity that continues to be associated with their creation myths and the celebration of the four annual rituals. Their adoption of some of the Hindu rituals and practices are superficial and sporadic, done more to 'fit in' when the host community is around, rather than a real deep questioning of their own beliefs. For the Vasava, the integration of some of these plains rituals does not mean that they are eroding or being disloyal to any fixed notion of their 'true' Vasava identity. The community believe that people must constantly negotiate and interact with the sphere of the supernatural, rather than accept it, which is the underlying norm in mainstream Hinduism (see also Bhagvat 1968). The Vasavas are open to adopting some of the practices of their host community, as they know it will demonstrate their willingness to adopt to a new way of life, thereby helping forge good economic and social relationships with their hosts.

Religious behaviour as a 'way of life': linking the supernatural to social morality

Vasava cosmology consists of a unique pantheon of gods. Appeasing them (and indirectly the forces of nature) takes place through rituals where the *badvo* (powerful shaman) cajoles a god into granting a wish or holding back her/his wrath. The community has no religious philosophy in the sense of a code of moral conduct decreed the 'right one' by myth, god/s or prophets as is the case of most major religions. In fact, moral conduct implicit in everyday actions is derived from social rather than religious custom, and references to the supernatural in most Vasava people's daily activities are minimal. The realm of the supernatural is closely tied up with what are viewed as 'natural' activities. Weather, birth and death are regarded as completely within the control of the pantheon of gods and goddesses; other spheres such as crop yields and illness are regarded as being partly controlled by the supernatural, and some human control over these areas is acknowledged. Daily activities such as dietary habits, dress, social hierarchy and social relationships are not viewed as reflective of 'morality', and are regarded as outside the sphere of the supernatural or any related philosophies and rituals.

In contrast, Hinduism as practised in the plains host communities associates a large number of daily activities and social relationships with religious piety and sanctions. Hence, whether you consume meat and alcohol, go to the house of a lower or higher caste, or marry outside your clan, and how one dresses, all go to indicate how pious, good or bad a Hindu you are, which in turn has bearing on your afterlife. There is hence social pressure on the resettled community to adapt to the eating habits, dress code and rituals (such as marriage) of the host communities, all of which are loosely tied up within the structure of religion as indicators of social and moral hierarchy. Attempts to 'Hinduize' the hill Vasavas are often viewed by host groups as their 'duty', and often take on a moralistic tone of 'improving the lot of the ignorant Vasava'. Social (and caste) hierarchy in the plains is linked to moral 'piety' and is influenced by variables such as food habits, the practice of marriage and other customs, religious practices and the behaviour of women. These daily activities, which in the hills are devoid of moralistic undertones, and seen merely as social relationships, are given a deeper significance and moral 'value' amongst host communities (especially the higher caste groups) in the plains of south Gujarat.

The 'potential' Hindu

The Vasavas of the Satpura Hills, like other relatively isolated Adivasi groups, are often referred to, in documentation and common parlance, as 'backward Hindus' (Ghurye 1963) or 'potential Hindus' who need to be 'purified' (Padel 1992:2).[1] However, there appears to be a contradiction in their inclusion in the Hindu grouping. Whilst most plains communities are quick to stress the 'primitiveness' of the hill tribes and to emphasize that they are different from them in every way (including religious practices), they will simultaneously agree that hill Vasavas are in fact Hindus, and should aspire to become 'proper' Hindus like themselves. In popular terms this usually means giving up meat and alcohol, stressing hygiene, worshipping in temples, hanging pictures of the Hindu pantheon in one's hut and being married by a Brahmin. The hill Vasavas in Makhadkhada never referred to themselves as Hindus, and they did not worship, nor were familiar with even the most popular deities of the Hindu pantheon such as Brahma, Shiva and Vishnu. However, one can trace elements of Hindu ritual within Vasava culture. The use of coconuts in rituals, the *lingam*-shaped stones that are symbols of the village pantheon of gods, and the strong belief in the history of regional deities such as Dev Mogra that is shared by other Hinduized plains groups are indicators of cultural exchange between Vasava and Hindu groups. The extent to which these traits have

---

1   Please note that explanations of certain key vernacular terms in what follows are included in a glossary following the main text.

been borrowed from outside or developed within the culture is difficult to determine.

Adivasi groups have always lived on the margins of dominant society; the fuzziness of the margins allowing them simultaneously to be a part of it and retain a strong distinctiveness. To try and determine whether hill Vasavas in Makhadkhada are really Hindus would be an irrelevant and futile exercise. The challenge lies in trying to understand the dynamics of the complexity of their link with the supernatural, and the manner in which this expresses itself in their daily lives.

Gods and goddesses: Vasava identity and the implications of resettlement

Labelled as 'stone worshippers' and 'pagans' by plains communities, the Vasavas of the Satpura Hills cannot be regarded as such. The community believes in the existence of Bhagwan or Malik (a supernatural being), who is considered the supreme power and who controls all the *devs*. Thus it would be wrong to refer to them as polytheistic. A *badvo* explained to me the relationship between Bhagwan and the *devs* as follows:

> *Bhagwan* is all powerful. He is the same for all people. The four winds,
> the stones, the *devs* are in fact all part of the same thing we call Bhagwan.
> Bhagwan works through different means, which we call *devs*. Each one
> has a name and an area that they function within such as Gam no darvajo
> *dev* (the god of the doors of the village), Raja Phanta (the god who controls
> the world of the living) and so on. But in essence they are all Bhagwan.
> Bhagwan, humans, trees, earth, *devs* were all created by a *mata* (mother
> goddess) called Vadi Ya ('Big Mother').

The Vasavas' relation with the world is based on the assumption that Bhagwan and the *devs* control most phenomena (natural and man-made), and can be appealed to, to exercise power over the domain controlled by that *dev*. Most of the communication with gods and goddesses is in the form of propitiations to ask for favours or offerings in appreciation of favours received. These are the institution of *manta* and *poonja*. The former is performed on behalf of an individual, and the latter is aimed at the larger social unit. Village and household-level *poonjas* are performed on a yearly cycle, and are prescribed in their frequency, unlike the individual-focused *mantas*, which take place as and when the need arises (for example, when an individual falls sick or is thought to be bewitched).

The pantheon of *devs* can be roughly divided into three categories. Firstly, those *devs* who are physically represented and territorially inalienable.

Secondly, those who are physically represented but not territorially linked. Thirdly, those who have no physical representation and no territorial link. These categories became very important with regard to the community's proposed resettlement. Since resettlement meant a physical move and access to the submerged village was cut off, each category of *dev*s was impacted in different waysa. The *dev*s falling into the first category – physically represented and territorially inalienable – are somewhat problematic in the context of resettlement. These included some of the mountains surrounding Makhadkhada, which were submerged in the reservoir. Vasavas identify strongly with being 'mountain people', which gives them a different way of life from those living in the plains. The move from the hills to the plains is an important factor in restructuring Vasava identity as both they and the plains peoples have always linked the community's identity to the hills. Vasava identity as hill people (*dungris*) is evident in the emphasis they place on self-sufficiency in production and consumption. It is the geographical location of the hills that both enables and necessitates this self-sufficiency.

The Vasavas' strong association with the hills is very evident in the respect and supernatural status that they attribute to them. Most of the more prominent mountains have a name and they are all referred to as *dev*s. From one hamlet in Makhadkhada, a *bhua* (shaman) pointed out over twenty mountains that were regarded as *dev*s. All Vasava show respect and great love for the mountains, and are familiar with the most well known of them, such as the mountains of Hirazu Baba (Father Hirazu), Pavu and Phenai. Although the mountain *dev*s have a fixed physical form, their sphere of influence is not restricted to their physical location and their help can be invoked anywhere, be it Makhadkhada or the resettlement sites. Vinya Lekji, another *bhua*, explained:

> The government may submerge a mountain with this dam, but that does not
> imply that the *dev* will no longer function. And besides, if it comes to that,
> the *dev*s can surely live below the water. We will continue to respect them
> and believe in them as we do now. I believe we will continue our ways in the
> new land.

The term 'stone worshippers' used by outsiders and casual observers when referring to the hill Vasavas has arisen from the village pantheon of *dev*s who are represented by *lingam*-shaped stones placed in a kind of sacred grove within each village. However, the hill Vasavas never associate the stones with Lord Shiva. The stones they use are naturally shaped by river water and found in river beds. Unlike the Shiva *lingam*, which are of black stone, these are grey in colour, containing pink streaks. The pantheon in Makhadkhada consisted of the village god Rojan *dev* and his helpers. Although the power of the village god is territorially linked to the boundaries of the village, and to that extent is territorially inalienable, the stone representations are moveable to the extent that they are simply viewed as a 'representation' of the *dev*.

The Vasavas responded to the issue of resettling the stone representations in what would appear to be an extremely logical manner. Since Rojan has his sphere of influence only in Makhadkhada, he will be of no use in the new land. They will no longer need to propitiate him, but will instead take on the *dev* of the new village. That the host community has a very Hinduized pantheon of gods, and propitiates them in a different way, did not seem to concern the Vasava much. An important reason for this is that Vasavas do not see themselves as following a different religion, with a different pantheon of gods. They believe in the universality of their religious beliefs, with only superficial changes such as different names of gods in different areas. They assume that differences in religious practices of different communities are just variations along the same continuum. Hence, they did not expect to have difficulty adapting to plains (*deshi*) rituals and practices.

Prior to resettlement, no one in Makhadkhada was sure about what would happen to the pantheon of stones. A young leader told me to ask the village priest, or *poonjaro* (village priest). The *poonjaro*, however, told me:

> Who am I to take the decision on my own? I am the feeder of the gods, that is my duty; but these are village gods, and the older men will have a meeting and decide when the time comes. Why are you fretting now? Perhaps they will decide to split the stones amongst the different new sites. Anyway, the stone is only the physical representation.

An observation of how different submerged villages dealt with 'resettling' the village pantheon reveals that there was no thought-out strategy regarding what should be done with the *dev* stones; there was no 'correct' behaviour as dictated by what one may refer to as Vasava religious philosophy. Some submerged villages, such as Danel and Sinduri across the river, left the *dev* stones behind and found new stones to erect in Somavale resettlement site. In contrast, the villagers of Gadher (downstream from Makhadkhada) transported their stones in a truck to the new site at Sitpur. The stones in Makhadkhada were simply moved to higher ground to prevent their submergence. The *poonjaro* like a few others continued to live in Makhadkhada, having rebuilt his house above the water level of the dam.

In the first year following resettlement, no stones from the pantheon were moved and the priest and some people went back to Makhadkhada to carry out the consecration rituals at the original site. The sacrificial goat meat was brought and distributed in the new sites. The following year however, no meat from Makhadkhada was distributed in the new sites. Smaller resettlement sites celebrated Divaho and Divali (see below) with the host village, on an appropriate day of the Hindu calendar recognized by the government as a public holiday. However, there was no ritual to mark the festival (as no pantheon had been erected), and families simply cooked a meal of rice, lentils and in some cases meat. Larger resettlement sites continued to time their celebration and ritual feasts with the hill calendar, on a different day than their hosts. In the hills, decisions regarding sickness or crop failure in the village determine when a celebration can take place. It is hence not on any fixed date, and the Hindu calendar plays no role. Interestingly, a recent visit showed that even smaller resettlement sites have now erected a pantheon of stones nearby, some doing this even ten years after their original relocation.

The second category of *dev*s also has a physical representation, but this is territorially alienable, and their powers are not restricted to a specific territorial area. These *dev*s are also represented by stones, which are placed at various places within the hills.[2] The most important is Vaghan *dev* (tiger god). Vaghan *dev* is believed to exist everywhere, and his powers of protection can be appealed to any town, village or city. Thus, unlike Makhadkhada's village god Rojan *dev*, whose sphere of influence is territorially limited, *dev*s such as Vaghan can be called upon and can function in new sites too. Prior to resettlement, it remained unclear what would be done with the existing stone representations of these *dev*s. The young headman claimed that they would simply find new stones from a nearby stream at the new site and leave the old ones to be submerged in Makhadkhada. Others suggested that perhaps the stones would also go in the big trucks to the new sites with them, and they would be distributed amongst the various resettlement sites. The stones have remained in the hills and no new ones have been erected in any of the new sites.

Although the physical transportation and the submerging of some stones has become an issue in the context of resettlement, what is more significant is that the *dev*s (except the village god) can be appealed to in the new sites. Some even have new physical representations in the form of replacement stones. Each *dev* may have several stone representations, and some may be called upon even if their stone/physical representation is not there. Thus, unlike other cults, such as the Gwembe 'cult of earth' in modern Zimbabwe (Colson 1971), the hill Vasavas' basic pantheon of gods continues to be appealed to

---

2   Pallit and Mody (1992:40–58) provide detailed documentation of similar Bhilala shrines but do not analyse fully their role and meaning in everyday life.

from the new sites.[3] Mountain *dev*s, however, are more difficult to conceive of without form. I was told:

> The mountain *dev*s are somewhat different from the others as their role is not as clear cut. We live amongst them; they give us our identity and our history. Our creation myths are embedded in them. Living amongst them and seeing them everyday reminds us how closely our identity is tied up with these hills. But they no longer surround us once we move to live in the plains. Hence, they are less in our conscious mind, especially for the young ones. We will always respect them; the possibility of going on a pilgrimage up Paavu or Phenai will always be valued. But our relationship with these mountains and hills will change albeit in a subtler, inherently less visible way. Not being constantly amongst them, often not even seeing them, will, to some extent, lessen their impact on our daily lives.

The third category of *dev*s, having neither a physical representation nor an obvious physical link with a particular territory, provide the least difficult dilemma for resettlement. Most of the community's *dev*s fall into this category. The most frequently invoked *dev*s are Karhun *mata* (to ensure a good grain harvests), Gaman *mata* (for the prosperity of livestock), and others like Raja Phanta and Hukal Bukal, who play an important part in creation myths and legends about the supernatural world. Religious practitioners invoke these *dev*s when their help is needed in the new site, just as in Makhadkhada.

Ancestors fall into this third category and are regarded as being somewhere between *dev*s and living humans. Vasava believe that some humans can achieve the status of *dev* upon dying. This is evident in their many myths, where the *dev*s appear to have many human traits, and even deceive one another like humans. Hence, the line dividing people and the supernatural is not an impenetrable one. Ancestors are remembered and offered a meal of *dangar* (hand-husked rice) and *tuver dal* (split pigeon peas, *Cajanus cajan*) with sacrificial meat on the three days of *tyohar* following the consecration of the village pantheon on Divaho, Divali and Geem. On these occasions, the common Vasava deals directly with his ancestors. The food given to them is in lieu of respect for one's lineage, rather than as a propitiation to avoid harm and gain benevolence, as is the case with most *dev* offerings. Vasavas do not believe in rebirth in the Hindu sense of a cycle of life from which one must be freed, nor do they have a concept of *karma* that will determine whether

---

3   Among the Gwembe, rituals and shrines were attached to inundated territories. These did not survive resettlement and were replaced by new ritual prophets. See Colson (1971).

and how one will be reborn. Cremation is the norm, and this is done on the edge of a river or a stream. The actual site is rendered sacred only for three days, until the rites have been completed. After that, the area is not marked nor is it considered sacred anymore. It is similar to the Ghanaian situation, where it is believed that the physical and the supernatural worlds exist closely side by side and, if a geographical move becomes necessary, it follows that the ancestral spirits must be called upon to make their move at the same time (Moxon 1969:163).

Vasava religion finds much of its symbolism in nature, on which the Vasava depend and are hence vulnerable to. Religion is considered important for maintaining people's way of life and ensuring their economic survival. Hence, what is important to their survival (such as the mountains, threshing ground, cattle) acquires a supernatural protector. To some extent, Vasava religion is need-based. The concept of praying daily for health and happiness, or simply as a preventive against disaster, is far less evident in this society than among many of the devout, temple-going Hindus of the plains.

Jatras and temples as sacred arenas

*Jatra*s (fairs) play an important role in the social life of the community. They provide an opportunity to meet other Vasavas as well as other communities who may attend the same festival. Although all the venues of the *jatras* (with the exception of the Surpan *jatra*) are located outside the area to be submerged, the community's resettlement has implications for the role these festivals will play in their lives. Resettlement has placed some locations out of reach, forcing people to frequent other fairs that were previously not attended by their community.

A large number of festivals in the hills around Makhadkhada are also popular amongst other Adivasi groups, such as Ratthwas and Bhilalas. While some plains rural communities and high-caste Hindus also attend some *jatra*s, the role these fairs play for Adivasi groups such as the Vasavas, and their interpretation of them, is significantly different from that of plains Hindu groups. This was clearly observable at the Shoolpaneshwar *jatra*, which attracted a wide range of groups. Most plains Hindu groups view the Shoolpaneshwar *jatra* as a 'religious' occasion: it is held in the village of Manibeli, which has a sacred temple with a Shiva *lingam* and is located on the banks of the holy Narmada River. For the Hindus, a visit to the shrine, the singing of *bhajan*s (devotional songs) and a cleansing dip in the Narmada are the highlights. My Vasava companions, however, focused on a totally different aspect of the *jatra*. All night they roamed amongst the many stalls selling jewellery, clothes and *deshi* food such as *gulfi* (Indian ice-cream), *dalya* (small local variety of chickpea) and *jilbi* (a sweet). Interestingly, the vendors at these *jatra*s are all plains Hindu petty traders who trade in particular jewellery, cloth and other items that are popular with Adivasis, designs and objects that plains Hindus would not buy. For young Vasavas, the *jatra* provides a social arena in which they can get to know potential marriage partners, the crowd, chaos and relative anonymity of the fair providing some private space. *Jatra*s, along with wedding celebrations, are the most common spaces in which potential marriage partners are identified and where marriage by capture takes place.

None of my companions visited the famous Shoolpaneshwar temple. For many devout Hindus the main event of the *jatra* is the bathing of the holy *lingam* in the Narmada, which takes place on the second day, and some only arrive on that day. By this time the stalls are packing up and the Vasavas are on their way home, exhausted after their exciting night at the *jatra*, and eager to get started on the long trek to the hills before the sun gets too hot.

The most popular *jatra* is that of Dev Mogra or Ya Mogi (Mother Mogi), held at the village of the same name, a seven hour journey from Makhadkhada. Legend has it that Ya Mogi, the mother of Vaghan *dev* and wife of Raja Phanta, roamed the whole world and eventually chose this village to settle in. Once a year, in the month of February, there is a huge gathering at the village to view the image of the goddess. She is believed to bring fertility, and many make vows to her in the hope of begetting a child. Upon the wish being granted, they must return with the child, sometimes already several years old, and make good their promise. Thus crowds of people wait to view the goddess, and give her grain, cocks and goats, as well as *mahuda*, a locally distilled spirit. Many stay for all five days of the fair, enjoying the shows and stalls, and socializing with friends. The site of the Surpan *jatra* has been submerged and a new site established. Unlike the new venue of the Surpan *jatra*, which is far from many new sites and was not attended by any resettled Vasavas from Makhadkhada, the Dev Mogra festival is easily accessible by bus from the new sites and continues to be frequented by many.

Celebrated in spring, Holi is the most popular festival, and all Vasavas participate in it and many walk two days in the hills to the Holi *jatra* at Molgi. Holi is celebrated almost all over mainstream India. People young and old throw coloured powder and spray water on one other, along with the consumption of intoxicants like *bhang* and the lighting of an effigy of 'Holika' based on a popular Hindu story. It signifies the end of the old year and the birth of the new cycle. Whilst the underlying rationale for the festival appears to be similar in the hills and the plains, Holi amongst hill Vasavas takes on a different picture. There is singing and dancing for five nights before the appointed day of Holi, whose date is totally different from that of the Hindu calendar. Men and boys dress up as *bawa*s. Some do this as a result of a previously taken vow; others do it just for fun and what little money they may collect. Troupes of *bawa*s, accompanied by drummers, travel through the Satpura Hills and gather on an appointed evening at Molgi. This is a rare occasion where the larger bond of the entire tribe is visibly acknowledged. At around 4 a.m. a huge bamboo pole is set alight, and the *bawa*s dance in a frenzy around its leaping flames, watched by thousands of Vasavas, scattered on the surrounding hillocks. The following day Makhadkhada celebrates its own Holi, the *poonjaro* lighting the bamboo, around which *bawa*s and other men, women and children dance to a frenzied rhythm.

The trip to Molgi is no longer possible by foot from the resettlement sites as it was from Makhadkhada. The year following relocation, only one person went to Molgi and only two Vasavas dressed up as *bawa*s, but there were not enough houses in the resettlement sites to go around dancing and getting money. A few host villagers gave some money but they did not join in the dancing as is the custom when a *bawa* visits one's home. The second year following relocation, no one went to Molgi and there were no *bawa*s. On the day appointed by the Hindu calendar, some children copied their hosts and played with a bit of colour, but for the large part, there was none of the atmosphere that characterized the Holi celebrations I had participated in at Makhadkhada. A recent visit several years after relocation showed that people had started dressing up as *bawa*s again and increased economic prosperity meant that more people could afford to pay for transport to Molgi.

It is the 'individuality' of the Vasava festivals that has begun to fade with resettlement. Most of the Vasava festivals have some equivalent among those celebrated by plains Hindus, and hence it is unlikely that they will totally 'give up' any festival. However, observation shows that resettled groups are beginning to frequent a different range of *jatra*s depending on the location of their new site and the influence of the host community among whom they are resettled. Far more Vasavas from the resettlement sites of Vadaj and Sitpur visited the *jatra*s of Bhadarva and Chanod (which were never frequented from Makhadkhada) than went to Dev Mogra. The main reason is the relative proximity of these festivals, which implies minimum transport costs. These *jatra*s are dominated by *deshi* Hindu groups, and lack the special location, music, stalls and goods that characterize festivals like Molgi. Although a few Vasavas did go into the temple at Bhadarva, none of them offered a vow but watched with curiosity as other communities danced with offerings of *jowar* seedlings (millet, *Sorghum bicolor*) carefully balanced on their heads in baskets. Being unfamiliar with much of the Hindu pantheon and its associated symbolism and ritual, most Vasavas were more at ease roaming among the stalls below. The dispersal of the community due to resettlement means that Vasavas in different resettlement sites are being introduced to different *jatra*s. Thus the opportunity to meet other Vasavas has declined.

*Jatra*s are decreasingly the arena where Vasava community strength is reinforced. However, the plains *jatra*s continue to play an important role in the socialization of young couples.

It is the 'sacredness' associated with most plains *jatra*s, their inclusion in the religious arena, that differentiates the hill Vasavas' perception of these events from that of plains Hindu groups. With the exception of the Dev Mogra *jatra*, Vasavas view *jatra*s as outside the sphere of religion, with their social and economic functions being the main factors. They are an opportunity for the young to meet others, a break from the routine of agricultural work and a chance to buy a range of goods in a relaxed and jovial atmosphere.

The exclusion of the hill Vasavas from the sacred arenas of plains Hindu groups is not overt, nor is it a physical exclusion. In fact, host villagers in resettlement sites often try to encourage resettled Vasavas to visit the temples in the host village, in an attempt to 'uplift' themselves both spiritually and materially. None of the Vasavas had ever entered a temple prior to resettlement, and they were reluctant to enter them in the resettlement sites.

> We don't know what to do there, we don't feel comfortable there ...
> Occasionally we are told to go in, but the same voice implies that our dress
> is not respectful enough, that entering the arena of the temple warrants
> a change in our wider social behaviour, and that we are not ready to
> implement such changes.

Even prior to resettlement, the community did not regard the temples along the Narmada as sacred arenas. These were only visited by pilgrims who walked the banks of the Narmada and had nothing to do with the tribes living along the banks that formed the route of the pilgrimage.

Temples are an important component of the overall image that is increasingly being viewed as the role model for the resettled community. Although a few Vasavas (especially men) are beginning to familiarize themselves with some of the Hindu pantheon, to some extent the resettled Vasavas have not embraced it in their daily lives. For plains Hindus, religious philosophy strongly influences daily behaviour and associated morality and purity: what one eats, how one dresses, behaviour between the sexes, rituals like marriage – all of these are indicators of one's religiosity and morality. For hill Vasavas, however, the religious sphere is largely associated with the unknown, deeply entrenched in the natural world that they are vulnerable to, but need to exist within. To associate mundane ritual and social behaviour with religious intent would be to make the sacred profane. To bring religion into everyday behaviour and conscious thought would be to dilute its strength. For most Vasavas, belief in the power of their pantheon and the associated rituals is closely linked to the fact that much of the religious sphere cannot be touched or fully understood by common Vasavas. Keeping one's distance from these sacred aspects of the religious arena is the basis for a secure belief in its efficacy.

A more recent visit to the resettlement site shows that a few Vasavas have now visited Hindu temples, though not in the resettlement site but occasionally at a distant *jatra* where they are relatively anonymous and their new plains clothes do not reveal their identity clearly. But it has taken several years for even this minimal entry of the hill Vasavas into the sacred sphere of the plains Hindus. This development continues because of curiosity on the part of the Vasavas, rather than due to the adoption of Hindu ritual or religion as practised by host communities.

Feeders of the gods: Vasava religious practitioners

The pantheon of *devs* described above is never approached directly by any Vasava, nor are Bhagwan and the *devs* offered daily prayers, as is done in the homes of most plains Hindus and most religious traditions. In fact, there is really no concept of daily prayer or any everyday ritual connected with appeasing or thanking the supernatural. Vasavas communicate with their *devs* only when their help is needed, their protection is sought or when they have to be repaid for granting a request. At such times – for example when illness strikes – Bhagwan or the *devs* (who are seen to control an area) is/ are approached by a 'religious practitioner'. There are three broad categories of such specialized people, whose functions may overlap, depending on each individual's skill and knowledge.

The term *bhua* is often used as a generic category to include all religious practitioners. *Bhua*s in Makhadkhada are not regarded solely as 'priests', at least not as this is understood in relation to Hindu Brahmins or Christian clergy. They are also shamans, have child-birthing skills and work as medicine men, these roles being closely linked to their ability to communicate with Bhagwan to ask him for favours and appease him through the institutions of *manta* and *poonja* (see below).

Meanwhile, a *badvo* is simply a more powerful *bhua*. The distinction is one of degree, and no absolute line separates the two. *Badvo*s are universally acknowledged to be *bhua*s as well, although some *bhua*s cannot become *badvo*s, whilst others choose not to do so. The talent of being a *bhua* and/or *badvo* is not inherited. As I was told, one is believed to have been 'chosen by Bhagwan'. To be a *badvo* one has to know every grass, tree, even the parents of every goat. It is very demanding, therefore Bhagwan reveals it only to few people'. Some *bhua*s choose not to become *badvo*s by consciously not developing powers of witchcraft detection: 'I can detect if an illness is the result of witchcraft, and if I pushed myself I could detect the witch, but I don't, as it simply causes enmity. I do not want to develop my powers to become a *badvo*, as there is more risk involved in such powerful work'.

The *poonjaro* is the caretaker of the village pantheon and the only one who can consecrate or 'feed' it on the occasions of Divaho, Divali and Geem. Unlike the other practitioners, the position of the *poonjaro* is hereditary, and the *poonjaro* trains one of his sons to take on his role. Although most *bhua*s and *badvo*s are men, women can also be 'chosen' for the role. The *poonjaro*, however, is always male.

Whenever illness strikes, its origin must be determined before treatment can proceed. Illness and misfortune are attributed to both natural causes and supernatural intervention. It hence demands a dual remedy: herbs plus *manta*, a ritual to appease the supernatural. This gives the *bhua*s their hold over their profession and over doctors. *Bhua*s claim that even if they revealed a medicinal plant to the layman, the latter would not know when to pick it, how to treat it nor when and how to administer it to the patient. Moreover he/she would not be able to invoke and appease the spirit of the supernatural (the *manta* part of the treatment). The medicine without the *manta* has no effect. While the former attacks the symptoms of an illness (such as pain or a wound), it is the latter that is the antidote to the cause (such as witchcraft). One without the other is ineffective.

In many cases of illness that I observed, the cause was detected as witchcraft, which calls for stronger *bhua* powers if the witch is to be detected and the evil removed. One night, Makti Chima awoke with terrible stomach pain. Vinya Lekji, a *bhua*, was summoned from the neighbouring hamlet. Upon his asking, Makti informed him that during the afternoon she had weeded Jerma Veshta's fields as part of a kin labour exchange. Vinya asked for *urad* (mung beans, *Phaseolus mungo*) and put them on a *khakhra* leaf (*Butea monosperma*) 'to read'. The sick or harmed individual (or cattle) is made to touch the beans, thus conveying information regarding their illness. 'It is all written here, the picture is acted out before my eyes, just like a story. But one has to know how to read it'. As Vinya reads, he describes what he sees, slowly building the situation from a few objects to a recognizable scene. The process can take from ten minutes to an hour depending on the seriousness of the case. If the need arises, the *bhua* may appeal to the supernatural to help him along; as enticement he may promise a chicken or some locally distilled *mahuda*. Only in very rare cases does he reveal the name of a *dhakan* (witch). In most cases he focuses on trying to find where the evil (embodied in a few stones) is buried, letting the images lead him to the spot where the stones will be dug up and disposed off appropriately. After the divination, some of the mung beans are tied in a cloth, which the patient carries until s/he recovers and the promised *manta* is fulfilled.

In this case, the stomach ache was attributed to jealousy. 'You Makti, are a hard worker and a quick weeder. This afternoon you weeded faster than the others and someone put evil on you at sunset. It is no use spending effort trying to find out who it is, but I will cure you by removing the evil'. Vinya traps the evil by pressing his thumb on the point of pain. He blows ash on the spot, while Makti coughs out the evil. He then asks for *jowar* (millet) and *mahuda* to increase the potency of the offering, and offers this to the *dev*s. He then asks me for a headache tablet and includes this in the offering, instructing Makti to swallow it. After an hour Makti falls asleep. The pain does not return, and a few days later a *manta* involving some *mahuda* and *jowar* is carried out.

Prior to resettlement, Vasavas rarely used the government or private dispensaries in town, due to the time and money involved. However, Vasavas are not opposed to the use of modern medicine. In fact, while in the hills, police crime cases and modern medicine were their greatest expenses. They do not see modern medicine as inconsistent with traditional medicine. The *bhua*s themselves may frequent the town doctors, and so do not discourage others from going. The allopathic treatment of modern medicine targets the symptom. But it needs to be accompanied by a *manta* to target the cause of the illness/misfortune for any treatment to be effective.

Resettlement has decreased the use of the traditional medical practitioner for several reasons. Access to a *bhua* is not always easy. Resettlement sites are scattered and many sites do not have a *bhua*. Access to government or private health centres is often easier than calling a *bhua*. Further, the *bhua* does not have access to the medicinal plants that he finds in the hills. This was initially an issue, but with time the *bhua*s have located similar plants in their new habitat, and many travel back to the hills on a regular basis to source what they need. In addition, government and private clinics are nearby and the community has always respected the potency of what is referred to as *deshi dava* (medicine of the world beyond the hills). Resettled Vasavas spend a substantial amount of time and resources frequenting these clinics, especially for minor illnesses. However, any major illness or long-term condition necessitates the intervention of a *bhua* or *badvo* and the accompanying *manta* ritual.

The *bhua* has retained his position as a unique combination of doctor and priest. Vasava religious practitioners (*bhua*s, *badvo*s and *poonjaro*s) do not form a separate clergy, as is found in Hinduism and Christianity. In plains Hindu communities, there is a much clearer distinction between the Brahmin or priest (who is seen as the link with the supernatural) and the doctor (who cures illness). During a ritual, the *bhua* appears similar to the Hindu Brahmin priest; it is he alone who communicates with Bhagwan and makes him offerings. However, at all other times, the *bhua* is difficult to distinguish from any other Vasava and does not command the same degree of social status, nor does he observe separate rules of purity and social interaction with other members of his community as does the Hindu Brahmin. An important reason for this is that the *bhua*, unlike a practising Brahmin, is not limited in his activities to dealing with the supernatural. He is a farmer first and has to till, sow and reap his crop, cut wood, build houses and make baskets like all other men. His role as a *bhua* is performed over and above his role as a contributor to the economy of the village. The more popular *bhua*s in their old age may spend a smaller proportion of their time farming, as demand for their religious and medicinal skills are high and a *bhua* cannot deny his skills to anyone. Other members of their family thus take over his share of agricultural labour.

Within Vasava society, there is the respect and awe that regulates the relationship between the clergy and the common man in most societies. However, although the *bhua* commands respect during his performance, there are no benefits for his family either economically or socially. Hence *bhua*s interact with the rest of the society on an egalitarian basis, sharing the same experiences, and subject to the same economic hardships, unlike the Brahmins of *deshi* Hindu society, who enjoy a superior economic and social position than people from lower-caste groups. In fact, a *bhua*'s family is often at a disadvantage as they have less of a claim on his time, and any reward he gets (alcohol and food) is only available to him as an individual.

Manta and *poonja*: the implications of resettlement on rites and rituals

The ritual of Divaho in August is performed for the forest, rain and cattle. It is one of the three occasions when the village pantheon is consecrated, the others being Divali in December and Geem in February. On these occasions, villagers collect around the *lingam*-shaped stones which are otherwise carefully avoided, as the *dev*s must not be disturbed unnecessarily.

In a ritual that I observed, two of the *poonjaro*'s assistants hold the chosen goat by strings tied to its neck. The *poonjaro* puts some *jowar* (millet) and *mahuda* (alcohol) on its head, asking that it be accepted as a sacrifice. The goat, however, refuses to shake its head. After several unsuccessful attempts the *poonjaro* becomes impatient, his voice rising as he attempts to reason and bargain with the *dev*. 'Why won't you accept this goat? It is a large one; we have contributed towards it. What wrong has the village done you? We do Divaho, Divali and Geem every year. You don't want it? That's up to you but I tell you it is a good goat. Have we not fed you well all these years?' The plea goes on, the tone switching from one of supplication to bargaining to threats: 'Do you wish that we desert you?' Finally the goat shakes its head vigorously and one of the assistants raises his *kuvad* (axe) to bring it down heavily on the goat's neck, but the handle breaks, the blade catching the goat on the neck causing it to bleat even more loudly. The *poonjaro's* voice rises. 'You are getting greedy now. Why won't you take what we are offering you? Who says I am not *bhua* enough to make the *dev* accept our offering … He is just playing games, my powers can overcome such behaviour'. Finally, the head is severed and the *poonjaro* relaxes, his place in society once again secure, the villagers assured by his conviction and power.

This mixture of supplication and bargaining highlights a duality in the Vasava relationship with the supernatural, and it is the reason why Brahmin priests view Vasava *bhuas* as disrespectful towards Bhagwan. *Bhuas* communicate with *devs* through rituals which involve propitiation: asking for a favour or offering thanks for a favour received. There is no direct link between the common Vasava and the pantheon of gods, nor is their any concept of daily prayer for general well-being. In fact, it is advised that the supernatural be left alone unless occasion arises to call upon a *dev*. 'Bhagwan is there always, he is always alert, but has a lot to do. Bhagwan controls everything and gives both happiness and sorrow. But we must not disturb him unnecessarily. It must not be treated like a casual relationship. Why disturb him if things are fine with you?'

The community thus communicates with Bhagwan and *devs* only through two kinds of rituals: *poonja* and *manta*. The term *poonja* is the equivalent of *puja* amongst *deshi* caste Hindus, a generic term for most Hindu rituals (see Fuller 1992:57–82). Both refer to an offering made to the supernatural, usually by a priest in the case of (Vasava) *poonjas*, and always by a priest in case of (Hindu) *pujas*. However, they differ in some very essential ways. Firstly, *poonja* is not done in front of any deity, while Hindu *puja* usually requires the presence of an idol (or a symbol) of the god being worshipped. Secondly, the Vasava ritual of *poonja* invariably involves the sacrifice of an animal and the offering of alcohol, whereas in the Hindu plains communities surrounding Makhadkhada, *puja* is vegetarian and devoid of alcohol.[4] Thirdly, Hindu *puja* involves the chanting of *mantras* (chants, prayers) from the sacred Sanskrit texts, while Vasava rituals have no texts backing them, and communication between the *bhua* and *dev* is more like a dialogue around the specific purpose of the ritual at hand. Moreover, the *devs* and myths of the hill Vasavas are not

---

4   Hardiman (1987:99–128) describes similar rituals amongst other South Gujarat tribes, showing a variation in how *poonja* is performed, in some cases, it closely mirrors that of Hindu *puja* unlike in Makhadkhada where Vasava *poonja* is distinct from plains Hindu *puja*.

known to the plains Hindus, and most Vasavas are unfamiliar with even the more popular gods of the Hindu trinity. Thus, whilst the plains communities conform in general to Fuller's image of a *puja*, Vasava ritual appears to have greater similarity with what Fuller terms sacrifice or *bali* (ibid.:46, 83–5) with regard to the items offered and, to an extent, to the manner in which they are offered and killed.

Poonjas are performed at the village and household level. Village *poonja*s 'ritually express village unity'. Some *poonja*s are prescribed in their frequency while others are performed as the need arises. For example, *Kholo poonja* is done in the *kholo* (threshing ground) of every family, once a year, preferably during harvest time. *Karhun* and *Gaman* are larger rituals, involving the sacrifice of more than seven fowl and are performed every five and eight years respectively, to ensure the prosperity of cattle. *Attham* is performed when a household has had a run of bad luck with regard to crops, cattle or personal health.

Whilst *poonja*s are normally prescribed in their frequency and performed for a group (such as the village or household), *manta*s are performed for the individual (human and animal). In most cases *manta*s are aimed at counteracting illness or bad luck, such as the death of several cattle. Thus they are not prescribed in their frequency and take place as the need arises. A *manta* is the promise or vow made to a particular *dev* or *mata* (female *dev*), or to Bhagwan at large, that he or she will be given a specified sacrifice consisting of grain, meat and alcohol if the illness or bad luck is cured. The promise is not carried out until the ill luck or sickness passes. The individual is instructed to wear some blessed grain tied in a cloth around the neck or arm or observe some food taboos. If there is no sign of improvement, the *bhua* may increase the value of the earlier *manta* assuming that the *dev*s are not satisfied. *Manta*s thus offer scope for bargaining with Bhagwan by increasing the amount of sacrificial offering promised. Hence these rituals can be costly (a goat, eight chickens and a pot of *mahuda*) and are fulfilled only when the family can afford the expense, often even several years after the illness or ill luck has been mitigated. There is a strong belief that if the *manta* is not fulfilled when the family can afford it, the illness will strike again and ill luck will multiply.

The items offered to the supernatural are seen as the objects through which dialogue and bargaining with the supernatural take place. Prior to resettlement, *bunti* (mountain millet, *Echinochloa crus-galli*) was the most common grain used in *poonja*s and *manta*s, followed by *jowar* (millet) and occasionally *dangar* (hand husked rice). This ritual grain hierarchy corresponds to the consumption value of grains in Vasava society. In the hills, *dangar* is scarce and its consumption reserved for special occasions. Thus a *bhua* may start a *manta* with *bunti*, but if it is not successful (for example, if the patient's stomach does not stop hurting), then he may go on to offer *jowar* or *dangar*. Similarly, chicks, hens, cocks and goats have a hierarchy in terms of their potency to make a *manta* effective. Later the food is cooked and consumed by the *badvo* and other men of the extended family. Women are excluded from the consumption of 'pure' foods after the commencement of menstruation. *Mahuda* alcohol accompanies every ritual and is consumed by men, women and children.

Resettlement has resulted in changes in rituals, stemming from the reorganization of social groups (which formed the unit for village *poonja*s), the unavailability of certain ritual items such as *bunti, mahuda* and *bili (Piliostigma racemosum)* leaves, and the stigma attached to meat and alcohol by plains Hindus. These are crucial elements in Vasava rituals, but considered 'vices' and 'impure' amongst many host groups. During the transition period, no rituals were carried out in the new sites and all *manta*s and *poonja*s continued to be done in Makhadkhada. Initially, there was a hiatus of these *poonja*s at several sites, but over time each resettlement site has erected their own pantheon of stones, and a less elaborate version of the hill rituals continue in the new sites. Interestingly, this has demanded that a wider set of *poonjaro*s become practitioners to serve the many new sites. In the hills, just one son became *poonjaro* after his father. However, the scattering and increased distance between resettlement sites has provided opportunities for several sons and even nephews to develop their skills.

The unavailability of certain materials has resulted in rituals becoming Hinduized in many ways. *Bunti* is not grown or available, as this coarse millet is looked down upon in the plains. The plains Hindus prefer rice as an offering in their ritual, along with *ghee* (clarified butter) and milk, which are often poured into a sacred fire. I observed the increasing substitution of rice in rituals, but this was consistent with the philosophy that the commonly available grain (now rice, earlier *bunti*) is used for the more common rituals and the more valued grain reserved for special rituals. 'The hosts live with the same uncertainties and problems we face, and if they can satisfy the *dev*s with *suka* (machine-husked white rice), that should work fine. We are not so dogmatic about that level of ritual detail'. Similarly, *bili* leaves were substituted with *peepad (Ficus religiose)*, while the *bhua* had declared that two or three chickens would suffice for *manta*s that required a goat; the sharp decrease in livestock made the large offerings I observed in the hills impossible for the resettled community.

The lack of *mahuda* trees in the resettlement sites was seen as more problematic. Resettled Vasavas adapted by distilling alcohol from jaggery (brown raw cane sugar). This is a valuable source of income as it is sold to host farmers and widely used for social drinking. Vasavas stress that *mahuda* is *chowkhu* (pure), where as jaggery alcohol is not considered as such, and hence cannot be offered to the *dev*s. However, with time this too has become adapted. *Bhua* Mangji Chaman who relocated from Gadher to Vadaj, a new site, rationalized:

> Our situation in the resettlement site is different. People don't have as many resources. Look around you … Families that had ten cattle, fifteen goats and seven chickens now have just three cattle and two chickens. We had huge pots of *mahuda* in our stores, now the pots lie empty. I may have prescribed a chicken and two bottles of *mahuda* for Hamsa's ritual in the hills. But here we fulfilled it with one glass of jaggery alcohol and some *jowar* … I don't know, but we assume the *dev* will also adjust and will accept this instead. For larger *manta*s, *mahuda* is still needed. Some of us get it from kin in the hills, or buy it from sites where there are *mahuda* trees.

Rituals in the plains follow a different, more rigid calendar, closer to the Hindu calendar as compared to the hills, where each village set its day taking into account issues such as sickness in the village, a recent death and so on. Vasava village-level *poonja*s such as Divali, Divaho and Holi have equivalent celebrations amongst the *deshi* (plains) Hindu villages, but the form they take is often different. With time, certain aspects of the ceremony that are considered 'primitive' (such as the application of white ash and adornment with leaves, the wearing of loin cloths by men after the Divali ritual) are becoming discarded (Chaudhuri 1980). Vasava songs, which are such an important part of village rituals in the hills, have undergone tremendous change. The young copy songs of the host villagers, who often make fun of songs sung in the Vasava dialect. The new songs, aside from being in the state language of Gujarati, reflect plains Hindu morality and values, unlike hill Vasava songs, where there was immense scope to be creative and often explicitly sexual, and they brought out the relatively free and egalitarian relationships between men and women.

For the large part, *poonja*s and *manta*s in the new sites remain a purely Vasava affair; host villagers are rarely invited, and the rituals take place in the privacy of the new site. However, my recent observations showed that things are changing as some of the resettled Vasavas have made deep friendships with some of the host groups, especially Tadavis. The resulting change is more along the lines of the adoption of certain plains Hindu rituals, rather than any serious alterations in the nature of the *poonja*s and *manta*s. Over time, many Vasava rituals are becoming Hinduized. Nowhere is this more evident than in the marriage ritual, which has been totally transformed. But marriage in Vasava society, unlike in most societies, was never associated with the realm of the supernatural. It was a purely social contract, and many couples simply eloped or men 'captured' their bride at a festive gathering. It is not that Vasavas are copying the dominant host groups in every aspect. This may have appeared as a risk in the early stages of resettlement. However, over the years it has been fascinating to see how Vasava ritual has managed to adapt without its philosophical basis being threatened. Adopting a ritual poses no threat. Devji Hamji was only around nine years old when he moved to a resettlement site. He grew up spending substantial time with host villagers, had made some good relationships with them and was recognized as the most 'integrated' in his site. When he died unexpectedly, his parents decided to hold a *bhajan* session (singing Hindu devotional songs) to which they invited his host villager friends. It was the first time this ritual was performed in the resettlement site and it is totally alien to Vasavas, most of whom do not know the songs nor understand them. However, it was felt that a ceremony was needed at which the host villagers could pay the deceased their respects. The next day, his parents carried out the traditional Vasava death ceremony, replete with alcohol and traditional wailing.

Similarly, Vasava are happy to adapt the more superficial parts of a ritual (such as grain and alcohol substitution). This is clearly brought out in the increasing acceptance of allopathic medicine without diluting the belief in the efficacy of the accompanying *manta*. Those aspects of ritual retained by the Vasavas are more likely to be those that are approved by the hosts.

Concluding remarks: change as an aspect of Vasava philosophy and culture

Resettled Vasavas' desire to 'mix in' with the dominant host communities has meant that the resettled community is very cognizant of, and vocal about, the changes that are taking place in the spheres of religion and consumption – the two areas that in the past had played a pivotal role in emphasizing their distinctiveness from plains (now host) communities. This should not be taken to mean that resettled Vasavas are blindly copying the host communities. The changes I observed in these areas are much more selective: the desire to 'fit in' does not stem from an inherent feeling of inferiority amongst the Vasavas (as is the case with many minority communities), but from a desire to be seen as adaptive and willing to change. In fact, I observed that Vasava philosophy and culture encourages people to adapt to change. It is not limited to the younger generation; it goes beyond the popular 'change/fashion receptive' areas of clothes, jewellery and music; and it is primarily a result of a 'push' rather than a 'pull' factor – that is, the community makes the effort to adopt a new way (push) rather than 'giving in' to something imposed by the dominant outside group (pull). The openness to adaptation was evident even while Vasava were in the hills, where outside contact and related 'pull' factors were marginal.

This ease of acceptance of different kinds of behaviour across different aspects of life has been crucial in helping the hill Vasavas adapt to involuntary resettlement. My research shows that whilst the hill Vasavas were the most isolated group to be affected by the Sardar Sarovar Dam, their experience of resettlement shows them to be (relatively speaking) receptive and hopeful. This is not to deny or belittle the numerous issues that have been a tough battle in this process. Nor is it to imply that the process of resettlement has been smooth, or that it has not deeply impacted many aspects of this community's life and lifestyle. Changes in production patterns following resettlement in the plains are eroding the economic self-sufficiency of the hill Vasavas. As noted above, plains agriculture requires a mix of food and cash crops, a good knowledge of market prices and the ability to handle middlemen. The resettled community's newly emerging production patterns increasingly resemble that of other plains communities and can no longer serve as a distinctive marker of resettled Vasava identity.

However, it is interesting that, compared to other groups who have always been more exposed to plains communities (such as the Tadavis and Ratthwas), and hence for whom the move can be assumed to have been less 'traumatic', the hill Vasava groups I worked with showed a much stronger mental acceptance of their situation. They tended to focus much less on the overall 'trauma' of the move itself, and discussions and debates were largely about the details: who had 'black' land and who had 'white' land, how would they learn the bus routes to visit relatives in the hills and in other new sites, who had successfully managed to find an honest middleman to sell cotton to and so on. This was unusual considering that the learning curve of new ways was steepest for this group compared to the more exposed Tadavi and Ratthwa settlers.

The resettled community is not resistant to adapting to these changes as they see it as necessary to make a success of their lives in the new sites. They do what is needed to fit in, without really compromising their core belief system, or undermining their identity as Vasavas. That is, they do not see the new ways of doing things as demanding, nor as an imposition forced on them by the host groups. The changes are viewed as a consequence of the practical implications of moving (the different availability of grains, distance from hill festivals and so forth); and they view it as necessary to be accepted by dominant plains groups.

Religion (demonstrated through the institutions described in this chapter) was one of the most visible ways that plains groups differentiated themselves from hill Vasava. Hence plains communities welcome changes in this area as a sign that the resettled community is making a willing effort to adapt to 'developed' ways of the Hindu plains groups. It appears almost convenient that changes in the aspects of religion that get the largest 'pay offs' (in terms of positive recognition from hosts) are those that the Vasavas are least resistant to changing, as they are not seen as a significant threat to their self-identity. Aspects of their religion that are highly valued such as their creation myths, the stories of how some ancestors became *dev*s and their link with the mountain *dev*s are the less 'visible' aspects of religion and are not threatened.

However, more recently, some concerns are beginning to be voiced as the next generation of Vasavas grows up in the resettlement sites with a different set of experiences to those of their kin who remain in the hills. For example, they rarely visit *jatra*s like Dev Mogra, where their identity with other hill Vasavas is re-enforced. Similarly, rituals such as Divaho that draw hill Vasavas from other villages are replaced by more local Hindu festivals, which are celebrated according to the Hindu calendar rather than other criteria as in the hills, and there are less opportunities for *bhua*s to pass on their knowledge of the creation myths. With time there is a risk that the resettled Vasavas' strong and conscious link to the physical and spiritual world of the hills, which is the bond between different hill Vasava clans, lineages and villages, may fade.

My recent visit to the resettlement site showed that resettled Vasava are making a more conscious effort to revive some of these fading links. This was the first time they urged me to bring photos and drawings and so forth of their lives in the hills. 'You know more about our lives in Makhadkhada than some of these children. It is not their fault. They grow up here amongst the cotton fields and travel by transport. We feel sad they know so little of our land and our hills'. In the last few years there has been an increase in people dressing up as *bawa*s at Holi and travelling between resettlement sites for entertainment. Parents are making the effort to take their children to *jatra*s like Molgi. There is an increasing trend for resettled households to choose marriage alliances with households in non-resettled hill villages. This is in contrast to the trend that started prior to resettlement, where alliances were largely restricted to other resettlement sites.

It would be premature to label these observations as a conscious revival of Vasava identity. They are partly a result of the increasing economic prosperity of resettled Vasavas, leading to a greater sense of security of self. Their economy has transformed and settled into a new pattern. Until now this was the major focus. The resettled Vasava are just beginning to feel they can recreate their own identity in the plains, an identity which does not have to copy that of the dominant host groups. It appears to be an identity that will celebrate their being Vasava, but one which will contain differences from that of their kin in the hills. The practical limits of resettlement and people's children's experiences require this.

Glossary

bawa   A term used to refer to those men and boys who dress up in fancy costumes during the festival of Holi. Some wear dried gourds or bells on their waists, tall bamboo top hats, peacock feather head-dresses and masks. Some men dress up as women and behave in a way that is considered feminine.

bhua   A shaman who is less powerful than a *badvo*, and deals largely with childbirth and other illnesses.

bili leaves   Leaves of the *Piliostigma racemosum* tree.

deshi   Of the dominant plains (Hindu) culture.

dev   A god who has a particular area of control and may have a physical symbol, but who is viewed as being under the supreme god (Bhagwan or Malik). Devs may be male or female, neither one being assumed to be more powerful solely by virtue of its sex.

dungri   Of the hills (implies backwardness).

lingam   A phallic-shaped representation or symbol of Lord Shiva.

mahuda   Alcohol distilled locally from the flowers of the tree *Bassia lactifolia* or *Madhuca indica*.

manta   A promise made to the *dev*s to sacrifice certain offerings following receipt of certain favours.

peepad leaves   Leaves of the *ficus religiose* tree popularly known as the *peepal* tree.

poonja   A generic term for village and household rituals among Vasava.

poonjaro   Village priest.

tyohar   The day following the three village rituals in Makhadkhada during which special food is cooked and offered to the ancestors.

References

Baviskar, A. 1995a. 'Displacement and the Bhilala tribals of the Narmada Valley'. In J. Drèze, M. Samson and S. Singh (eds), *The Dam and the Nation: Displacement and Resettlement in the Narmada Valley*, pp. 103–35. Delhi: Sage Publications.

——— 1995b. *In the Belly of the River: Tribal Conflicts over Development in the Narmada Valley*. New Delhi: Oxford University Press.

Bhagvat, D. 1968. *Tribal Gods and Festivals in India*. Bombay: D. Bhagvat.

Chaudhuri, B. 1980. 'Changing religion and ethnic cycle of the Mundas'. In L.P. Vidyarthi, B.N. Sahay and P.K. Dutta (eds), *Aspects of Social Anthropology in India*, pp. 165–84. New Delhi: Classical Publications.

Bradford, M. and Berger, T. 1992. *Sardar Sarovar: The Report of the Independent Review*. Canada: Resource Futures International (RFI) Inc.

Colson, E. 1971. *The Social Consequences of Resettlement: The Impact of the Kariba Resettlement on the Gwembe Tonga*. Manchester: Manchester University Press.

Fuller, C.J. 1992. *The Camphor Flame: Popular Hinduism and Society in India*. Princeton: Princeton University Press.

Ghurye, G.S. 1963. *The Scheduled Tribes*. Bombay: Popular Prakashan.

Hakim, R. 1996. 'Vasava identity in transition: some theoretical issues', *Economic and Political Weekly of India*, special issue, 31(24):1492–9.

——— 1997. 'Resettlement and rehabilitation in the context of Vasava culture: some
        reflections'. In J. Dreze, M. Samson and S. Singh (eds), *The Dam and the
        Nation: Displacement and Resettlement in the Narmada Valley*, pp. 136–67.
        New Delhi: Oxford University Press.

——— 2000a. 'From corn to cotton: changing indicators of food security amongst
        resettled Vasavas'. In M.M. Cernea and C. McDowell (eds), *Risks and
        Reconstruction: Experiences of Resettlers and Refugees*, pp. 229–52.
        Washington: World Bank.

——— 2000b. 'Identity, resettlement and perceptions of change: the Vasava Bhils of
        Gujarat, India'. Goldsmiths Anthropology Research Papers, No 3. London:
        Goldsmiths College, University of London.

——— 2000c. 'Agricultural land: the case of Hill Vasavas displaced by the Sardar
        Sarovar Dam, India', *Eastern Anthropologist* 53(1/2):73–94.

Hardiman, D. 1987. *The Coming of the Devi: Adivasi Assertion in Western India*.
        Delhi: Oxford University Press.

Moxon, J. 1969. *Volta: Man's Greatest Lake*. London: Andre Deutsch.

Padel, F. 1992. 'The position of tribal people in India'. In M. Bradford and T. Berger,
        Sardar Sarovar: The Report of the Independent Review, p. 2. Canada:
        Resource Futures International (RFI) Inc.

Pallit, C. and Mody, P. 1992. 'On the tribal path: a study of the SSP affected villages of
        Kakrana, Jhandana and Anjanwada, Madhya Pradesh'. In M. Bradford and
        T. Berger, *Sardar Sarovar: The Report of the Independent Review*, pp. 40–58.
        Canada: Resource Futures International (RFI) Inc.

5

The impact of attempted resettlement on the Konda Reddis, South India

Thanuja Mummidi

Research on development-induced displacement and resettlement has been steadily increasing, bringing to light the diverse development projects that cause displacement (e.g. Baviskar 2002; Dwivedi 2002; Fernandes 2001; Mehta 2009; Parasuraman 1999; Ramanathan 1996; Thukral 1996). The most common development initiative that has led to large-scale displacement, especially in India, is the construction of dams (e.g. Baviskar 1995; Dhagamwar *et al.* 2003; Dreze *et al.* 1997; Thukral 1992). To this list can be added displacement due to industrialization and infrastructure projects, natural resource extraction and the setting up of biosphere reserves. Further, research on development-induced displacement has, since the late 1980s, moved on from 'descriptions to prescriptions, and from academic analysis to operational research' (Cernea 1996b:263). This is closely linked to the development of two theoretical frameworks proposed as ways to understand the impact of displacement. The first model proposed by Scudder and Colson (1982) was applicable only to voluntary resettlement and those involuntary relocations that successfully move through the four stages of 'recruitment, transition, development, and incorporation/handing over' (Cernea 2000:5). This model, focusing on settlers' stress and behavioural reactions to each stage of resettlement, was not very useful as most displacements were involuntary and did not successfully pass through the four stages.

In the 1990s, Cernea (1990, 1995b, 1996a, 1997, 1998) proposed the impoverishment risks and reconstruction (IRR) model to understand the cumulative impact of failed resettlement. In assessing impoverishment as a result of displacement, the model suggests nine risks that need to be examined for reconstruction: landlessness, joblessness, homelessness, marginalization, food insecurity, increased morbidity, loss of access to common property resources, community disarticulation and education. This model has been used widely in assessing the impact of development-induced displacement, and importantly in suggesting avenues for post-displacement reconstruction. However, more recently the applicability of the model has been critiqued on the grounds that it:

> ignores the differences within communities as well as the implications
> of indirect changes arising from shifts in livelihood patterns ... [I]t does
> not consider the changes occurring in an area independent of the project,
> be they the results of other state policies or issues concerning the wider
> political economy.
>
> (Mitra and Rao 2009:38)

Similarly, Mehta argues that the model falls short of testing the 'dynamics of social differentiation amongst the resettled populations' (Mehta 2009:14). Taking the case of the Tadvi and Vasava groups regarding displacement and resettlement in the Sardar Sarovar Project, she analyses the relevance of each of the impoverishment risks listed by Cernea (1997), concluding that:

> risks and losses cannot be reduced to simple variables or causal relationships
> as put forward in a positivist model (for example, land for land; jobs for
> jobs). ... The multi-causal relations between land, livelihoods and identity,
> and their links with overall well-being, thus, cannot be reduced to a model.
>
> (Mehta 2009:27)

Another critique that has gained ground in the displacement and resettlement literature is the distinction between voluntary and involuntary displacement (e.g. Baviskar 2009; Mitra and Rao 2009). Baviskar (2009) argues that rural–urban migration has been classified as voluntary simply because it is not a mass displacement triggered by development projects, when in fact the causes of rural–urban migration from the migrants' perspective are forced and therefore it is incorrect to classify it as voluntary displacement. Given the fact that the IRR model is prepared especially for involuntary or forced displacements, is it right to assume that, displacement classified as voluntary does not suffer from impoverishment. On the contrary, if they do, then is it justified to classify such displacement as voluntary?

This chapter compliments these two critiques using the case of resettlement among the Konda Reddis of South India. The resettlement of the Konda Reddis is a case less reported in the list of diverse reasons for development-induced displacement. The government of India's stated objective for Konda Reddis resettlement is the 'development' of the community given their constitutional status as a '"weaker section"[1], and not the common rhetoric of "people's sacrifice for the larger good; for the nation's development". The chapter juxtaposes the uniqueness of their case, one in which people have not lost access to their traditional resources and have been given a choice to resettle or stay on in their traditional habitats. This means that it is possible to classify the displacement as voluntary, even though the impact of the resettlement shows signs of equating to an impoverishment, leading to a situation similar to involuntary resettlement. Using this case study, the chapter reveals that impoverishment can also be found in situations of 'voluntary' displacement even though access to traditional resources is not restricted. I question the issue of 'informed consent' and 'choice' in classifying such displacement as 'voluntary'.

The following section opens with a discussion on the constitutional status of the Konda Reddis and then gives the details of the sequence of development planning and implementation for the community. The chapter then moves on to discuss the impact of resettlement, and the changes it has brought to the social dynamics of the community. The chapter concludes with a discussion on the classification of resettlement as voluntary and involuntary with reference to the Konda Reddis, arguing that this simplistic binary classification does not hold good, and irrespective of the case there is a risk of impoverishment.

Why resettlement? The constitutional status of the Konda Reddis

Forest-dwelling communities like the Konda Reddis have been listed separately as scheduled tribes in the Constitution of India, and are of special concern to the development agenda of the state. In the 2011 census of India, 705 tribal communities are listed as scheduled tribes, and collectively they constitute 8.6 per cent of the total national population. The main purpose for creating this category was to provide special provisions for safeguarding the rights and interests of these communities, who are classified as part of the larger group of weaker sections. The identification, enumeration and special provisions for the category of the scheduled tribe are part of the affirmative action towards development. The policy for protection of the rights of scheduled tribes, especially their access to livelihood resources, as in land and forest, has been

---

1   The reference to weaker sections by the Constitution of India, relates to those communities (tribes/castes) that have suffered deprivation as a result of denial of access to livelihood resources/opportunities, that live in regions with poor infrastructural facilities or/and have been socially excluded through practices of 'untouchability' or other forms of discrimination.

debated from colonial times. Independent India adopted the policy of the 'integration' of this population with the larger nation to undo the colonial administrative approach of 'isolation' for these groups (Xaxa 2003).

Many committees and commissions were set up to further the process of integration of the scheduled tribes and of raising the levels of their development indicators (education, health, livelihood) to match the national averages. Careful development planning evolved to facilitate this process, including special schemes for scheduled tribes within the five-year plans of the government of India. With time it was realized that the level of integration was markedly varied within the category of scheduled tribes. This led to the creation of another category, the 'particularly vulnerable tribal group' (PVTG), on the recommendations of the Shilo Ao Committee, set up in 1969.[2] The category of 'particularly vulnerable tribal groups' was created to include those groups that lived in relatively isolated geographical regions, had a stagnant or diminishing population and whose subsistence depended mainly on the use of 'pre-agricultural' technology, with low levels of literacy in comparison to the national average.

The Konda Reddis are one among the seventy-five communities belonging to this category, and live mainly in the Schedule V[3] region of northern central and western parts of Andhra Pradesh in South India. The government of India looked at the inaccessibility of Konda Reddis hill hamlets, and their practice of shifting cultivation was viewed as contrary to state development policy. This policy proposed resettling the hill dwellers in the plains, and replacing shifting cultivation with settled agriculture as the only hope for improving the community's living conditions.

The sequence of resettlement planning

Little is known about development planning and implementation for the Konda Reddis prior to the fifth five-year plan (1974 to 1979). The period of the fifth five-year plan coincides with the first exclusive development plan drafted for the Konda Reddis by the Tribal Cultural Research and Training Institute (TCR & TI) in 1978. The plan contained the usual contempt for the traditional knowledge and practices of the community. This is especially reflected in the

---

2   When framed in 1969, the category was called '"primitive" tribal groups' with the acronym PTG. This was changed to '"particularly vulnerable" tribal groups' in 2006 through the first draft national policy for tribes in India, taking into consideration objections made by the public to the use of the term 'primitive'.

3   Schedule V regions are notified in the Constitution of India under Article 244 as those with a preponderance of scheduled tribe populations. They are largely forested, and contain many areas demarcated as reserved forests.

main focus of the plan, which was to discourage shifting cultivation through resettlement in the plains.

The plan was drafted under the pretext that,despite decades of development intervention, the Konda Reddis remained the most backward tribe in their region. This situation is related to previous development interventions, which had benefitted only the easily accessible villages inhabited by advanced sections among the tribal population and immigrant non-tribal population. The integrated plan identified 52 per cent of the Konda Reddis in three districts as shifting cultivators and, focusing on the hill-dwelling Konda Reddis, proposed establishing settled agriculture by discouraging shifting cultivation and replacing it with horticulture. Livestock development and cottage industries were to be introduced to check pressure on land and to provide a source of supplementary income.

The plan to discourage shifting cultivation was based on the contention that it resulted in low production and thereby low consumption, and that its effect on the local ecology was deleterious. This contention was supported by India's national forest policy, which advocated its ban. It was thus suggested that the comprehensive programme to wean people off shifting cultivation should involve persuading people that shifting cultivation was not good for their ecosystem.

The planners were determined to change everything that existed. They not only wanted shifting cultivators to change to settled cultivation, but their entire seed bank was to be replaced by high-yielding varieties, and cash crops were to be introduced to compete with the production of food crops. There were even proposals to transform traditional practices in the rearing of livestock. The absence of milking, consumption of milk products or rearing of milch animals among the Konda Reddis was seen as a major constraint for dairy development. As with settled cultivation in opposition to shifting cultivation, rearing milch animals for the dairy market was part of the livelihood development schemes promoted by the government. To overcome the absence of milch cattle rearing among the Konda Reddis, they were to be 'educated' on its benefits. Upgrading the local stock of goats and poultry was also proposed, by introducing improved stock to the Konda Reddis. Since pig-rearing was found to be popular among the Konda Reddis, upgrading local breeds by replacing males with Yorkshire boars was also proposed.

Thus development here meant replacing all local breeds. There are no reports on how the Yorkshire boars survived in the hills of the Konda Reddis, or how the people took to these new breeds. The planners do not seem to have seen this replacement as a threat to biodiversity, which will eventually lead to the extinction of local breeds.

Although the integrated plan was conscious of development benefits not reaching the remote areas, most of the schemes failed to reach areas such as the hill villages in Khammam district that the Konda Reddis of this research belong to. Then, during the ninth five-year plan (1997 to 2001) a comprehensive plan of action for the development of the Konda Reddis in Khammam district was prepared by the government's Integrated Tribal Development Agency (ITDA) in the municipality of Bhadrachalam, and submitted to the Tribal Welfare Department of the government of India.

The plan was designed to cover 1,379 households, of which 237 households belonged to twenty-one hilltop settlements.[4] The plan proposed schemes for housing, agriculture, irrigation, drinking water, horticulture, infrastructure, health, malnutrition and food security, education, training in model farming and community awareness, along with a community-based training programme.

The plan for the hilltop population was to resettle them in the plains. This seemed to follow the trend set by the 1978 plan. The ITDA felt strongly that, through resettlement, the isolation of the Konda Reddis in the hills could be overcome, and that this would make the land for shifting cultivation inaccessible and automatically promote the integration of the community into the mainstream society.

The implementation of the ITDA resettlement plan

The hilltop settlements were grouped on the basis of proximity to each other, and people were scheduled for resettlement in seven colonies in the foothills. The first colony, with twenty-one houses, was ready in 1996, and it was occupied by fourteen households from two hill settlements. The construction of the other colonies followed, and by 2003 six colonies were ready for occupation.[5] Except for the colony at Tekulodi, which was established in an existing Konda Reddi village in the foothills, the other six colonies were built either in or next to the villages of the Koya, a scheduled tribe subsisting mainly

---

4   My research is concerned with nineteen of these twenty-one hill settlements. However, the numbers quoted here are based on an ITDA survey and do not correspond to a research survey (see Thanuja 2005b).

5   The seventh colony at Gandikothagudam, for the Konda Reddis of Pedavagu hill settlement, was to be built in 2000. Twenty households from Pedavagu settled in Gandikothagudam in early 2000, but they continued to stay in their huts in the colony until September 2002, when the construction of concrete houses began and they were shifted to Ayyavargudam. The construction of the colony in Ayyavargudam did not start until January 2003. Three households from this colony settled in Challakavam colony, while the rest resettled at the foothill of the original hill settlement. The construction of this colony was later abandoned.

by settled agriculture. The presence of non-tribal or other tribal populations in these villages in the foothills is negligible.

Of the twenty-one hill villages listed by ITDA for resettlement, two fall outside the study region and one village, Goddladoddi, is uninhabited. Six villages have refused to be resettled. Of the remaining twelve villages, five were to be resettled in Tekulodi. There are a total of thirty-four households in these five villages. However, in January 2003 only twelve houses were under construction. In the remaining seven settlements that were resettled, 67 households shifted to the colonies from a total of 131 households (64 households remained in the hill settlement). In 2003, the total number of households in the seven colonies corresponded to 29.82 percent of Konda Reddi (hilltop) households. This reflects their receptivity to the resettlement programme.

It is important to note here that ITDA officials tried to lure the hill-dwelling Konda Reddis to settle in the plains by promising housing, agricultural land and other infrastructure, but no force was used to bring all households to the colonies. In fact a list of households willing to resettle was prepared and housing was constructed only for this number, although the ITDA plan had estimated costs for all hilltop households. Also, those households who opted for resettlement did not always move to the colonies when they were ready. From its inception, settlement in the colony has not been permanent, with some households living both in the hills and in the colony according to seasonal livelihood activities; while others have lived more permanently in the colonies, yet continue with livelihood pursuits available in the hills. This situation was feasible as the majority of households remained in the hills, thus permitting the continuity of traditional social structure, beliefs and practices.

Resettlement was the main focus of the development programmes planned by the ITDA for the Konda Reddis. Other schemes involving agriculture, drinking water, irrigation, horticulture and so on were complementary to the resettlement programme. The ITDA plan for agriculture proposed allocating 5 acres of land per household in the resettlement colony. This scheme also included provision for agricultural implements, livestock, seeds, fertilizers, pesticides and land development. It was assumed that this would wean the population away from shifting cultivation. However, no colony was allotted 5 acres per household, and each colony was left to cultivate the land allotted collectively. The lack of implementation of the promised agriculture scheme and along with it changes in traditional social dynamics pushed the colonies' inhabitants to resort to shifting cultivation in the hills. The events leading to this situation can be seen through the case of one of the seven colonies discussed below.

The impact of attempted resettlement

The Boddugudem colony was occupied by ten households who were allotted 12 acres of land for collective cultivation. In the very first year of cultivation in July 2002 there resulted some tension with respect to the division of labour among the resettled households. The labour input for shifting cultivation is quite different from the labour demanded by settled agriculture. In shifting cultivation, nuclear families usually cultivated their own plot, thereby allowing them to decide on their labour input. Even though certain activities like weeding demanded communal labour, the time required for this was no more than half a day in a cultivation cycle (for one year). Further, cooperation was engaged in on a reciprocal basis. But the case of collective agriculture was different. Giving 12 acres of common agricultural land to the ten resettled households demanded great levels of cooperation, making labour input more intensive from the Konda Reddi perspective.

One household belonged to a couple who were the first to resettle. Apart for them, the rest of the households were quite out of place in the colony and often shuttled between the hills and the colony. The initial couple had undergone training in making bamboo handicrafts at the ITDA training centre a year earlier. They acted as the head of the colony on the insistence of ITDA officials, as they were economically dependent on the sale of bamboo handicrafts through ITDA-organized stalls in nearby towns at regular intervals. They were also expected to act as the agents of ITDA in convincing the rest of the community of the benefits of resettlement and settled agriculture. The role of colony head played by the couple with the backing of ITDA was resented by the other inhabitants of the colony, and this made labour cooperation difficult. This was because the other households had not severed their ties with their hill settlement and continued to enjoy access to resources in the hills. Further, the colony was recognized as part of, or belonging to, the hill settlement. For this reason the settlers in the colony did not see the need for a new headman as they continued to accept the traditional power structures, beliefs and practices of the hills.

The other problem with receptivity to agriculture was also related to the land allotted. In acquiring land for the Konda Reddis, the ITDA had not looked into all the details of the acquired land. The land had been bought from a Koya of Boddugudem and had an important history. An ancestor four generations back of Sathyanarayana, the original owner of the land, had created a sacred place by erecting a stone at one end of the 12 acre plot under the shade of a tree. This place was worshipped as the dwelling place of the village god, Pothi Raju. The land, being sacred, was believed to ensure good harvests and health for its cultivators, provided appropriate sacrifices were made. Such sacrifices were not necessary for the remaining cultivable land of the Koyas. Three rituals had to be performed for the newly acquired land. The first took place before sowing, when four chickens had to be sacrificed; the next took place before harvest, when a pig had to be sacrificed. The final ritual, when the harvest was to be threshed, required a coconut, turmeric and vermilion powder, rice powder, two eggs, incense sticks, cooked rice and four chickens. The ITDA officials who monitored cultivation among the Konda Reddis were not informed about these rituals by the Konda Reddis themselves as they felt it was difficult to make the officials understand the power of their belief system. Though the Konda Reddis have a similar practice of sacrifice for shifting cultivation, they are the responsibility of the lineage. The political and religious heads of each lineage arrange for the sacrificial animals to be obtained from lineage members and perform the rituals. In the case of the colony, the ten households were expected to contribute to the sacrifices. Not being members of the same lineage, and in the absence of their political head, cooperation and coordination was a failure. Further, these rituals posed great financial strain on the resettled Konda Reddis. In fact, they had no money to buy a pig for the second ritual, and they instead agreed to give 80 kilogrammes of millet after the harvest to a Koya, from whom they procured the pig.

The other problem experienced during the first year of agriculture was the authority of the ITDA officials. The colony settlers were provided with two electric generators for the agricultural land, one which had not worked since installation and one that was often out of order, and the Konda Reddis had to wait for the ITDA official to have it repaired. Though the village was supplied with electricity, the power supply was very irregular. Finally, irrigation was inadequate and one patch of paddy had dried out, and on the plot where seeds had been sown none had sprouted. The Konda Reddis complained that the soil in this plot was not suitable for maize, but they were forced to sow it on the insistence of the ITDA official. The harvest of red gram sown along with great millet was minimal. The Konda Reddis again felt that the harvest could have been better if cultivated in a separate plot, but they were not allowed to do so by the ITDA official. This highlights the disregard of the ITDA officials for traditional experience and knowledge combined with the execution of a rigid top-down approach.

During the second year in the colony in 2003 all households (except for the one dependent on making handicrafts, mentioned above) had gone back to the hills to practise shifting cultivation. Though there was good rainfall that year, which could have ensured a good harvest, agriculture was not possible as they were told to wait for seeds and required to have the land ploughed under ITDA supervision. These inputs, promised by the ITDA, though not implemented promptly, were provided only for the first two years of resettlement. The Konda Reddis were left on their own to manage the high input cost of agriculture from the third year. However, since this time agriculture has not been practised collectively. On and off, a couple of households have got together to cultivate a fraction of the 12 acre plot, while the rest have continued with shifting cultivation in the hills. A similar situation applies to all the resettlement colonies.

There are therefore important questions that need to be answered to understand the situation described above. First, why did ITDA make resettlement optional? Did those who opted for resettlement give 'informed consent'? If so, or even otherwise, what was their motivation, especially when the majority of Konda Reddis refused to relocate? Was there conflict within the community between those who opted for and against resettlement? Why the strong preference for shifting cultivation?

The dynamics of resettlement

Both the 1978 and 2000 development plans drafted exclusively for the Konda Reddis stressed the importance of resettling hill Konda Reddis in the plains and the introduction of agriculture as the only way to wean people off shifting cultivation, thereby promoting better living standards. But resettlement was offered as a choice to people. How did this come to be? Since the recognition of the Konda Reddis as a 'particularly vulnerable tribal group' in 1980, ITDA received funds from the government specially allocated for the development of the Konda Reddis. Using the 1978 plan as a reference point, the officials started to prioritise interaction with the Konda Reddis in their attempt to convince them to resettle in the plains. Officials had refrained from heading to the hill settlements for a long time, and they tried to make contact with the Konda Reddis during the latter's weekly visit to the plains on market days. Eventually government officials did trek into the hills to convince the Konda Reddis of the benefits of resettlement. The opinion of a headman of one hill settlement reproduced below reflects the popular consensus of the Konda Reddis to these interactions with ITDA officials:

> We have all that we need for survival and have survived till now without
> external support... We understand our forests, own and protect them
> and know how to utilize them to ensure our food supply... We do not
> understand why officials volunteer to help us when we have not asked for
> help, and insist on satisfying all our needs, which we have already done for
> ourselves.[6]

---

6   Kadala Chinam Reddy, Jinnethogu settlement, 2000.

Such statements were also made directly to ITDA officials, who were finally forced to change their strategy and ask the people what they would like the government to do. This question may elicit responses from the Konda Reddis today, but in the early 1990s there was no response. The ITDA officials found it challenging to negotiate and convince the Konda Reddis to participate in the development programme. Besides the community's attitude towards external intervention, their settlement pattern in the hills also posed an important obstacle for the ITDA officials. This was because the Konda Reddis would not gather in one settlement for the visits of officials, forcing the officials to trek to each hill settlement, which range in size from two to thirteen households. Further, with householders busy with different livelihood activities such as hunting and gathering, the officials were often greeted with empty settlements. Also, because of frequent transfers among ITDA officials, the initiative took its time. It was finally out of desperation that ITDA went ahead with its plan, leaving it to people to volunteer for resettlement.

Even before the resettlement programme a few development programmes were initiated in the hills, such as the 'hilltop primary residential school' and the 'health programme'. Both these programmes offered jobs to the Konda Reddis. A total of seven residential schools were established across the hills, and for each school a cook and helper were recruited from the settlements. The health programme recruited a community health worker from each of the ITDA-listed hill villages. All three positions were provided with a monthly salary from ITDA, and the employees were also used as messengers, communicators and, slowly, as ambassadors of ITDA development plans. The resettlement project continued to be at the forefront of ITDA development planning as their experience in negotiating with the Konda Reddis only convinced them that the inaccessibility and consequent isolation of the hill settlements contributed to people's indifference to development intervention. They believed that once the community resettled in the plains, frequent access to the people would be possible and other development plans could be initiated. ITDA thus went ahead with resettlement knowing full well that the majority of households in the hills would not be interested. They were, however, confident that the programme would attract the households who were employed by ITDA and newly established households of young married couples. Not only were there exceptions even in these categories, but at the same time some older households did opt for resettlement.

So what motivated those who opted for resettlement? One of the classic ways that the government approaches the implementation development policy is to inculcate disrespect for local culture amongst a community. The policymakers manage to do this as they totally disregard the need to understand local culture. The first volunteers for resettlement came from those households who had a member employed by ITDA. This employment had increased interaction with ITDA officials, slowly making these Konda Reddis buy into the rhetoric of the underdevelopment of the hills and the development of the plains.

As stated earlier these, households eventually turned into ambassadors of the ITDA development plan, convincing other households, especially newly married couples, to establish their households in the resettlement colonies. Complementing this situation was the easy accessibility of the resettlement colonies to navigable roads, and thereby weekly markets. These weekly markets were an important attraction for the Konda Reddis, where relatives from different hill settlements met and exchanged news and treated each other to alcohol. The resettlement colonies provided relief from trekking over the hills after a day out at the market.

However, for the majority, the resettlement colonies were just an extension of territory in the hills. The colonies were viewed as part of the traditional practice of setting up new settlements in search of land for shifting cultivation or building temporary field houses in the plots they used for shifting cultivation. Similarly, they chose to occupy their dwellings in the plains during the summer, when no cultivation activities took place in the hills, or they were occupied by those households that skipped a year or two of practising shifting cultivation. But the new livelihood opportunities of the plains –both agriculture and other wage labour– were not a motivation for these households. The overruling motivation remained the fact that they did not lose their membership and rights in the hill settlements and could always resettle in the hills.

How is this possible when there is a clear difference of opinion between those who opt for resettlement and those who do not, creating the potential for conflict? And how is this resolved so as to give the settlers the advantage of claiming territory in both the hills and plain? It is noteworthy that the majority (70 per cent) of households did not opt for resettlement. Significantly, these included the households of the lineage political and religious heads. Opting out of resettlement, which was the majority choice, reflects the importance of the hills in Konda Reddi identity. This was voiced by one elder:

> We see ourselves as people of the hills. We are Konda Reddis, heads of the
> hills; we do not see ourselves as agriculturalists. We have always practised
> hunting and gathering along with shifting cultivation; they go together. And
> bamboo – I do not know how we learnt to weave bamboo into baskets, but

our elders did it and we learnt it from them. As we watched our elders do it, we got into the practice of doing it too. We live in the hills because we have a lot of resources to live on.[7]

The hills and their abundant resources are revered by the Konda Reddis as much as they look down on the plains and agriculture. So the access to agricultural land and housing in the plains gained by the settlers is not envied by the hill dwellers. The only source of conflict that did erupt initially and on and off was when settlers indulged in setting up parallel power structures. This, as discussed above with the case of Boddugudem colony, was backed by ITDA, who wanted to make the resettlement colonies autonomous. But the traditional positions of authority in the hills are not created haphazardly. There are two offices of authority: first, the village headman responsible for all political affairs in the village and the lineage; second, the religious head of each lineage, who is responsible for performing all harvest rituals and communicating with the hill spirits. Though each village is occupied by members of different lineages, it is recognized that the lineage who first established a hill village will hold the headship of it (Thanuja 2005b). As people revere the hill spirits and the resources of the hills, access to them can only be enjoyed by paying reverence through cooperation to the lineage heads.

The close linkage between the belief system, natural resources, livelihood activities and the social organization of the Konda Reddis makes relocation from the hills to the plains difficult if not impossible. It is this connection to the hills and the continuity of membership to the hill settlements, rather than the support of parallel power structures, that prevented conflict between non-settlers and settlers in the plains. This linkage also explains the resilience of the practice of shifting cultivation. It is important to recollect here that while giving up shifting cultivation is an important objective of resettlement, almost all resettled households continued with shifting cultivation.

The resilience of shifting cultivation can be attributed to the fact that it allows for the management of time, space and labour in practising cultivation, hunting, gathering, rearing livestock, maintaining kitchen gardens and making bamboo handicrafts (Thanuja 2005b). Shifting cultivation for the Konda Reddis is a system that together includes all these livelihood activities. It is a strategy that allows the optimal use of the abundant resources of the hills referred to above. Further, these diverse livelihood activities can be carried out at the individual and household level, so that cooperation across larger units is not mandatory. Unlike agriculture, the main input cost for these activities is human labour, giving the Konda Reddis autonomy in decision making

7   Valla Bhima Reddi, Chintagandi settlement, 2006.

regarding whether or not to practise these livelihood activities at any given time. These factors contribute to the continued practice of shifting cultivation even after resettlement.

Voluntary or involuntary displacement: is there a case for impoverishment?

In the preceding sections, this chapter has looked at the details of the history, implementation, motivation for and impact of resettlement among the Konda Reddis. The case has been discussed to question the logic behind the simplistic position between voluntary and involuntary displacement/resettlement. Further, in line with objections raised by Mehta (2009) and Mitra and Rao (2009), the case of the Konda Reddis is used to critique the IRR model of Cernea (1997). Here I argue that irrespective of the type of displacement there is a risk of impoverishment.

As stated above, the Konda Reddi case is unique since the settlers did not lose access to their traditional hill resources and community membership. In fact, the resettlement colony has also been perceived by them as an extension to their hill territory, giving them the option of settling once again in their traditional hill habitat. According to this perception, the present case cannot be classified as one of displacement. On the other hand, not all households opted for resettlement. In light of this, this case can be viewed as one of voluntary displacement. However, the most important aspect of the case, and the basis on which it should be judged, is the cause of resettlement, which came from an external source.

The hidden agenda of ITDA's resettlement policy was to remove the community from its traditional lifestyle and resource base and incorporate it into the plains with settled agriculture as its mode of living. This implies a shift from the hills to the plains, from autonomy to dependency on the government, and with it the loss of traditional knowledge and practices. This disregard for local culture is intended to develop disrespect and a sense of shame amongst the community, especially the younger generation, who are lured with material inputs by the development agent. Such a situation has the potential of instigating internal conflict. It thus becomes crucial to strike a balance between changes brought about by external intervention and traditional practices.

The Konda Reddi resettlement, thus, holds good as a case of involuntary, not voluntary, displacement, as the initiative for resettlement had been taken and carefully planned by an external source. Further, the objective behind this initiative was based on a disregard for traditional knowledge and practices, and the hope that eventually the community's dependency on the external source would increase. ITDA went ahead with resettlement even though the number of households opting for it was minimal, and it anticipated that more households would in time be motivated to resettle. However, the post-resettlement situation is not at all the one ITDA expected. The resilience of shifting cultivation and the fact that Konda Reddi identity is linked closely to the resources and livelihood practices of the hills has kept the majority in the hills, with more resettled households practising traditional livelihoods than settled agriculture. This situation has helped to keep in check internal conflict and maintain a balance between adherence to traditional practices and participation in opportunities created by external intervention.

It is relevant to return here to some of the impoverishment risks listed by Cernea (1997). The first impoverishment risk suggested by him for reconstruction/rehabilitation is the lack of provision of land. Though the Konda Reddis did not lose access to traditional cultivation land in the hills, agricultural land in the plains was provided. But the risk of impoverishment is not addressed simply with the provision of land. The case of agricultural land provided for inhabitants of Boddugudem colony discussed above shows how factors of collective labour, new leadership, the authority of the external agent and increased financial and ritual commitments can cause the land provided not to be used, leading to impoverishment. While in this case impoverishment is avoided thanks to access to traditional resources, it is clear that, as argued by Mehta (2009), mere provision of land will not necessarily avoid impoverishment.

Another important aspect overlooked by the IRR model is change brought about by policies independent of resettlement programmes (Mitra and Rao 2009). The case of the 'public distribution system'(PDS) of the state government,which provides 35 kilogrammes of rice per month at a cost of 2 rupees per kilogramme, requires discussion here. The regular dependence on purchase and consumption of PDS rice among the resettled households has a bearing on the neglect of not just agriculture, but also of shifting cultivation, leading to a risk of morbidity and food insecurity due to impoverishment.

Though the PDS provision is common to all Konda Reddis, the risk of impoverishment is strong among the inhabitants of the resettlement colony. This is because PDS rice is dominant in their dietary intake. This has interlinked causes: the subsidised price of the rice, the quantity being sufficient for the predominantly nuclear households, and their increased cash income (the result of higher prices for commodities sold by them, amongst other opportunities).

The replacement of millet varieties, pulses and vegetables produced by shifting cultivation by a single cereal (white rice) in the dietary intake of the Konda Reddis can be correlated with the increased morbidity that is visible among the settlers. Along with this change, households in the resettlement colony have shown increased dependence on other nutritional supplements provided by the government for infant and maternal health, corresponding with a lack of storage and procurement of multiple food products from the forests, thus leading to food insecurity.

This case is a clear demonstration of how the resettlement goal of transforming settlers from a situation of autonomy to dependency can be achieved. Changes induced by the state and market threaten the nutritional security of the Konda Reddis, making them vulnerable in many ways. As stated above, it is crucial to maintain a balance between changes brought about by external intervention and adherence to traditional practices to avoid impoverishment.

References

Anon. 1952. *The National Forest Policy of India, 1952*. Delhi: Government of India.

Baviskar, A. 1995. *In the Belly of the River: Tribal Conflicts over Development in the Narmada Valley*. Delhi: Oxford University Press.

———2002. 'States, communities and conservation: the practice of ecodevelopment in the Great Himalayan National Park'. In V. Saberwal and M. Rangarajan (eds), *Battles over Nature: Science and the Politics of Wildlife Conservation*, pp. 267–99. Delhi: Permanent Black.

——— 2009. 'Breaking homes, making cities: class and gender in the politics of urban displacement'. In L. Mehta (ed.), *Displaced by Development: Confronting Marginalisation and Gender Injustice*, pp. 59–81. Delhi: Sage.

Cernea, M. 1990. 'Poverty risks from population displacement in water resources development'. *Harvard Institute for International Development, Development Discussion Paper* 355. Cambridge, Mass.: Harvard University Press.

———1995. 'Understanding and preventing impoverishment from displacement: reflections on the state of knowledge', *Journal of Refugee Studies* 8(3):245–64.

——— 1996a. 'Bridging the research divide: studying refugees and development oustees'. In T. Allen (ed.), *In Search of Cool Ground: War, Flight and Homecoming in Northeast Africa*, pp. 293–317. Boston: UNRISD.

———1996b. 'Public policy responses to development-induced population displacement', *Economic and Political Weekly* 31:1515–23.

———1997. 'The risks and reconstruction model for resettling displaced populations', *World Development* 25(10):1569–87.

——— 1998. 'Impoverishment or social justice? A model for planning resettlement'. In H.M. Mathur and D. Marsden (eds), *Development Projects and Impoverishment Risks: Resettling Project-Affected People in India*, pp. 42–66. Delhi: Oxford University Press.

———2000. 'Risks, safeguards and reconstruction: a model for population displacement'. In M. Cernea and C. McDowell (eds), *Risks and Reconstruction: Experiences of Resettlers and Refugees*, pp. 11–55. Washington: World Bank.

Dhagamwar, V., De, S. and Verma, N. 2003. *Industrial Development and Displacement: The People of Korba*. New Delhi: Sage.

Dreze, J., Samson, M. and Singh, S. (eds). 1997. *The Dam and the Nation*. Delhi: Oxford University Press.

Dwivedi, R. 2002. 'Models and methods in development-induced displacement', *Development and Change* 33(4):709–32.

Fernandes, W. 2001. 'Development-induced displacement and sustainable development', *Social Change* 31(1/2):87–103.

Mehta, L. (ed.). 2009. *Displaced by Development: Confronting Marginalisation and Gender Injustice*. Delhi: Sage Publications.

Mitra, A. and Rao, N. 2009. 'Displacing gender from displacement: a view from the Santal Parganas, Jharkhand'. In L. Mehta (ed.), *Displaced by Development: Confronting Marginalisation and Gender Injustice*, pp. 34–58. Delhi: Sage.

Parasuraman S. 1999. *The Development Dilemma: Displacement in India*. Baring Stoke: Palgrave Macmillan.

Ramanathan, U. 1996. 'Displacement and the law', *Economic and Political Weekly* 31(24):1486–91.

Scudder, T. and Colson, E. 1982. 'From welfare to development: a conceptual framework for the analysis of dislocated people'. In A. Hansen and A. Oliver-Smith (eds), *Involuntary Migration and Resettlement: The Problems and Responses of Dislocated People*, pp. 267–87. Boulder, CO: Westview Press.

Thanuja, M. 2005. 'The Konda Reddis in transition: a study on social organisation, shifting cultivation and development'. PhD thesis. Madras: University of Madras.

Thukral, G. 1992. *Big Dams, Displaced Peoples: Rivers of Sorrow, Rivers of Joy*. Delhi: Sage.

——— 1996. 'Development, displacement and rehabilitation: locating gender', *Economic and Political Weekly* 31(24):1500–3.

Xaxa, V. 2003. 'Tribes in India', *The Oxford India Companion to Sociology and Social Anthropology*. Delhi: Oxford University Press.

6

Displacement, language loss and identity in two villages in eastern Nicaragua

Mark Jamieson

In this chapter I consider reasons for the recession of the Ulwa (Southern Sumu) and Miskitu languages in Karawala and Kakabila, two villages on Nicaragua's Mosquito Coast.[1] In Karawala, Miskitu has all but displaced Ulwa; meanwhile, in Kakabila, Creole English is apparently displacing Miskitu. I first examine the history of language and identity in the wider region. Second, I present the communities of Karawala and Kakabila. I then consider changes in the linguistic habits of Karawala and Kakabila villagers. Finally, I claim that language change in each case can be explained to a considerable extent by single occurrences in the histories of these communities. I conclude by arguing that, often enough, relatively spectacular demographic events, rather than gradual processes, produce tipping points (Gladwell 2000; see also Wolf 1963) resulting in the abandonment of, or modifications in the social uses of, autochthonous languages.

---

1   I use the term Sumu as a term of reference to encompass both Mayangna (Northern Sumu) and Ulwa (Southern Sumu). Some, though by no means all, Mayangna regard the term 'Sumu' as an ethnonym with insulting connotations that has been imposed on them by others. Others, however, regard the term 'Mayangna' as 'inauthentic' and have reclaimed the term 'Sumu'. I do not use the term 'Mayangna' as an all-inclusive substitute for 'Sumu' since this term (meaning the inclusive 'we' in the Panamahka, Tuahka and Tawahka languages of the north) does not exist in Ulwa (inclusive 'we', according to Green, being 'mining'). Green suggests that the term 'Muih' would be a better ethnonym for the Sumu in general since this word means 'person' in both Panamahka-Tuahka and Ulwa (Green 1999:11). See Hale and Benedicto (2004) for discussion of these issues.

A history of language and identities amongst the Miskitu and Sumu

The conquest and hispanicization of western Nicaragua was fast, brutal and complete. Today, no minority languages remain in this part of the country, though 'Indian' identities persist in such towns as Masaya and Nindiri. From the country's western region settlers pushed rather more tentatively eastwards into the central highlands in the nineteenth century, incorporating Matagalpan speakers and others into Nicaragua's Spanish-speaking majority, but as they continued to push the frontier of settlement further into the eastern lowlands they found both a considerably more challenging environment, characterized by poor soils, a lengthy rainy season and inhospitable flora and fauna, and hostile locals – some 'Indians', others Caribbean English speakers – who regarded 'Spaniards', as they called Spanish speakers, as enemies (Newson 1987).[2]

The Caribbean coast of Nicaragua and eastern Honduras, known as the Mosquito Coast, lying beyond the range of early Spanish settlement, had early in its history become a refuge for English speakers: first, buccaneers; then settlers known as Shoremen, some of whom kept slaves of African and Amerindian descent; and, finally, Caribbean English-speaking Blacks who came looking for land and freedom. Members of these groups took local Indian women and by the early nineteenth century a society and culture had emerged from their descendants that came to be known as Creole. The members of this society, so-called Creoles, spoke a distinctive variety of Caribbean English, and during the late nineteenth century embraced Moravian Christianity. Many regarded themselves as 'English' or kin to the English, and most were antipathetic to the Spanish empire and later Spanish-speaking Nicaragua, both of which they viewed, successively, as threats to their independence and way of life.[3]

When the first of these European settlers (English, French and Dutch buccaneers) came to the Mosquito Coast during the course of the mid to late seventeenth century, they found groups of speakers of Misumalpan languages. Since these arrivals came not to conquer or proselytize, but rather to refit and reprovision, they were able to establish friendly relations with native people, particularly those in the area near the mouth of the Rio Coco, on the present-day Nicaragua–Honduras border (Holm 1978:29–41). This group of

---

2   I have some reservations with the term 'frontier' as it has been applied to the Nicaraguan context and more generally. See Hale (1994) for discussion of 'Anglo-affinity' and hostility towards 'Spaniards' among the Miskitu in the late twentieth century.

3   British governments meanwhile vacillated between recognizing the Mosquito Coast as sovereign Spanish or Nicaraguan territory and regarding it as an unofficial protectorate of Britain (Floyd 1967:26–38; Gordon 1998:30–50). See Dozier (1985) and Naylor (1989) for discussions of this history.

Indians came to be known as Mosquito (later Miskito or Miskitu) and they became active partners with their mainly English-speaking allies, giving them locally produced goods, services as provisioners, rights of access to their women, and slaves from other groups, in exchange for cloth, iron goods and, importantly, firearms. Miskitu society, which seems almost certainly to have been comparatively egalitarian, now acquired a class of entrepreneur warlords on whom their English-speaking partners conferred such titles as general, governor, admiral, captain and, for the most important, king. During the eighteenth century these warlords controlled supplies of slaves to Anglo-Jamaican buyers and weapons to their followers, organizing (sometimes in conjunction with their English-speaking allies) raids and tribute-taking expeditions deep into the Central American interior. The Miskitu even raided Spanish settlements, sacking Granada on at least one occasion, and seem to have visited, and demanded tribute from, the Spanish cacao plantations on Costa Rica's Matina Coast on a more or less annual basis. The Miskitu also kept many of the slaves that they captured, and these were absorbed into Miskitu society as more or less ordinary members (Floyd 1967:55–69; Helms 1983; Noveck 1988).

The eighteenth century was characterized by considerable Miskitu geographical expansion, as the members of the group's growing population, troubled by weakening soils caused by overuse (and hurricane damage), sought sites for settlement away from the increasingly overpopulated Cape Gracias and Sandy Bay areas where they mainly lived. A number of these people founded communities near river mouths and around the coastal lagoons, close to the incipient Creole communities with whose members they established increasingly intimate relations of exchange. Marriages cementing trading relations between Miskitus, Creoles and visiting traders seem to have been common. Meanwhile, Indians who inhabited districts into which Miskitu and Creole settlers arrived gradually disappeared, becoming enslaved or absorbed by the new arrivals (Floyd 1967:55–69; Naylor 1989:27–53; Roberts 1965:116–17).

As the British traders pulled out of the region in the late 1780s following formal cession of the Mosquito Coast to Spain, the two communities – Miskitu and Creole – became increasingly dependent on one another. With the absence of an export slave market, Miskitu raids ceased, but by this time many of the groups whose members had been victims of Miskitu slaving were disappearing or had retreated into the interior beyond the range of their predatory enemies (Helms 1983, 1986; Jamieson 1998:716). Many of these groups were, like the Miskitu, speakers of Misumalpan languages, and came to be known by Miskitu and Creole alike as Sumu. Even into the nineteenth and twentieth centuries, after the cession of raiding, many Sumus regarded the Miskitus with fear or apprehension, because, it was widely claimed, the latter tended to look down on and dominate them. Indeed Charles Napier Bell, a nineteenth-century British resident on the Mosquito Coast and a fluent Miskitu speaker, reports the existence of a 'silent trade' between some fearful Sumus and the Miskitu in which the two parties would not meet, instead leaving goods and miniature tokens of goods desired from the other party at a pre-arranged place (Bell 1989:266–7; see also Roberts 1965:120).

From the mid nineteenth century to the mid twentieth century (and to some extent beyond), logging, banana and mining companies, mainly North American, came to the Mosquito Coast offering employment to Creoles, Miskitus and Sumus alike (Dozier 1985; Vilas 1989). Most of these companies came and left shortly afterwards, once the exploitation and extraction of resources in the district became too expensive. Consequently the region experienced a series of extremely localized booms and busts, resulting in considerable movements of manpower, as men moved from district to district, getting laid-off in some places and seeking work in others. The North American companies favoured Creoles over Indians because they spoke English, and consequently they gave them the best jobs, resulting in the consolidation on the Mosquito Coast of an English-speaking elite that had already emerged during the course of the nineteenth century (Helms 1971:27–35). From the 1960s onwards, markets have appeared for marine resources (Nietschmann 1973) and some Creoles have been able to use their relative wealth to purchase outboard motors, skiffs, gill nets, lobster pots and diving equipment, thereby generating further wealth. Jobs offered to young men and women in the region on cruise ships by companies such as Celebrity Cruises and Royal Caribbean give Creoles another advantage over non-English speakers. While these jobs are generally menial, they are well paid by local standards, and many young men and women are able to use their salaries to build prestigious cement homes rather than the commonplace timber houses. Demonstration of competence in English by employees is considered essential by the cruise ship companies, since the tourists on these ships usually speak at least some English.

From this history there emerged over time a hierarchy amongst the region's languages, in which English was valued more highly than Miskitu, and Miskitu more so than the Sumu languages. Miskitus found that they had to learn at least some English while Sumus learned Miskitu and sometimes English, competence in these languages affording speakers access to resources that were otherwise unobtainable (Freeland 2010:244–9).[4]

---

4   As early as the late seventeenth century, Miskitus had used English to facilitate access to the trade with buccaneers, Shoremen and traders, as well as jobs with English-speaking employers (Jamieson 1998:714).

Trade also shaped Miskitu engagements with English speakers into ones characterized by affinity, as the Miskitu secured partners by offering traders their sisters and daughters, a practice that continues to this day (Jamieson 1998). Orlando Roberts, a smuggler working the Mosquito Coast in the early nineteenth century, discussed this tendency in some detail:

> By this licentious and immoral conduct [sexual partnerships with local
> women] they [English-speaking traders] have, however, so identified
> themselves with the natives [the Miskitu], and with some of the principal
> people on the coast, as to obtain a sort of monopoly in the sale of goods,
> which it would be difficult for any stranger, not possessed of an intimate
> knowledge of the Indian character, to shake.
>
> (Roberts 1965:109–10)

As linguist John Holm has perceptively written, 'the Englishman became the Miskito's kinsman, with all the little-dreamt-of political, cultural and linguistic consequences' (Holm 1978:37), and English speakers in Belize, the Bay Islands and the Cayman Islands came to refer to the Miskitu as Waika, from the Miskitu word *waik* or *waikat*, meaning classificatory male cross-cousin or brother-in-law. *Waik* connotes 'potential exchange partner' and is still used as a form of address between Miskitu-speaking strangers hoping to establish friendly relations. Roberts indeed refers to one of his exchange partners as Whykey Tarra (Roberts 1965:55), almost certainly his orthographic rendering of *waiki tara* ('my big brother-in-law' in Miskitu).

Over the course of this history, hundreds of English words entered the Miskitu language, from which the extent of this intercourse can be gauged. Amongst these are items such as *rakbus*, deriving from 'arquebus' but now meaning 'rifle', which demonstrate the earliness of the English influence on Miskitu (Holm 1978:334–42). Miskitu, owing to its association with the English trade, became the lingua franca amongst all the Indians of the region, and, it seems, came to be understood by both Miskitus and Sumus alike as an important signifier for a way of life that in local imaginations was rather more 'English' than 'Indian'.[5] For Sumus wishing to insinuate themselves into the Miskitu-dominated English trade, it was important to learn the anglocentric lexicon of the trading Indians (the Miskitu), and it is very likely that these borrowings from English played quite a large part in effecting a conceptual

---

5   The Miskitu habit of dressing 'right English gentleman fashion' must have
     also distinguished them from the Paya and Sumu groups in the interior to a
     considerable extent (Naylor 1989:36). For a detailed account of the Miskitu
     adaptation to culture contact, see Helms (1971).

linguistic distinction between Miskitu on the one hand, and the other Misumalpan or Sumu idioms on the other.[6] Acquiring Miskitu identity, quite probably understood in part as a project of reinventing oneself as 'English', was therefore a strategy that many Sumus employed.

Bell describes this process of becoming Miskitu among the mid-nineteenth-century Toongla (or Tungla), a group of probably Prinzu Sumus from the districts around Tungla, Layasiksa and perhaps Quamwatla. The Toongla, he writes, 'seem to be a mixed race between the Smoos [Sumus] and Mosquito Indians, and their dialect is nearly pure Mosquito with a large mixture of Smoo words' (Bell 1862:258). Elsewhere Bell notes:

> The village I am staying in is a Toongla village, and the Toonglas are a sort of non-descript people. They claim to be the same as the Mosquito Indians, but although they speak the Mosquito language, they do not quite resemble the Mosquito men. But neither do they resemble the interior and riverine tribes, such as the Smoos [Sumu], Twakas, Ramas, etc. The Mosquito men are prone to domineer over the Toonglas in much the same manner as they do over the Indians of the interior.
>
> (Bell 1989:267)[7]

Thus, just as the Miskitu aspired towards an English identity, the Sumus, or at least some of them, seem to have sought Miskitu identity through abandonment of their own languages and claims to be Miskitu (Green 1999:22). Interestingly, in some districts these processes continue to this day. I present two case studies that demonstrate this. One considers the displacement of Ulwa by Miskitu identity and language in the Rio Grande community of Karawala. The other examines the inroads that Creole English language and identity have made in the traditionally Miskitu village of Kakabila in the Pearl Lagoon basin.[8]

---

6   Distinctions between Miskitu on the one hand and the closest Sumu groups like the Bawihka on the other were quite possibly anything but clear-cut during the pre-contact and early post-contact period, particularly in view of the fact that the Sumu languages are almost identical in syntactic structure to Miskitu (Hale 1991:40–1).

7   See also Anon. (1929:319) and Heath (1950:28).

8   Much of what I describe for Kakabila and Karawala is based on first-hand knowledge obtained through intensive fieldwork and remains therefore unreferenced. I have conducted fieldwork in Kakabila during 1992/3, 1997, 1998, 1999/2000, 2002 (twice), 2004, 2005/6, and 2009/10; fieldwork in Karawala was conducted during 2006. Green's contextualizations of his accounts of the Ulwa language has also been exceptionally valuable (Green 1996, 1999:1–28).

Karawala and Kakabila

The Mosquito Coast today remains one of the most isolated parts of Central America, and there are still very few roads that connect the region to other parts of Nicaragua. Transport throughout much of the region is mainly waterborne, and the dugout canoe, known as a dory, is still the principal means of personal transport. Although some people in the region own small outboard motors, the majority still rely on the paddle and sheet sail to reach neighbouring communities and places of work. For longer journeys people buy rides in passenger skiffs known as *panga*s, transporting larger or heavier goods in the commercial freight boats that ply their trade in the intricate waterways that characterize much of the region. Members of local communities have traditionally been hunter-horticulturalists, cultivating sweet cassava and other tubers on swidden plantations, to which plantains and bananas have been added in post-contact times. They also raise fruit trees, including mango, soursop, cashew and lime, as well as coconut and breadfruit, in yards surrounding their houses, most of which are of timber construction. Almost all families raise chickens, but those who are comparatively wealthy sometimes own cattle, horses or pigs. Men also periodically hunt, usually with dogs but sometimes with rifles, for deer, armadillo and wild peccaries, while women and children gather foodstuffs from the forest and water's edge.

Kakabila: the Miskitu village

Kakabila, a predominantly Miskitu village, is situated on a high bank on the shores of Pearl Lagoon. Surrounded by dense rainforest and swamp, for much of the year it can only be reached by waterborne transport. In the past, villagers travelled to and from Kakabila in dugouts with sheet sails. Today, about one-third of the seventy or so households own small outboard motors with which they power their canoes. Village men employ gill nets to catch snook, coppermouth, drummer and catfish, and casting nets to catch white shrimp and sea shrimp, which they sell to commercial buyers for cash. Fishing with gill nets, mainly in the waters in front of the village, is the main source of income in the village. Some men also go to sea outside the lagoon bar in order to catch turtles, the meat of which is generally sold in the village. The exploitation of marine resources mainly takes place during the rainy season between mid May and the end of December. During dry season months, January to mid May, villagers prepare and plant their swiddens. The Kakabila *centro* (the lands used for planting) is close to the village, and consequently about 85 per cent of household units are engaged in horticultural work for subsistence.[9]

---

9   I do not have space in this chapter to consider issues to do with the use of the ethnographic present. I remain in continual contact with Kakabila people by

Life in Kakabila is thus comparatively similar for most households, albeit differentiated internally by age and gender. Most villagers are involved seasonally in gill-net fishing for cash and horticulture for subsistence, supplemented in a few cases by teaching work in the small primary school, raising cattle or the small-scale selling of commodities such as flour, sugar, cooking oil and coffee, and good food, often in the form of fish and cassava, is rarely scarce. In Karawala there is considerably more variation. A few households, those who have members in regular employment or who own businesses, are demonstrably wealthier than any one might find in Kakabila, and eat well, albeit mostly store-bought foodstuffs. Many others, however, are poorer than any one would find in Kakabila. In these cash is scarce and household members often eat only 'rice so-so' (rice with nothing else).

Karawala: the Sumu village

Karawala, a mainly Ulwa village, is located close to the mouth of the Karawala River, which flows into the Mosquito Coast's Rio Grande about six miles from the river bar. The village is situated on a small series of connected ridges rising out of a swamp close to the river, meeting a large savannah as one travels away from the river's edge from which it is possible to walk to the Miskitu villages of Sandy Bay Sirpi and Walpa. In contrast to Kakabila, few of the Karawala men are fishermen. Although there are locations in the district that are suitable for gill-net fishing (the waters near Rio Grande Bar and Toplock Lagoon), these are not close enough to Karawala to prevent the theft of villagers' nets. Consequently, few villagers participate in this activity. The community of Karawala claims land in the savannah and swamps close to the village, along the Karawala River and at various locations further up the Rio Grande, quite a bit of which is suitable for swidden horticulture. Few households (about 10 per cent by local estimates), however, actually cultivate land. Many villagers say that they are unable to plant crops successfully close to the village because these are all too often stolen and sold for cash by crack-cocaine addicts. They also point to the fact that upriver in places like Betania, Spanish-speaking farmers are slowly taking over land formerly farmed by Karawala people. Other villagers claim that with the arrival of logging companies the village

---

telephone and feel that my current knowledge of the state of affairs in that village justifies my use of the present tense. I am less comfortable using the present in the case of Karawala, as I am less up to date with developments there since my fieldwork in 2006. I beg the reader's indulgence in allowing me to use the present for stylistic reasons, while asking him or her to remain aware of the distinct possibility that much of what I write for this community (and indeed Kakabila) may have changed, even as this book is published.

men have become lazy and too dependent on wage labour, which at the time of fieldwork was offered by a Costa Rican logging company operating on community lands and a church-sponsored house construction project.

Karawala is now the capital of the Desembocadura de Rio Grande municipality, and the village has a police station, a magistrate's office, a health centre employing eleven people and an *alcaldía* (town hall), and large primary and secondary schools. More than half the employees of these are from Karawala or neighbouring villages, but the remainder, particularly those in senior positions, are Spanish-speaking Nicaraguans, which along with the logging company workers constitute a fairly sizeable Mestizo minority in the village. Quite a few villagers make a little income from these Mestizos by taking in laundry, cooking meals or performing one-off tasks (*chamba*), and the greater penetration of cash in the Karawala economy permits the existence of two large shops and a small *pensión*.

Language change
Language attrition in Karawala
There are today perhaps 11,000 people that might be classified as Sumu living in Honduras and Nicaragua. Around 9,500 of these are Northern Sumus, now usually called Mayangna, a category that includes speakers of the closely related Tuahka and Panamaka dialects of Mayangna in Nicaragua, and the Panamaka-speaking Tawahka in Honduras. Perhaps another 1,500 are Southern Sumus (though numbers are hard to guess), some competent in Ulwa, a language related to, but quite distinct from, Tuahka and Panamaka (see Green 1996, 1999:11–17). The great majority of Southern Sumus live in the village of Karawala situated near the mouth of the Rio Grande. Smaller numbers live in the predominantly Miskitu villages of Kara and Tumarin on the Rio Grande, in smaller hamlets and on isolated farms along the Rio Grande, Kuringwas and Wawashan rivers, and in similarly isolated communities along the upper reaches of the tributaries of the Rio Escondido to the south (Green 1999:15–17). Many of those living in Karawala, like the Mayangna to the north, have rejected the name Sumu, which they regard as having been bestowed on them pejoratively. Most, though by no means all, now refer to themselves as Ulwa, though this term seems to be unknown to other Southern Sumus nowadays, especially those living on the tributaries of the Rio Escondido. Since the majority of Southern Sumus now live in Karawala where the term Ulwa is preferred, I will henceforth refer to all the people of this group as Ulwas, including those living outside Karawala.[10]

---

10   The most informative and thoughtful discussion of the history and distribution of the Ulwa, I have found, is Green (1999:10–22). The most authoritative account

I noted above that members of the Southern Sumu population are for the most part 'competent in Ulwa' rather than 'Ulwa speakers' because almost all use either Spanish or Miskitu far more often than they do Ulwa. Along the tributaries of the Rio Escondido, as well as on the Wawashan and Kuringwas rivers, waves of Spanish-speaking farmers have all but absorbed the Ulwa. In these districts only the villages of Virgen and Kahmi Tingni seem to have majorities of inhabitants who identity as Sumu or Ulwa, and even in these communities Ulwa is now heard much less often than Spanish.[11]

In Karawala, use of the Ulwa language is also receding, though in this case it is Miskitu rather than Spanish that is displacing it. The population of Karawala is about 1,400, most of whom identify as Ulwa, though many of these are semi-speakers or non-speakers of the Ulwa language. There is also a smaller number of villagers, probably less than fifty, who identify themselves as Tuahka, most of whom regard themselves as at least competent in Ulwa. Most of these Sumus (Ulwa and Tuahka) generally speak Miskitu nowadays, and most regard themselves as only partially competent in Ulwa. Even fluent speakers of the language hardly use Ulwa at all, though a few elderly residents still use it amongst themselves, remembering a time before the 1950s when Ulwa was the language used by almost everyone in the village (Green 1996).

There are many reasons why Karawala might be 'losing' the Ulwa language, and all these have, I argue, contributed towards its gradual displacement by Miskitu. One of these is the proximity and relative importance of large numbers of Miskitu speakers. The lower Rio Grande district, the so-called Desembocadora, is home to four other villages – Rio Grande Bar, Sandy Bay Sirpi, Kara and Walpa – where Miskitu is the first language or the lingua franca. Rio Grande Bar is a predominantly Creole-speaking community that came to prominence as a place where the peoples of the Rio Grande could bring goods for sale and purchase manufactured items brought up by freight boat from Bluefields, the regional capital nearly 60 miles to the south. This trade has receded and manufactured goods are now almost all brought up

---

of the Sumu peoples in general, as far as I am aware, is Houwald (2003). See Hale and Benedicto (2004) for issues surrounding the ethnonyms 'Mayangna', 'Sumu', 'Tuahka', 'Panamahka' and 'Ulwa'.

11   Because of its age, the rapid advancement of the campesino frontier into eastern Nicaragua and the disruptions occasioned by the Contra War during the 1980s, the survey by Houwald and Jenkins (1975) of the distribution of the Sumu peoples, including the Ulwa, must now be regarded more as a fascinating historical document than as an accurate account of the present-day locations of the Ulwa and other Sumu groups. Whether the mysterious and partly Ulwa-speaking community of Santa Isabel on Mahogany Creek described by Palombieri (1967) is the same community as Virgen is unclear.

through the channel made in the 1950s to connect Pearl Lagoon with the river. As a centre where turtle, fish and shrimp are bought and exchanged by coastal fishermen, commercial buyers and purchasers from upriver, Rio Grande Bar retains some importance, and the inhabitants, most of whom are involved in this trade to some degree, are all fluent in Miskitu as a second language. Most use this language with the people of Karawala, many of whom speak little Creole English.

The other communities in the Desembocadura are predominantly Miskitu speaking. Of these communities, Kara has the closest ties with Karawala, and is home to a small Ulwa minority, a few of whom (the so-called Sûtak or 'calabash people') arrived in Kara from Kahmi Tingni on the Kuringwas River during the Contra War and settled as refugees (Green 1996). This group has since been joined by others fleeing incursions by land-hungry Spanish-speakers on the Kuringwas, Sequia and Pilan rivers. Most people of Kara, however, consider themselves to be Miskitu and have no competence at all in Ulwa. Walpa, situated on an estuary of one of the Rio Grande's tributaries, though relatively small, is almost entirely ethnically and linguistically Miskitu. It is said that Karawala people enjoy good relations with the inhabitants of Walpa, just as they do with those of Rio Grande Bar and Kara.

More vexing is the relationship between Karawala villagers and the people of Sandy Bay Sirpi, a large ethnically Miskitu community of similar size, situated on the Caribbean shore a little north of the mouth of the Rio Grande. Sandy Bay Sirpi, home to families involved in fishing, catching lobster and the finding and sale of cocaine thrown overboard by smugglers, is said to be much wealthier than Karawala. It is said in Karawala that Sandy Bay Sirpi people resent the fact that Karawala, home to the Sumus whom they allegedly despise, is now the municipal capital. Karawala villagers often depict Sandy Bay Sirpi as a dangerous place, especially after dark, where rape, violence and theft by *rakman*, men addicted to crack cocaine, are commonplace. Many Ulwas say that violence and aggression are traits that are characteristic of the Miskitu, and maintain that in this respect Sandy Bay Sirpi is typical. This view of Sandy Bay Sirpi aggression is, no doubt, partly inherited from ancestors who experienced Miskitu domination of the Sumu in previous centuries. However, it is also couched in the knowledge that the appearance from the early 1990s onwards of large amounts of cocaine has brought many problems to coastal villages like Sandy Bay Sirpi, where men's work at sea brings them into regular contact with both the drug itself and others involved in trafficking.[12]

---

12 See Dennis (2003, 2004:260–70) for discussion of the role of cocaine in the transformation of Miskitu communities to the north.

Josefa, a woman in her seventies, blames much of what she saw as dysfunctional in Karawala – theft, violence and drug abuse in particular – as being 'Miskitu' practice. One part of Karawala, the side of the village nearest the savannah known as Twi Said (literally 'by the grass'), is the home to a number of Miskitu families from Sandy Bay Sirpi and communities to the north. One man told me that much of the trouble in Karawala emanated in this particular part of the town, adding with some venom that this was because they were 'Miskitu'.

Mindful of supposed Miskitu aggression towards Sumus and the fact that the former are said to despise the latter, many Ulwas in recent decades have, Karawala people say, become ashamed to speak the Ulwa language (see also Green 1996). As Josefa, who still sometimes speaks Ulwa with her husband and other elders, vehemently explained, '*Miskitu pulisa*' ('they play at being Miskitu'). Sarah, a woman in her fifties, explained that although her mother was actually Miskitu, she (Sarah) learned to speak Ulwa as a child and used it as a joint first language during her childhood. She told me that her daughter Rosa, now in her thirties, refused to speak Ulwa as a child, because she thought people from other places laughed at it. Many villagers echoed Sarah's view that children are to blame for refusing to learn it, but there is also a substantial body of opinion that blames parents for refusing to 'teach' (*lan munaia*) it to their offspring.

Jorge, a young man in his twenties, explained the loss of Ulwa in Karawala in rather more sociological terms. Jorge lives in the 'Miskitu' Twi Said part of Karawala, but both his parents are Ulwa. He understands the Ulwa language but does not use it himself since hardly anyone else does. Like the great majority of villagers, Jorge uses Miskitu exclusively. He attributes the impending loss of Ulwa to the fact that so many Karawala girls establish conjugal unions with Miskitu men from outside the village. Since Karawala Ulwas speak Miskitu but Miskitus rarely speak Ulwa, Miskitu (the district lingua franca) consequently becomes the language of the household, and children raised in such households therefore feel more at ease using Miskitu. It is widely reported by social scientists following Conzemius (1932:147) that the Sumu as a whole rarely allow their sons and daughters to marry people of other groups such as the Miskitu, but as Jorge pointed out this is certainly not true for people of Karawala.

The existence of 'mixed' Miskitu–Ulwa households and the supposed Miskitu denigration of 'Sumu' language and culture no doubt contributed to the displacement of Ulwa by Miskitu. However, Karawala children born into 'mixed' conjugal unions at one time invariably grew up speaking Ulwa, as was the case with Sarah. Indeed, as Green (1999:19) notes, until 1950 Ulwa seems to have been surprisingly resistant to displacement by Miskitu. In hindsight, as

Green argues, it was a single circumstance that produced a tipping, or turning, point (ibid.:21–2) – one that set in motion the processes that, sadly, will almost certainly bring about the eventual disappearance of Ulwa.

This circumstance was the appearance of the Nolan Lumber Company, known to Karawala people simply as Nolan. As I noted above, capitalist enterprises, and in particular logging companies, have been active on the Mosquito Coast for much of the last century and a half. Between 1950 and 1957, Nolan, one of the biggest of these companies, set up an operation extracting mahogany, pine and other kinds of timber from the lands around the lower Rio Grande. Nolan's centre of operations was Karawala, previously a rather sleepy village of (as noted above) predominantly Ulwa speakers centred on a Moravian Church mission. Until then the population of Karawala was probably less than 400. Nolan needed a large workforce of men to work both in their camps along the river (between Karawala and Makantaka) and in their headquarters in Karawala. Men seeking work came to the village from all over the region, increasing the population to at least 800 and probably more than 1,000 (4,000 by one local estimate!). Some were Creoles, a number of whom, by virtue of their competence in English, worked in administrative and supervisory capacities; others were Mestizos, mostly unskilled Spanish-speakers from the interior; others, who came to set up stores, were Chinese. The great majority, however, were Miskitus, mostly unskilled workers who had little to offer but their labour power. This expanded population of mainly men was serviced by a number of shops (most run by the Chinese), a company airstrip, a cinema and a brothel. And so for seven years the Ulwa became more or less a linguistic minority in their own town, outnumbered by a Miskitu majority. When, in 1957, Nolan pulled out of Karawala, most of the Miskitu workers also departed, and the community shrank to its former size, but by then a death blow to the future of Ulwa had already been dealt.[13]

The Miskitu language, already spoken as a second language by the Ulwa and, thanks to the Moravian Church, the community's language of liturgy, became Karawala's lingua franca during the Nolan period. The town's children, cognizant of the despised status of the 'Sumu' language, took advantage of the opportunity to acquire Miskitu. Most, both then and subsequently, decided to abandon the Ulwa language, as did Sarah's daughter Rosa. Many adopted a Miskitu identity that had now become readily available. By the time Nolan pulled out of Karawala in 1957, the majority of children aged ten or less were primarily Miskitu speakers. Most were passively competent in Ulwa, but many refused to speak it. A linguist working in Karawala in 2006 told me of Angela, a woman in her sixties with whom he spoke Ulwa, a language that she had

---

13 See Green and Hale (1998) for speculation on the future of the Ulwa language.

not otherwise spoken in nearly half a century. He also told me that only one person under the age of twenty spoke Ulwa with any fluency.

It was thus a single circumstance, the arrival of Nolan, that ushered in Miskitu as the community's mother tongue and initiated the processes that are leading, apparently inevitably, to the eventual loss of Ulwa in Karawala and, therefore, in Nicaragua. It was similarly a single circumstance that has led to the abandonment by children of the Miskitu language in Kakabila, to which I now turn.

Language shift in Kakabila

There are today about 140,000 speakers of Miskitu, mostly living between Pearl Lagoon in eastern Nicaragua and Ibans Lagoon in north-eastern Honduras, as well as along the Rio Coco. Almost all consider themselves to be 'ethnically' Miskitu. Although there are regional dialectal variations, these are generally by no means great. In most Miskitu villages, other languages are comparatively rarely heard and those people who acquire fluency in other languages, most often Spanish, generally only do so once they reach adulthood. The Pearl Lagoon basin Miskitu villages, the southernmost of the diaspora, are, however, rather different in this respect. In these communities, children now grow up bilingual, speaking either both Miskitu and Creole (Mosquito Coast Creole English) or as apparently monolingual speakers of Creole.

Kakabila is one of the six traditionally Miskitu villages in the Pearl Lagoon basin that are experiencing a process whereby Creole has apparently been displacing Miskitu. In another of these communities, Haulover, villagers abandoned the Miskitu language about a hundred years ago and, though many still insist that they are 'Indians' (and therefore Miskitu), others consider themselves to be Creole. In the larger village of Tasbapauni and the neighbouring hamlet of Set Net Point, Miskitu is still spoken, but only nowadays by elders aged fifty or more. Most children growing up in these villages have no or little competence in Miskitu, and it is safe to say that the Miskitu language is likely to disappear in these villages in the next thirty or so years. In Raitipura and Awas, children still grow up speaking Miskitu but, like their parents, they are also fully fluent in Creole. Added to this, the distinctive variety of Miskitu spoken in these two villages demonstrates a particularly strong lexical and syntactic Creole influence.

In Kakabila the situation is quite different to that in Haulover. Here adults aged twenty-five or more generally speak Miskitu to one another, and report that at one time only Miskitu was spoken in the village (though villagers were universally fluent in Creole, which they deployed when speaking to non-villagers). Today, however, children of eighteen years or less almost universally use Creole with one another as well as with adults. Between the ages of eighteen and twenty-five, the language habits of villagers are less predictable, varying more widely according to context. These data suggest that Kakabila is abandoning the Miskitu language and that Creole is displacing Miskitu, as it has done in Haulover and is evidently doing in Tasbapauni and Set Net Point. Longitudinal study of bilingualism in Kakabila, however, reveals a different and more interesting picture. I return to this below.

There are a number of factors that have contributed to the loss of Miskitu and the adoption of Creole amongst Kakabila children, some of which are necessary but not sufficient conditions. Creole is much more prestigious than Miskitu since it recognized as being a variety of English and consequently a language of international importance; in local terms the English language, and its Creole variant, represents 'advancement'. Thus Kakabila parents, though offered the Miskitu–Spanish primary school bilingual education programme by the Nicaraguan Ministry of Education, have chosen to receive the English–Spanish equivalent. They say that their children, already passive Miskitu speakers, have no need to learn how to read and write the language. Acquisition of the arcane English spelling system, however, is important. This is particularly the case for those boys who wish to get work on the cruise ships, since the company representatives looking at applicants insist on demonstrable competence in English. In any case, Kakabila people have regular, often close, dealings with Creole speakers in Pearl Lagoon, Bluefields and other places, but comparatively few with Spanish-speaking Mestizos, few of whom speak Miskitu. It is therefore important that they speak Creole and this is the reason, according to some Kakabila people, why parents talk to their children in Creole and not in Miskitu. Some villagers regard this as a necessary evil. The children are very possibly 'losing their language' but they are acquiring a skill that they most definitely need, for although Kakabila people have spoken Creole for generations, they have previously done so as a second language.

Until the mid 1980s Kakabila children almost uniformly spoke Miskitu, both with one another and with adults, just as most adults in the village speak it with one another today. This all changed in 1985 during the Contra War when the people of Kakabila were evacuated following a fierce battle that took place in the village. The villagers, already traumatized by repeated incursions of government soldiers and MISURASATA insurgents during the previous months, were told that the town was no longer safe to live in. They were consequently evacuated to Pearl Lagoon town, an almost uniformly Creole-speaking community, where most remained for two years until returning to Kakabila in 1987. Some villagers subsequently spent their time as refugees in other communities, though these also were mainly Creole speaking, but most remained in Pearl Lagoon, living with friends or relatives. For two years, therefore, Kakabila children grew up and engaged with Pearl Lagoon's majority Creole English-speaking people. Kakabila people regard adults and children (defined in social terms) as being quite distinct, and members of the two groups converse remarkably infrequently.[14] This being so, the Kakabila children who, comparatively speaking, socialize themselves to a considerable extent, rather easily acquired their language habits from their Creole-speaking age mates rather than from their parents. By the time they returned to Kakabila in 1987, those less than four or five years old had become, or were destined to become, Creole speakers. Children born and raised in the village since 1987 have also become Creole speakers. Other children speak Creole with them, as now do their parents. Older children who had already acquired Miskitu as their mother tongue by 1985, however, continued to speak Miskitu with one another and adults, though not with younger children, but by the mid 1990s, these older children had become young adults; Miskitu was now the language of adults, and Creole had become, for Kakabila people, a children's language, a state of affairs that remains the case today (Jamieson 2007).

It is interesting to note that in Kakabila there is a more or less readily discernable cut-off point in terms of age. Almost all villagers older than 24 or 25 habitually use Miskitu with one another (though not with those who are younger), while those younger than about 23 tend to speak Creole with others. In other words, the switch from Miskitu to Creole was neither gradual nor staggered. This supports the assertion of many villagers that it was during their period of exile in Pearl Lagoon that Kakabila children 'stole' (*implikan*) the Creole language from their Pearl Lagoon hosts, bringing new language habits back to the town during the re-occupation of Kakabila in 1987. Evidently, children exiled to Pearl Lagoon when more than about two years old retained Miskitu as their mother tongue, while those who were younger became primarily speakers of Creole.

With few children or young adults apparently speaking Miskitu, visitors to Kakabila often speculate that the Miskitu language will eventually disappear in the town. Many villagers, however, do not agree. The village's children are almost all clearly passively competent in Miskitu, they say, and will speak it when they get older. It is easy to argue that this is wishful thinking, that Kakabila adults voicing this opinion do not want to believe that the community's 'proper' language, Miskitu, is being abandoned. Closer examination, however, reveals that there is, in fact, evidence that supports this view. As Kakabila adolescents younger than 23 approach social adulthood, defined by villagers to some extent in terms of the attainment of parental

---

14 I have explored the significance of the stark distinction made by Kakabila people between adults (*upla almuk*) and children (*tuktan*) in Jamieson (2001).

responsibility, many acquire new linguistic habits, and begin to use Miskitu with other socially defined adults. The distinction that Kakabila make between those socially defined in terms that may be glossed as 'children' (*tuktan*) and 'adults' (*upla almuk*) is so absolute that adolescents engaged in the process of attaining social adulthood find they are usefully served by speaking Miskitu, the language of adults, with their would-be peers, rather than Creole, which in intergenerational contexts is perceived as the language of childhood. Kakabila adults often make the point that they do not 'talk' (*aisaia* or *laka paskaia*) with children, and chase them from locations where they are talking with other adults. Children thus reinvent themselves as adults by turning from Creole to Miskitu, perpetuating a situation in which Creole has become a children's language and Miskitu an adults' language.

Sociolinguists often find that 'adults' and 'children' use different sociolects or registers of the language of a speech community. Rarely, however, do they find that completely different languages represent generationally distinct registers as they do in Kakabila. Of course, it may be the case that analogous forms of inter-generational diglossia exist in similar contexts of language shift, and indeed instances of this do turn up in the sociolinguistic literature. However, I have been unable to find any instances of such radical distinctions between adults' and children's languages persisting over time, the assumption being that reports of these are time-bound snapshots of particular moments during the process of language loss. This lacuna in the literature may be due to the fact that anthropologists and sociolinguists rarely do fieldwork for more than two years and therefore are unable to get much sense of how speech communities change over time. I have now been working in Kakabila for twenty-one years and have been impressed by the durability of the linguistic distinction between adults and children, as Creole-speaking children in significant numbers over the years consistently switch to Miskitu while they negotiate their passage to adulthood. Whether this peculiar diglossia will persist far into the future, however, is a question that is impossible to answer, and there are already some indications that in the part of the village close to the wharf, Creole immigration may bring about the eventual loss of Miskitu. Adult–child diglossia may thus be said to be fairly stable for the intermediate future as village endogamy remains statistically significant, but it is quite likely to disappear within a matter of decades.

A number of factors may therefore have encouraged the emergence of Miskitu–Creole bilingualism and diglossia in Kakabila. Among these, one may point to the sense that Creole is a variety of English and therefore an internationally important language that children should be encouraged to master. One might also consider the fact that Creole is the dominant language in the Pearl Lagoon basin, in terms of both the number of speakers and its relationship with economic and political power. One might also consider the role of the English bilingual education programme in Kakabila's primary school, and also the general disapproval in the community of children conversing with adults. These factors, however, while perhaps necessary conditions for the appearance of distinct intra-generational sociolects, were not sufficient. Rather it took a two-year period of exile in Creole-speaking Pearl Lagoon to bring these into existence, a single historical interlude that, like the arrival of Nolan in Karawala, produced a tipping point that changed the linguistic landscape of the community forever.[15]

Conclusion

The evidence from Karawala and Kakabila suggests that relatively marginalized languages in many speech communities are often surprisingly resistant to change if left to themselves. Karawala, for example, was primarily Ulwa speaking for generations in spite of the fact that it was essentially an enclave, isolated from other Ulwa communities, in a district of predominantly Miskitu-speaking villages. Kakabila, similarly, was Miskitu speaking for centuries despite the economic and political dependence of the community on neighbouring Pearl Lagoon, a larger Creole-speaking town. In Karawala, Ulwa persisted until the arrival of the Nolan Lumber Company, while in Kakabila Miskitu continues to persist despite its abandonment by children because the use of these languages index(-ed) community, as opposed to individual, values (Jamieson 2003, 2008, 2010). What eventually initiated the changes described above in both cases were extraordinary events that produced tipping points after which local language landscapes were forever altered.

Minority languages are often surprisingly resistant to displacement by the languages with greater socio-political or economic power that beleaguer them, particularly if the former remain the languages of community. In this way Karawala and Kakabila successfully resisted, respectively, linguistic displacement by Miskitu and Creole English for many generations. In instances of this kind it is instead demographic displacements in which populations of such communities find themselves as minorities within their places of residence, whether in exile as with the people of Kakabila between 1985 and 1987 or at home as in Karawala during the mass immigration of labourers during the Nolan period between 1950 and 1957, that result in dramatic changes to language habits.

---

15   For the complexities of Miskitu–English–Spanish multilingualism on Corn Island, see Minks (2013).

References

Anon. 1929. *Periodical Accounts Relating to Moravian Missions*. London.

Bell, C.N. 1862. 'Remarks on the Mosquito Territory, its climate, people, productions, etc', *Journal of the Royal Geographical Society* 32:242–68.

––––– 1989 [1899]. *Tangweera: Life and Adventures among Gentle Savages*. Austin: University of Texas Press.

Conzemius, E. 1932. 'Ethnographic survey of the Miskito and Sumu Indians of Honduras and Nicaragua', *Bulletin of the Bureau of American Ethnology* 106.

Dennis, P.A. 2003. 'Cocaine in Miskitu villages', *Ethnology* 42:161–72.

––––– 2004. *The Miskitu People of Awastara*. Austin: University of Texas Press.

Dozier, C.L. 1985. *Nicaragua's Mosquito Shore: The First Years of British and American Presence*. Tuscaloosa: University of Alabama Press.

Floyd, T.S. 1967. *The Anglo-Spanish Struggle for Mosquitia*. Alberqueque: University of New Mexico Press.

Freeland, J. 2010. 'Gaining and realizing language rights in a multilingual region'. In L. Baracco (ed.), *National Integration and Contested Autonomy: The Caribbean Coast of Nicaragua*. New York: Algora Publishing.

Gladwell, M. 2000. *The Tipping Point: How Little Things Can Make a Big Difference*. New York: Little, Brown.

Gordon, E. 1998. *Disparate Diasporas: Identity and Politics in an African-Nicaraguan Community*. Austin: University of Texas Press.

Green, T. 1996. 'Perspectivas demográficas e históricas del idioma y el pueblo Ulwa', *Wani* 20:22–37.

––––– 1999. 'A lexicographic study of Ulwa'. PhD dissertation. Cambridge, MA: Massachusetts Institute of Technology.

Green, T. and Hale, K. 1998. 'Ulwa, the language of Karawala, eastern Nicaragua: its position and prospects in modern Nicaragua', *International Journal of the Sociology of Language* 132:185–201.

Hale, C.R. 1994. *Resistance and Contradiction: Miskitu Indians and the Nicaraguan State, 1994–1987*. Stanford: Stanford University Press.

Hale, K. 1991. 'El Ulwa, Sumu meridional ¿Un idioma distinto?', *Wani* 11:27–50.

Hale, K. and Benedicto, E. 2004. '¿Sumos, mayangnas, tuahka, panamahka, ulwa? Lengua e identidad étnica', *Wani* 38:6–24.

Heath, G.R. 1950. 'Miskito grammar with ethnographic commentary', *International Journal of American Linguistics* 16:20–34.

Helms, M.W. 1971. *Asang: Adaptations to Culture Contact in a Miskito Community*. Gainesville: University of Florida Press.

––––– 1983. 'Miskito slaving and culture contact: ethnicity and opportunity in an expanding population', *Journal of Anthropological Research* 39:506–23.

——— 1986. 'Of kings and contexts: ethnohistorical interpretations of Miskito political structure and function', *American Ethnologist* 13:506–23.

Holm, J.A. 1978. 'The Creole English of Nicaragua's Miskito Coast: its sociolinguistic history and a comparative study of its lexicon and syntax'. PhD dissertation. London: University of London.

Houwald, G. von. 2003. *Mayangna: apuntes sobre la historia de los indígenas sumu en Centroamérica*. Managua: Fundación Vida.

Houwald, G. von and Jenkins, J. 1975. 'Distribución y vivienda sumu en Nicaragua'. *Revista Encuentro* 7:63–83.

Jamieson, M. 1998. 'Linguistic innovation and relationship terminology in the Pearl Lagoon basin of Nicaragua', *Journal of the Royal Anthropological Institute* 4:713–30.

——— 2001. 'Masks and madness: ritual expressions of the transition to adulthood among Miskitu adolescents', *Social Anthropology* 9:257–72.

——— 2003. 'Miskitu or Creole? Ethnic identity and the moral economy in a Nicaraguan Miskitu village', *Journal of the Royal Anthropological Institute* 9:201–22.

——— 2007. 'Estilos de habla e idiomas sécretos entre los niños de una comunidad miskita', *Wani* 50:75–90.

——— 2008. 'Sorcery, ghostly attack and the presence and absence of shamans among the Ulwa and Miskitu of eastern Nicaragua', *Journal of the Royal Anthropological Institute* 14:554–71.

——— 2010. 'Bloodman, Manatee Owner and the destruction of the Turtle Book: Ulwa and Miskitu representations of knowledge and economic power', *Journal of the Royal Anthropological Institute* 16:31–45.

Minks, A. 2013. *Voices of Play: Miskitu Children's Speech and Song on the Atlantic Coast of Nicaragua*. Tucson: University of Arizona Press.

Naylor, R.A. 1989. *Penny Ante Imperialism: The Mosquito Shore and the Bay of Honduras, 1600–1915. A Case Study in British Informal Empire*. London: Associated University Press.

Newson, L.A. 1987. *Indian Survival in Colonial Nicaragua*. Norman: University of Oklahoma Press.

Nietschmann, B. 1973. *Between Land and Water: The Subsistence Ecology of the Miskito Indians, Eastern Nicaragua*. New York: Seminar Press.

Noveck, D. 1988. 'Class, culture, and the Miskito Indians: a historical perspective', *Dialectical Anthropology* 13:17–29.

Palombieri, M. 1967. 'Les Sumus du Nicaragua: essai d'analyse de leur système phonologique'. Master's dissertation. Aix-En-Provence: Faculté des Lettres et Sciences Humaines d'Aix-En-Provence.

Roberts, O.W. 1965 [1827]. *Narratives of Voyages and Excursions on the East Coast and in the Interior of Central America.* Gainesville: University of Florida Press.

Vilas, C.M. 1989. *State, Class and Ethnicity in Nicaragua: Capitalist Modernization and Revolutionary Change on the Atlantic Coast.* Boulder, CO: Lynne Rienner Publishers.

Wolf, E.P. 1963. 'The tipping point in racially changing neighborhoods', *Journal of the American Institute of Planners* 29:217–22.

7

Displacing culture

Intervention and social change in Papua New Guinea's extractive industries

Emma Gilberthorpe

Ever since the demise of functionalism in anthropology, anthropologists have been concerned with the 'how' and 'why' of social change, whether it be the result of colonization, missionization or impacts from 'development'-oriented global agendas and goals. Yet, what still remains largely unexplored in the current climate, dominated by discourses of global challenges and collective action, is, on the one hand, the influence of encroaching industrial activity on social change, and on the other, how these impacts can illuminate the inherent value attached to indigenous conceptualizations of family, kinship, community and culture. This exploration is particularly illuminating in the extractive industries sector. Here, the encounter between multinational giants and small-scale indigenous communities represents a conflict of culture that is vastly unbalanced in terms of power, equality and access to resources. This imbalance is framed by the dominant [Western] paradigm of community, culture and change that informs corporate activity and facilitates extraction. Resource intervention strategies, supported by dominant discourses grounded in concepts of division, categorization and management, impinge on thought and action at the local level, affecting social organization and consequently the efficacy and sustainability of long-established social systems. The exponential spread of extractive industries in low-income, resource-abundant countries over the last two decades, largely in response to growing demand for the products of industry in the West (minerals, energy, metals), has occurred alongside the growing demand for accountability from multiple sectors (civil society, Indigenous groups, donor institutions, NGOs etc.) and subsequent emergence of regulatory frameworks and attention to corporate social responsibility. In this chapter, I examine how the key strategies employed by multinational corporations to address issues of accountability have a divisive effect on social relations and behaviour within host communities. I argue that this 'encounter' can provoke both physical and psychological types of displacement, the social and cultural implications of which represent a growing, even urgent, area of concern for anthropologists.

The socio-cultural impact of extractive industries is a particularly urgent area of concern for anthropology because global agendas and goals, and the associated trajectories of economic growth embedded in the so-called global challenges of, inter alia, poverty alleviation, gender equality, and climate action, are restricted from penetrating impacted areas and impacted communities because the encounter itself is essentially temporary. As a temporary encounter, the lineal structure (that is, where sustainability is conceived through processes of economic growth and sustained economic rise) required to achieve the ambitions of either regulatory frameworks or global agendas such the Sustainable Development Goals, is missing. As I and others have shown (Auty 1993; Benson and Kirsch 2010; Gilberthorpe and Papyrakis 2015; Humphreys *et al* 2007), whilst industry giants emphatically employ sustainable development rhetoric, extractive industries are deeply incompatible with 'sustainable development' for various reasons: (1) mineral resources are depleting assets ('non-renewable' or 'finite'); (2) the industry is capital- rather than labour-intensive; (3)extraction becomes less economically viable the more geologically embedded resources are, thus reducing project lifespan; (4) the production chain is short, creating productive enclaves that generate few economic and social linkages; (5) and consumption overcomes investment due to the nature of resource rents and consequent methods of capture and state distributive policy (see also O'Faircheallaigh and Ali 2007).

The incompatibility between the extractive industries and sustainable economic growth is theoretically represented by the 'resource curse', a theorem proposed by Richard Auty (1993) to address growing evidence (see Gelb 1988) that resource-abundant countries perform worse in terms of economic growth than non–resource-producing countries at the same stage of economic development (see Papyrakis 2017; Ross 1999; Sachs and Warner 1995). Numerous examples of 'the curse' have emerged from Nigeria, Angola, Sierra Leone, the Democratic Republic of the Congo, Venezuela, Ecuador, the Middle East and Papua New Guinea, where resource-curse theorists have identified trends of dependency, poor economic growth, human rights abuses, violent conflict and/or huge ecological devastation. A dominant discourse focused on macro-level economic and political factors locates explanatory variables for such negative outcomes in a range of sources, from revenue volatility (Auty 1998; Mikesell 1997), state corruption (Karl 1997; Kronenberg

2004; Sachs and Warner 1995), poor institutional quality (Atkinson and Hamilton 2003; Mehlum *et al.* 2006; Ross 2001), including inadequate policy and distributional management (Torvik 2002), poor education (Gylfason *et al.* 1999; Kronenberg 2004; Papyrakis and Gerlagh 2003) and embryonic technological systems (Buttel 2000; York and Rosa 2003).

Nigeria is a case in point. According to Watts (2008, 2010), Nigeria's high level of corruption stems from the capture of resource rents by governments and elites, which continue to reduce the flow of mineral wealth to local communities in the form of direct transfers, infrastructure and services, and/or development programmes. Intergenerational conflict and large-scale urbanization are additional problems that the Nigerian state is unable to address (Jike 2004; Okoko 1999; Ovadia 2016; Watts 2010).

The 'paradox of plenty' (Karl 1997) retains theoretical dominance in research on the extractive sector, lending itself to bourgeoning efforts by international donor agencies to monitor more closely and efficiently the activities of multinational corporations (MNCs) operating large-scale extraction projects in low-income countries. Some of the schemes borne of this concern are the 'performance standards' and 'extractive industry review' led by the International Financial Corporation, the UK Department for International Development's Extractive Industries Transparency Initiative (EITI), and the International Institute for Environment and Development's 'mining, minerals and sustainable development project'.

These schemes incorporate the central definition of sustainable development set down in the Brundtland Commission, ('development that meets the needs of the present without compromising the ability of future generations to meet their own needs' (WCED 1987:8)) and adapted in the Sustainable Development Goals. This is consequently embraced by MNCs operating in low-income countries, with industry giants such as Rio Tinto, BHP Billiton, Barrick Gold, Chevron and ExxonMobil all presenting themselves as sustainable development practitioners at the very basic level, and even as 'agents of development' at the more extreme (see Gilberthorpe and Banks 2012). Sustainable development activities endorsed and supported by MNCs, usually through a community affairs department, are done so under the collective banner of Corporate Social Responsibility (CSR). The employment of CSR as a strategy for mitigating local hostility and maximizing profits is well addressed in the literature, and I discuss the issue in more detail elsewhere (see Gilberthorpe and Banks 2012; Dolan *et al* 2018; Jacka 2018).[1]

---

1   For studies of CSR, see e.g. Banks (2009), Benson and Kirsch (2010), Blowfield and Frynas (2005), Cowell *et al.* (1999), Frynas (2005), Hilson (2007), Kapelus (2002), Kepore and Imbun (2010), O'Faircheallaigh and Ali (2008) and Trebeck (2008).

Suffice to say here that CSR underpins a 'business logic' that is very much acknowledged by the corporate sector itself, evident in a statement from the energy company Chevron:

> We recognize that business success is deeply linked to society's progress. Our investments in communities – developed in partnership with those communities – also are investments in the long-term success of our company ... We make community investments in the three areas that we believe are the foundation of working societies the world over – health, education and economic development.[2]

For the purpose of this chapter, I am more concerned with the implications of the interventions predicated on convictions of form and content embedded in CSR and sustainable development discourse. The discussion that follows highlights and addresses some of the key socio-cultural problems emerging from MNC interventions, focusing specifically on key strategies and their implications for processes of social change at the village level. Of particular concern is the way dominant concepts of 'development' provoke both physical and psychological displacement.

Physical displacement refers to either forced or voluntary relocation, forced relocation being in the form of relocation programmes, de rigeur in the extractive industries, especially the open-cast mining of hard-rock minerals (see Owen and Kemp 2015). Forced relocation imposes the physical displacement of individuals and, more often, entire villages from the site of extraction and supporting infrastructure. Relocation is justified by the need to isolate communities from the possible health and safety risks associated with the extraction and production processes (Owen and Kemp 2015). Voluntary displacement is a consequence of the migration that extraction projects inevitably attract through the provision of wage labour and access to the infrastructure and services that form part of large mining projects. Yet physical displacement is not the only type of displacement experienced by individuals and groups living in the shadow of industry. In this chapter, I focus on the effects of psychological displacement, a term I employ in reference to the impact of unfamiliar systems on perception, belief, emotion, motivation and awareness, and the ultimate affect this has on social behaviour and interpersonal relationships. I argue that psychological displacement is an importation of corporate intervention that imposes concepts and practices of

---

2   Quoted from Chevron's CSR statement, previously available from www.chevron. com/globalissues/corporateresponsibility/2010/ceomessage (accessed 12 August 2011).

division and membership onto traditional landscapes, causing indelible change to social systems. This multi-level displacement raises critical questions about the impact of extractive industries on the social and economic security established by socio-political exchange networks in non-market economies.

In this chapter I draw on case study material from two of Papua New Guinea's largest extraction projects: the Kutubu oil and gas field and the Ok Tedi copper, gold and silver mine. The indigenous hosts of these industries, the Fasu and Min respectively, have altered their conceptualizations of place, community and culture in response to the intervention of new principles pertaining to landownership and cash royalties. My aim here, is to highlight the multitude of problems and challenges emerging from processes of resource-based development to challenge assumptions about the efficacy of interventions and the discourse that informs them. I begin with an outline of the key intervention strategies emerging from the corporate sector's need to obtain a social licence to operate, followed by a brief outline of the context under discussion and an analysis of the impact and effect of psychological displacement.

Development and resource extraction: obtaining the social licence to operate

Social change brought about by global capitalist forces may be referred to as 'development', but what does a development encounter entail for the millions of indigenous groups confronted by it? Does 'development' follow a linear pattern of 'progressive' integration? Do indigenous populations displace tradition with the 'new' and the 'modern'? And can 'development' be effectively measured using quantitative indicators of education, standards of living, income and life expectancy? According to Hoben, development is:

> A process of change through which an increasing proportion of a nation's
> citizens are able to enjoy a higher material standard of living, healthier
> and longer lives, more education, and greater control and choice over
> how they live. Development is generally believed to rest on rising levels
> of labor productivity, which can be achieved through the application of
> science, technology, and more efficient forms of economic and managerial
> organization.
>
> (Hoben 1997:113)

This definition reflects typical development agendas that are finely tuned to and measured by economic growth indicators. This developmental approach is employed by states and international donor agencies under the precept of 'integration' where opportunities and resources are supposedly accessible to indigenous groups. However, when the development encounter is isolated from the market, as it so often is in the extractive industries sector, and there is no opportunity or resources to facilitate national/global integration, development agendas take on a new character.

Rather than following a neat pattern of linear, economic transition and a displacement of the traditional with the modern, the peculiarities of 'development' – from discourse to infrastructure – become part of dynamic, traditional systems. Unfortunately, as the Papua New Guinea case data presented below clearly show, these can threaten the long-term socio-economic security of individuals and groups. In rural Papua New Guinea, variables constituting development agendas such as 'a higher material standard of living', labour productivity, health service and education provision, become entwined in the activation of CSR and 'best practice' by MNCs. Emerging expectations attached to CSR and best practice tend to focus on elements of infrastructure such as schools, hospitals, roads and so on, as well as training and micro-credit schemes that seek to promote 'sustainable development' at local, regional and national levels. The problem with this approach in rural Papua New Guinea, and elsewhere, is that minimal opportunities exist for locals to develop skills and 'efficient forms of economic and managerial organisation' to maintain a capital-led economic base when projects cease production (see Ballard and Banks 2003; Biersack 1999; Ernst 1999; Filer 1999; Hyndman 1994; Jacka 2001; Jackson and Banks 2002; Jorgensen 2004; Kirsch 1997; Macintyre and Foale 2004).

Papua New Guinea's resource extraction pathway has been defined by a number of large-scale open-cast mines in Bougainville, Ok Tedi, Porgera, Misima and Lihir, as well as a number of smaller-scale oil and gas concessions at Kutubu, Gobe and Moran. More recent industries, including the Hidden Valley Gold Mine, the Ramu Nickel Project and the Papua New Guinea Liquefied Natural Gas Project have arguably established Papua New Guinea as a resource-dependent state (Filer and Macintyre 2006). The CSR interventions accompanying multinational extraction projects are executed through a compensatory system that disseminates cash royalties to indigenous landowners. Direct transfers of cash wealth have made a number of 'landowners' very wealthy by national standards. By way of example, Fasu landowners, hosts of the Kutubu oil and gas project and discussed in detail below, received in excess of 120 million kina (approximately £33 million) in royalties, compensation, land rents and equity dividends between 1992 and 2007 (Gilberthorpe 2007).

As I have discussed elsewhere, the principles guiding strategies for intervention heavily depend on a business logic grounded in profit maximization and the mitigation of local hostility (Gilberthorpe and Banks

2012; see also Frynas 2005). To ensure these outcomes, MNCs identify an 'affected community', a named entity or set of entities that can be referred to in the corporate literature and 'social impact assessment' reports. Cultural categorization of what are effectively fluid, unbounded units of affiliation presents a number of problems for indigenous populations. In the first instance, conceptualizations of 'culture' conflict with perceptions of 'cultural reproduction' at the village level (Gilberthorpe 2013). Whilst 'culture' and 'cultural reproduction' are theoretically ambiguous terms in anthropology because they assume a collective homogeneity that does not necessarily exist, the use of 'culture' has been central to Papua New Guinea's colonial and developmental trajectories. Across Melanesia the concept of bounded territory and delineated boundaries are inherently ambiguous. Groups fade into one another, languages overlap and traverse vast environments, and rituals and customs flow between groups (Gilberthorpe 2007). The colonial legacy of 'cultures' and 'language groups' are embraced by MNCs because they comply with a business logic by facilitating profit maximization through a reduced sphere of benefit provision (Gilberthorpe 2013).

Due to the geographical isolation of Papua New Guinea's rural interior, where many of its current resource extraction projects operate, state interest is very much qualified by the industry itself. The state has little concern for regions beyond the commercial extraction of resources. The government has employed a number of incentives to attract foreign investment, including the Tax Credit Scheme, an initiative allowing multinational corporations to develop basic infrastructure (classrooms, housing, medical centres and so forth) in place of the payment of tax. As such, MNCs take on a pseudo-government role, providing basic services such as health centres, classrooms/schools and road maintenance in a bid to maintain their social licence to operate. In Ok Tedi, the vast infrastructure (discussed below), developed through the Tax Credit Scheme, accommodates the mine community living in the central mining town of Tabubil for the duration of the project. What this means is that the infrastructure and the 'higher material standard of living', health services and 'education' it provides, is only available for as long as the project is in operation. The 2015-16 El Niño drought, which initiated the temporary closure of Ok Tedi mine and subsequent permanent withdrawal of its expatriate community (Gilberthorpe, forthcoming), is testament to this, driving the reality of a 'sustainable mining' strategy home for the indigenous populations living in and around the mine.

The infrastructure at Kutubu is typical of oil-producing regions. Operations and employee headquarters are located within secure compounds, and all infrastructure constructed outside the boundaries of corporate operations forms part of the company's CSR agenda and application of the Tax Credit

Scheme. Schools, aid posts, community centres and eco-tourism lodges have all been endorsed and/or sponsored by the MNC across the broader Kutubu region. Infrastructure is a small part of the sector's 'minimal footprint' strategy whereby CSR is implemented through 'benefits' and a presumed concomitant self-development through investment, entrepreneurial activity and capitalist gain rather than being constructed around housing and a township, as is the case in mining regions such as Ok Tedi.

In contexts of extractive industry, a number of critical factors, including the isolation of producing regions from the market, their dependency on extractive activity for 'development', the 'finite' and volatile nature of the industry itself, and ill-conceived interventions, mean that the peculiarities of development do not always have the desired effect. Case studies from Kutubu and Ok Tedi demonstrate this claim further.

Ethnographic background
Ok Tedi

Ok Tedi lies in the Star Mountains region of Western Province, an area characterized by rugged, steep limestone ridges, dense primary and secondary rainforest cover and one of the highest levels of rainfall in the country.[3] Elevations range from 300 to 3,000 metres, offering a range of resources and thus variety of subsistence activities including sago production, hunting (wild pig, cassowary and small game) and taro gardening. The mine is managed from headquarters in Tabubil mining town on the banks of the Ok Tedi River. For the majority of its life it was home to both expatriate and national mine employees, but since the 2015-16 drought expatriates work on a fly-in-fly-out basis rather than permanent residence in the mining town with their families. Still, the schools, hospital, supermarkets, bakeries, banks, hardware store, newsagents, post office and chemist, sealed roads, street lights, permanent houses, swimming pool and golf course, all developed for a largely expatriate population remain and flourish in a post-drought context. As do the hydro-electric power scheme and sanitation plant whilst the national airport and hotel, are busier than ever. This level of infrastructure and provision, however, is limited to the mining town itself and does not extend to the surrounding villages with the exception of the 'landowner' villages discussed below. Everything needed to keep the mine and town functioning arrives on a daily

---

3   Occasionally the area falls victim to the El Niño weather pattern that affects the central and east-central equatorial Pacific. From late 2015 to early 2016, Papua New Guinea suffered widespread drought and frost that threatened livelihood security. Western Province was particularly badly affected and the Ok Tedi mine ceased operating as a consequence.

lorry convoy that has travelled 140 kilometres on an unsealed road from the port town of Kiunga.

Rent-free, permanent houses with running water and electricity are built across the town for mine workers and government employees, whilst satellite villages catering for project beneficiaries provide permanent housing with running water and electricity, along with bathrooms and kitchens with white goods. Non-beneficiaries live in peripheral villages that are best described as shanty towns (see Gilberthorpe 2009b). Initially, mine employees lived in and operated from Tabubil township. Housing was organized into three categories: category A and category B houses exclusively for the upper echelon of mine employees, and category C houses for government employees such as teachers, postal workers and medical staff. Lower-level mine employees, mostly local and migrant workers, lived in dormitories known as 'dongas'. Post-drought, category A and B houses largely lay empty and the dongas, which provided free accommodation for mine employees, have been replaced with rental accommodation.

The extraction site on Mount Fubilan is located approximately 8 kilometres north-west of Tabubil town. This area was uninhabited during prospecting and project development, a fact implicit in the loose environmental conditions put in place at the time (Burton 1997:29–30). But ownership and user rights were firmly established by the Min ethnic groups to whom Mount Fubilan and the surrounding land have significant spiritual value (see Jorgensen 1996:98). Individuals from these groups moved to the mine site during its development phase and a steady flow of migrants has since ensued, including those claiming direct ownership of the land and those from further afield in search of wage labour and other benefits. The population of Tabubil is thus comprised of migrants, many of which have no access to gardening and hunting land. With subsistence secondary to a consumer lifestyle, cash is central to the local economy.

The ethnic groups around Ok Tedi include sociolinguistic communities living in the northern mountainous region: Telefolmin, Urapmin, Oksapmin, Tifalmin, Wopkaimin and Faiwolmin (Gardner 2004; Jorgensen 1996). In the southern foothills and valleys live Ningerum, Yonggom and Awin (Kirsch 2006). These large 'tribal' units are divided into smaller descent groups (glossed today as 'clans') who acknowledge variable degrees of biological kinship through shared substance (Barth 1987:13; Jorgensen 1986; Poole 1982). According to Barth, the larger 'tribal' groupings provided social and economic security for its members (Barth 1987:11).

The sociolinguistic groups sharing the suffix 'min' (literally 'people') lived closest to the mine site at the time of project development. Only one of these groups, Wopkaimin, laid claim to the mine site and signed a 'memorandum of agreement' during project development (Barth 1987; Brumbaugh 1990). Wopkaimin are sole recipients of cash royalties and other infrastructural benefits, receiving 30 per cent of the 1.25 per cent royalty rate (see Ballard 1997:55). Whilst anthropologists suggest that internal recognition of a homogeneous unit was unlikely in the past (Jorgensen 1996:192), the term 'Min' has been widely adopted to demonstrate collective identity and ownership by Min groups in the shadow of industry.

The Min (population 25,000) acknowledge a linguistic, cultural and geographic affinity (ibid.:190) through specific cultural features including cults, symbolic themes, rites, non-verbal expression and secrecy that show local variation but distinct interconnectivity. Prior to the mine, the Min inhabited more than thirty scattered villages, ranging 'from scattered households to shifting longhouses or fixed central villages' (ibid.:191). Political groupings ranged in size and organizational complexity, some groups observing exogamous marriage alliances, others observing endogamous affiliations (Barth 1987:11). Political groups were autonomous and self-sufficient, interacting very little with 'outsiders' (non-Min) and observing rules of trade and intermarriage within a defined territory. Social organization varied widely across the region with descent being reckoned along patrilineal lines in some areas and bilaterally in others (ibid.:11).

Interconnectivity between different descent groups is rooted in the mythology of a single female, widely known as Afek, who wandered into the region some eleven generations ago (Brutti 2000:102; Gardner 2004:108). Afek mythology is highly complex and varies amongst the different sociolinguistic groups inhabiting the Star Mountains. Due to limited space, the full extent of these variations cannot be fully addressed in this chapter (see Barth 1987; Craig and Hyndman 1991; Poole 1982). What is important to this discussion is how intrinsic Afek mythology is to perceptions of community and culture and the interweaving of relational trajectories, sustained over at least eleven generations to inform the way the peculiarities of mining are given meaning. A summary of Min interrelationality will thus suffice here.

The ancestress (or female wanderer) Afek imposed land boundaries, and marked ethnic territory, trade networks, customs, clan specialties, rituals and male initiation, and gave meaning to local landmarks such as Mount Fubilan (Brumbaugh 1990; Jorgensen 1996; see also Barth 1971, 1987; Hyndman 1990). These fixed markers and ritualized activities formed the cultural nexus of all Min groups and ensured the circulation of resources, valuables and people in the region (Barth 1971; Brumbaugh 1990). Specialization in taro farming, adze manufacture or other forms of production formed the basis of trade networks and formulated the trade paths that connected otherwise autonomous groups (Kaoyak 2003).

Male initiation, said to be established by Afek, was a particularly important activity, its complex and exclusive nature determining the patriarchal base of Min sociality (Barth 1987; Crook 1999; Jorgensen 2005). Prior to the mine, initiation houses were socio-political cores located across the region. They were exclusively for initiated males and contained powerful relics, including bones and ancestral remains (Jorgensen 1996:191). All important decisions were made within them and membership of them was based on a series of male initiation rites marked by complex systems of taboo and secrecy that varied between groups but were essentially founded on Afek's teachings (Barth 1987; Brumbaugh 1990; Jorgensen 1996; Kaoyak 2003).[4] Telefolip was the name of the central cult house, said to have been built by Afek and widely acknowledged as the most significant of all cult houses in the region. Telefolip (and the village that shared its name) was the centre of regional cult activity and provided the ethnic link between all Min. The cult house was rebuilt on the same site for many generations until it was destroyed by a religious movement in 2001 (see Brutti 2000; Hyndman 1990; Jorgensen 1981, 2005; Lohmann 2001; Robbins 1995, 2004).

Kutubu

Kutubu lies approximately 90 kilometres south-east of Ok Tedi in the fringe highlands of Southern Highlands province. The landscape is situated between 300 and 1,500 metres above sea level, offering a range of ecological conditions from sago swamp valleys and agricultural grasslands to dense tropical forest. The Kutubu Petroleum Development Project began commercially extracting oil in 1992 under the operatorship of Chevron. Chevron sold their stake to Oil Search Limited of Australia in 2003, who continue to lead a consortium in petroleum production, whilst ExxonMobil began extracting liquified natural gas (LNG) in 2014. There is no central township, nor are there facilities around the operations, which, along with employees, are secured within policed compounds. Infrastructure comprises a central production facility, processing plant, two company camps, a small international airport, a series of well heads and semi-permanent access roads all tightly controlled by the operators. The main camp has a number of employee cabins, a gym, a basketball court and a medical centre. A largely expatriate and non-local workforce operates on a 28-day fly-in, fly-out rota. Crude oil is processed on site and petroleum is exported via a 265 kilometre pipeline to a marine loading terminal in the Gulf of Papua. LNG is transported via two processing facilities connected by a 700-kilometre-long pipeline network.

---

4   These initiation rites are no longer practised, largely due to the impact that Christianity has had in the region.

The oil concession lies between the Hekikio (Kikori) and Soro rivers, a geographic enclave that is home to the Fasu language group. There has been no large-scale migration to the region as there has at Ok Tedi (with the exception of a strong Huli contingent in the northern region bordering Huli territory) and there is no provision of houses for project beneficiaries. Fasu villages remain isolated from project activity, houses are primarily constructed from bush materials and there is no electricity, running water or sanitation facilities. The value of infrastructure developed by the company through the Tax Credit Scheme is reduced through poor management by the state. One isolated school is barely accessible and the provision of equipment and supplies is negligible. Three aid posts are neither regularly staffed nor stocked. An access road that joins all but one of the thirteen Fasu villages is rarely repaired and inaccessible to most.

The Fasu and Foi ethnic groups inhabit the Kutubu region. The Fasu occupy the land on which oil project infrastructure is located and are primary project beneficiaries, receiving 90 per cent of royalties, calculated at 2 per cent of well-head value. The Fasu (approx. population 1,100) were, prior to project development, predominantly hunter-horticulturalists with a diet based on sago production and garden produce, supplemented by fish, game and sweet potato. Whilst the influx of cash has seen processed foods enter the Fasu diet to varying degrees (particularly tinned meat and fish), traditional subsistence activities retain their strong practical and cultural function. Sago production (exclusively done by females) is still prominent, but male hunting has declined and age-mate hunting parties are infrequent as a result. As subsistence remains the dominant economic form much of the burden on accumulation falls to females. Male activity, concentrated around 'business', is now far more village-focused, whilst female activity maintains a domestic theme. Domesticated pigs have retained their pre-project value and still represent an important part of Fasu exchange. They are raised in small numbers by both males and females, used as exchange items in ceremonies and consumed on ceremonial occasions (Gilberthorpe 2004).

The Fasu region is roughly divided to form three geographically and dialectically distinct groups, the Uri ('mountain'), Hekari ('by the water') and Yasuku ('by the bush'). Each group specializes in tradable resources – pigs, sago and shells respectively – the movement of which defined socio-political networks of exchange and intermarriage, creating a vast network of social kinship in the recent past. Although geographically isolated by the Hekikio and Soro rivers, a network of trade and intermarriage over generations of migration and activity ensured the maintenance of ties across a broad territory that included the Foi to the east, the Huli to the far north, the Kasua living on the other side of the Hekikio River and the Bosavi-Kaluli groups to the west.

Membership of a larger 'tribal' group (that is, the Fasu) is based on colonial efforts to categorize. As a collective group, the Fasu acknowledge an affinity with people who speak Namo Me (Namo, 'real'; Me, 'talk'), known as Namo Aporo (Aporo, 'people') rather than 'Fasu' (actually the name of a single clan/family unit). Like 'Min', however, 'Fasu' has come to represent connectivity in the shadow of industry, although the smaller groupings of Uri, Yasuku and Hekari are more readily used as markers of ethnic identity (see detail in Gilberthorpe 2007).

Unlike the Min, genealogical memory is shallow among the Fasu. It is, however, no less constrictive. Group membership is constructed around a strong sense of biological kinship that defines connectivity to place and ancestral lines. Whilst for the Min, biological kinship marks permanent connectivity (Barth 1987), for the Fasu, biological kinship must be maintained through ongoing obligatory, reciprocal processes. Connectivity is thus built on resource use and the fulfilment of obligation that can be severed as easily as it is established.

As for many Papua New Guineans, the Fasu have recently adopted the term 'clan', now used in reference to what were characteristically fluid units of affiliation. Exchange networks depend on a hierarchy of obligation with kinship terms distinguishing levels of patri-focal membership and responsibility beginning with the individual, then brothers and fathers, affines, parallel-cousins, cross-cousins and so on. A bi-generational, patrilocal unit of father and adult sons (known by the kinship term *kepo*, literally 'base of tree') forms the core of any clan grouping, and additions to this make up the broader clan group (*aporo ira*, literally 'man tree'). The metaphorical analogy between group membership and trees (the biological 'base' and extending 'branches') provides an excellent indication of levels of obligation and connectivity amongst the Fasu. The core, or base, of the group (the *kepo*) is bound by biological ties between a father and his productively mature sons. Ties are determined by conception – that is, shared substance – but maintained through the ritualized sharing of substance culminating in male initiation (no longer practised) and the ongoing exchange of resources (see Kurita 1994). Importantly, emphasis is placed on nurture, and it is ongoing exchange that defines relationships and, ultimately, kinship (Gilberthorpe 2007; see also Sahlins 2011).

Each *kepo* is headed by the eldest living male member, who is conceptually descended from a group founder. The headman along with his younger brothers or mature sons makes all decisions about land transfers, marriage and so forth. The headman inherits the obligation to maintain ties with other groups and individuals through the transfer of land and its resources (mainly of the primary resource, sago palms). This was done in the past by ensuring that enough non-agnates were recruited to support the group in warfare and the accumulation of bride wealth. Membership of the *aporo ira* was characteristically fluid, with land being easily transferred from one man to another through the transference of resources. All affiliations to the core are the result of either migration – of wives and non-agnatic males – or progeny, dependents making up the broader clan group. The relationship of others to land is through their connection to individual men as siblings, spouses, offspring, affines or allies.

Migration was central to the constitution of any named group at any time. Due to fluid migration patterns and principles of marriage and recruitment in the recent past, many of the 'clans' that exist today may be quite recently resident and the result of past migrations.[5]

Resource impacts

As we can see, forced displacement has not, to date, been an essential part of the development strategy for the MNCs operating at Ok Tedi and Kutubu. Voluntary displacement, however, has occurred on a large scale at Ok Tedi due to the extent and quality of infrastructure. However, in both Ok Tedi and Kutubu there is an overwhelming level of psychological displacement caused by discourse and action surrounding intervention strategies, most notably through policies regarding landownership and cash royalties. These policies form the core remit of Papua New Guinea's national sustainable development trajectory and the imposition of CSR through the corporate sector, and I address them in more detail here.

Land ownership

The landowner model confronting indigenous hosts of industry is a generic and all-encompassing one fashioned on Western methods of categorization and hereditary land tenure constructs (Gilberthorpe 2013). At Kutubu, the dissemination of cash royalties is organized and managed by the 'incorporated lands group' (ILG) system. The ILG is a self-registering unit where a single 'clan' represents a specific pocket of land (see Gilberthorpe 2007). The ILGs identified as 'beneficiaries' receive cash royalties, which are distributed via the government to the Fasu chairman, then to ILG headmen, then to ILG members and then female kin, affines and other affiliates in a system of redistribution. Due to a regional bias on patrilineality and patrilocality, landowners are always male. A critical difference between Ok Tedi and Kutubu is that Ok Tedi's 'landowner' list was not the result of the type of social mapping exercises carried out at Kutubu, but on an ambiguous first-come, first-served basis. As

---

5   See Gilberthorpe (2007) for an in-depth discussion of these issues.

the land around what is now Tabubil and the site of extraction, Mount Fubilan, was previously uninhabited, those who presented themselves as landowners (Wopkaimin) were entered onto a list (the memorandum of agreement) that has survived for over twenty years as the authoritative catalogue of local landowners.

The rigidity of the landowner model does not complement the characteristically fluid nature of traditional organizational features and it has created formalized division (Gilberthorpe 2007; see also Ernst 1999) by making a distinction between land (as commodity) and people (as consumers) that does not intrinsically exist. For the Fasu and Min, it is a fusion of social, political and economic constructs that determine access to and tenure of natural resources (Banks 2009).

As the case study data show, the Fasu are characteristically segmented, with identity firmly grounded in small, family groupings based on levels of biological and social kinship and the cultivation of ties within and without the immediate territory. The ILG system draws on long-standing values that place importance on the relationship between the *kepo* and a loosely defined and transferable area of land. In the past, mature brothers often divided to form separate *kepo* units either within the larger group's territory or in an area left vacant by group extinction or permanent migration. The grouping together of several *kepo* units to form the larger *aporo ira* was common during periods of endemic warfare.

In recent years *kepo* identity has sharpened to become synonymous with an exclusive ILG, and ILG status is legitimized by claiming genealogical links to a lineage founder, producing a level of genealogical depth that was previously ambiguous. Emphasis on the *kepo* as an impenetrable, exclusive unit controlling land as 'property' and 'commodity' has generated stratification, hierarchy and 'bisnisman' status.

Accentuation of the father/son unit (the *kepo*) as the primary mechanism for defining landowner status and rights to benefits in the shadow of industry attributes more value to biological than social kinship. Consequently, non-agnates are no longer recruited, but groups continue to segment as male children mature and form new *kepo* units and thus new ILGs. In 1992, fifty-four groups registered as ILGs, but by 2005 this number was closer to eighty-eight.[6] The fifty-four groups registered in 1992 were those resident at the time of initial registration, and have continued to fission in accordance with traditional principles of group membership based on reproduction of the kinship category *kepo*. This is seen by the corporate sector as 'greedy', 'lazy'

---

6   Due to incomplete up-to-date electronic records, the accuracy of this number is
     questionable. There is also an issue of some overlaps in group registration.

and 'opportunistic' (Goldman 2000; cf. Banks 2009:46) rather than as the activation of traditional networks of kinship and descent combined with the socio-political desire to maximize wealth, and thus status, for the kin group.

The intensified focus on biological over social kinship has caused a level of regional isolation imposed by significant changes to processes of marital coupling. As is typical in subsistence-based, exchange economies, marriage is an important cultural mechanism for maintaining ties between individuals and groups. Pathways are created by females when they leave their natal group on marriage, their movement establishing physical links between two groups. Obligatory gifts and trade goods continue to traverse pathways along with other females, establishing inter-group connectivity over several generations. Over the last two decades, however, female migration has expanded beyond traditional territories to the more wealthy and affluent regions, such as Port Moresby and Mount Hagen. This has caused the Fasu to become regionally isolated as long-standing social obligations established through marriage are frozen or even severed.

What is particularly important for anthropologists is that the formalization of membership and creation of social exclusion seen in the Fasu's response to interventions are informed by already-existing rules of membership and rights based on patri-focal biological kinship, the movement of females in marriage and the transference of valuable resources. This shows, as I have argued elsewhere (Gilberthorpe 2007), that identity within the core unit is valued over and above the collectivity of the larger *aporo ira* ('clan' grouping), but that at the same time the importance of biological connectivity has been intensified by development discourses (also Golub 2007). Yet it is the larger network that provides social and economic security over a vast area in a configuration of what I refer to elsewhere as rooted and extended identity (Gilberthorpe 2009a). The increasing importance placed on the core unit as the exclusive landholding lineage threatens the security provided by broader networks of social kinship, not only between Fasu but also with traditional trading and marriage partners at a regional level.

A similar case exists for the Min, for whom kinship and descent ultimately inform ownership rights. Whilst the term 'clan' implies a rigidity in group membership that did not previously exist, a conception of 'pure Min' did (Kayaok 2003). The Min have a restrictive form of cultural connectivity where 'pure Min' are internally recognized as collective inheritors of a culture developed by the female ancestress, Afek (see Jorgensen 1996). When the Wopkaimin sub-clans laid claim to the land around Mount Fubilan and signed the memorandum of agreement they voluntarily moved close to the mine site where they now live in three villages, all supplied by the mine operators with permanent housing, electricity and running water. Benefits are disseminated via chairmen, who have the authority to determine beneficiaries. Their ongoing refusal to share benefits more widely has created a division of 'haves' and 'have nots', along with a tangible level of hostility, jealousy and resentment and a break down in trade and marriage relations between groups. A non-landowner described the situation to me, saying that, 'it is as if they [landowners] are cooking a pig and the smell is wafting over to us, but they will not let us taste a bit of it.'

The cultural importance of kinship and descent underpins much of the resentment and conflict in the region, particularly in relation to the lack of obligation shown by Wopkaimin to share benefits. Members of clans that 'missed out' have left traditional villages and moved closer to Tabubil to assert their claims on what they perceive as shared territory. All Min consider themselves as 'custodians of Afek's legacy' (Jorgensen 2004:73) and the mine site as the mythological centre of Min society (see ibid.). Non-landowners living in shanty towns struggle to maintain their subsistence endeavours as the environmental impact of the mine has devastated waterways and local gardening land. Those living in Tabubil and surrounding landowner villages enjoy a Western lifestyle, living in houses with kitchens, bathrooms, gardens, washing machines and so forth; landowner royalties are used to purchase material goods from superstores and supermarkets in the town, which stock everything from clothes, pots and pans, bicycles and ice cream to TVs, barbeques, beds, lawn mowers and coffins. Many of the wealthier landowners (chairmen in particular) own four-wheel-drive vehicles and travel to and from the capital, Port Moresby, by air on a regular basis.

The overt stratification of wealth has caused a number of social problems for the Min. Not only have they been alienated from traditional lands and villages as a result of voluntary displacement, they have also alienated each other by propagating a division between 'haves' and 'have nots'. Loss of traditional knowledge is widespread, including traditional dress, exchange activity and the initiation processes on which much of Min cosmology is based. This is especially true for those living in and around the mining town itself, who have grown dependent on store-bought goods and produce.

What the data show is that the corporate strategy of categorizing and dividing, emulated in the landowner model and forming an intrinsic part of Papua New Guinea's developmental trajectory, can break down the long-standing networks of sociality, cooperation and obligation that ensured social and economic security in the past. At the same time, historical and cultural factors dictate the way agendas are modified. Both the Min and Fasu have restricted forms of biological kinship that shape the way that the landowner model is managed by individuals and groups at the village level. In other mining regions, most notably Porgera (see Filer 1999), kinship networks are far less restrictive, a factor facilitating a 250 per cent population increase between 1995 and 1999 and a 'watering down' (Banks 2007:262) of landowner benefits in the Porgera region. So whilst intervention strategies prompt very different outcomes, they consistently and indelibly alter the organizational constructs that provided sustainability and security in the past (see also Ballard and Banks 2003). The flow of cash linked to landowner identification exacerbates this situation even further and has an overall effect on people's perceptions, motivations and beliefs, which ultimately inform social behaviour.

The flow of cash royalties

The flow of cash in the form of royalties to landowners is perhaps the most overt cause of psychological displacement. The assumption held in economic and political spheres that mineral endowment can stimulate economic growth may prevail, but this does not take the nature of diverse social, economic and political environments into account. Ok Tedi and Kutubu, like many rural areas receiving resource-generated 'benefits', are isolated from the market. Cash provided as 'compensation' is not integrated into a typical capitalist economic system defined by labour, taxes and consumption.

Classical political economists theorized that this type of unearned income creates unsustainable economic systems. The circulation of cash royalties within the economic enclaves of Ok Tedi and Kutubu are typical examples of this economic anomaly. In Papua New Guinea, the phenomenal flow of cash is referred to as *mani ren* ('money rain'). This term symbolizes the magico-religious quality attributed to resource-generated cash that has initiated a type of cargo cult mentality similar to that well documented in the literature on the region.[7]

The indigenous analysis and use of unearned income generates tension between the state, MNCs and local communities. Whilst the state and MNCs expect cash to stimulate entrepreneurial activity and a more quantitative type of development, local communities use it to redefine socio-political exchange networks. Within traditional systems the passage of resources, including wealth items such as shells, pigs, cassowary and *tikiaso* oil, marked obligations between individuals and groups that were maintained through ongoing cycles of giving, receiving and reciprocating. As cash enters this system a number of unpredicted problems emerge stemming from the confinement of benefits, the role of MNCs in exchange relations and the status of those who engage with the capitalist principles confronting them.

---

7   See esp. Lawrence (1964) as well as Wagner (1981). For more recent studies, see Bainton (2008) and Bainton and Cox (2009).

Whilst the confinement of an 'affected community' is seen as a necessary step prior to any intervention by MNCs, because it facilitates the confinement of responsibility whilst maintaining a commitment to it (Frynas 2005), it is divisive to traditional socio-political exchange networks because it isolates beneficiaries within economic enclaves, stimulates the realignment of networks and, consequently, creates tension and hostility between traditional trade and marriage partners. As commitment is maintained within ever-decreasing circles, traditional exchange relations are neglected causing resentment and amplified risk for those not fulfilling traditional obligations. This risk is magnified even more by the fact that, as we have seen, extractive industries and the benefits they radiate are 'finite', 'non-renewable' and 'exhaustible'.

Those not receiving benefits seek answers to the exclusivity of cash flows. In Ok Tedi this has provoked a number of cults that link resource wealth with a Western form of witchcraft, portrayed in the esoteric creations of Western films (such as Frankenstein and Dracula) broadcast on the Australian television networks available in the region. Beneficiaries are believed to have harnessed this power enabling them to 'capture' resource wealth, and others seek to channel it by employing traditional methods (as well as more innovative methods based on religious belief). As a result, sorcery, and its effects, has intensified in the region (Gilberthorpe 2009b:38). The Fasu's good fortune is accounted for by neighbouring groups in a number of ways. In some circles it is attributed to a believed sorcerous power and fear linked to their cannibalistic past, whilst in others to their religious commitment and dedication to a Christian way of life, which neighbouring groups make every effort to emulate.[8]

As the source of cash wealth, MNCs form an unwitting yet intrinsic part of new exchange relations. MNCs, such as BHP Billiton, may claim 'to be a valued member of our host community',[9] but such a naive statement fails to acknowledge key obligatory principles attached to membership. The most notable failure of this principle is corporate withdrawal from regions in efforts to remove themselves from environmental devastation: BHP Billiton from Papua New Guinea, Chevron from Ecuador and Rio Tinto from Indonesia are just a few examples of this kind of corporate abdication. The severance of ties in this way has been condemned by academics (see Filer *et al.* 2008) and host communities who take corporate resignation as a sign that MNCs are reneging on their social responsibility.

---

8   This observation is based on my own fieldwork, but see also Freund (1977:134).

9   Quoted from BHP Billiton's statement about their 'sustainability framework', previously available at: www.bhpbilliton.com/home/aboutus/Documents/ourSustainabilityFramework2010.pdf (accessed 12 August 2011).

Stuart Kirsch provides one of the best examples of this. He states that the Yonggom, who live downstream from Ok Tedi mine, compare BHP Billiton to a sorcerer because the company has failed to fulfil their moral responsibility to them. As Kirsch explains:

> Like a sorcerer, the mining company refuses to take responsibility for its actions, including the social consequences of its environmental impacts. The analogy between the sorcerer and the mine appears in compensation claims against the mining company that follow the logic of sorcery accusations ... They [Yonggom] frame their dispute with the mining company in moral terms that invoke the absence of an appropriate social relationship.
>
> (Kirsch 2006:120–1)

The impact cash has on those who externalize themselves from traditional systems is an ongoing problem in need of greater academic research and corporate and institutional recognition. At Kutubu and Ok Tedi, a small number of 'entrepreneurs' immerse themselves in the capitalist world confronting them. These are the few, predominantly male, individuals who were able to build on opportunities made available to them, mainly through missionary patronage between the 1960s and 1980s, and who have applied their skills and knowledge to form ties with corporate and government bodies. These few individuals benefit from opportunities to develop business partnerships, participate in training schemes and engage in entrepreneurial activity supported by the state and corporate sector. Whilst one of the stipulations of Papua New Guinea's landowner remit is 'residence', local entrepreneurs struggle to consolidate business activity with traditional obligations within a traditional, localized economic setting.

The resilience of Papua New Guinea's cultural character is evident in the way the majority of the population retain an egalitarian, acephalous form of sociality where mechanisms are in place to ensure its reproduction. Individual self-interest is characteristic of social life in rural Papua New Guinea, but the individual acts in accordance with sets of obligations that are embedded within formal socio-political exchange systems. These systems ultimately ensure social and economic security but come into conflict with the individualizing and solitary pursuits underpinning the 'entrepreneur' (see Gilberthorpe and Sillitoe 2009). The fruit of entrepreneurial labour feeds the bank balances of individuals rather than the broader community, diametrically opposing traditional principles of sharing and obligation. Resentment is amplified when local obligations are not fulfilled at the village level, and hostilities, often leading to violent conflicts, emerge. Those who engage in capitalist activity risk permanently detaching themselves from the social and economic security of long-established social networks, and they expose themselves to the vulnerable, 'finite' cash economy characteristic of resource extraction (Gilberthorpe and Sillitoe 2009:16; Kirsch 2008).

The value appended to the term 'entrepreneur' in development discourse and intervention more broadly is symptomatic of how inequalities are accentuated by incompatible agendas that are poorly thought out and, as a consequence, inappropriate. For both the Fasu and Min, the encounter with industry has stimulated adaptation to a cash economy that defies traditional systems of exchange along affinal lines. The economic shift has forced local people to adopt the very Western and capitalist notions of property and ownership, for which they have drawn on traditional descent constructs. This has caused inequality between men and women, and between men, isolating individuals and tight family units from each other and from traditional neighbours.

Conclusion: impact implications

The general conclusion that can be drawn from this comparative study of resource development in Papua New Guinea is that the extractive industries exact various levels of displacement through the imposition of incompatible categories that threaten socio-economic security and cultural reproduction more generally. The encounter between indigene and industry is important to anthropology, not only because the presence of mineral, oil and gas exploration and extraction in areas inhabited by indigenous populations is now so widespread as to be almost unavoidable in ethnographic descriptions, but also because it presents social structures in a heightened and intensified context, where important underlying ideologies are intensified to reveal the cultural value and meaning attached to conceptions of interrelationality.

Perhaps more important, however, are the key socio-cultural problems emerging from intervention strategies, such as resource rents and infrastructure development, and the dominant definitions of development they employ. This is especially true in relation to the landowner and royalty models that form an intrinsic part of CSR objectives, discourse and action. The aim of this chapter has been to show the often abstruse and latent impact of extractive industries on social change, particularly their divisive effect on what are essentially sustained, efficient and complex socio-cultural systems that ensured economic and social security in the past. The most pertinent outcome of this aim has been the revelation that impacts felt at the psychological level, the impact of the development encounter on perception, belief, emotion, motivation and awareness, are impacts on the cultural tools that inform social behaviour and interpersonal relationships, and essentially human well-being.

References

Atkinson, G. and Hamilton, K. 2003. 'Savings, growth and the resource curse hypothesis', *World Development* 31(11):1793–807.

Auty, R. 1993. *Sustaining Development in Mineral Economies: The Resource-Curse Thesis*. London: Routledge.

——— 1998. *Resource Abundance and Economic Development: Improving the Performance of Resource Rich Countries*. Helsinki: United Nations University World Institute for Development Economics.

Bainton, N. 2008. 'The genesis and the escalation of desire and antipathy in the Lihir Islands, Papua New Guinea', *Journal of Pacific History* 43(3):289–312.

Bainton, N. and Cox, J. 2009. 'Parallel states, parallel economies: legitimacy and prosperity'. State, Society and Governance in Melanesia Discussion Paper 2009/5. Canberra: Research School Asia Pacific Studies, Australian National University.

Ballard, C. 1997. 'It's the land stupid! The moral economy of resource ownership in Papua New Guinea'. In P. Larmour (ed.), *The Governance of Common Property in the Pacific Region*, pp. 47–65. Canberra: Australian National University.

Ballard, C. and Banks, G. 2003. 'Resource wars: mining and anthropology', *Annual Review of Anthropology*. 32:287–313.

Banks, G. 2007. '"Money rain": indigenous engagement with business models in Papua New Guinea', *Development Bulletin* 72:36–9.

——— 2009. 'Activities of TNCs in extractive industries in Asia and the Pacific: implications for development', *Transnational Corporations* 18(1):43–59.

Barth, F. 1971. 'Tribes and intertribal relations in the Fly headwaters', *Oceania* 41:171–91.

——— 1987. *Cosmologies in the Making: A Generative Approach to Cultural Variation in Inner New Guinea*. Cambridge: Cambridge University Press.

Benson, P. and Kirsch, S. 2010. 'Capitalism and the politics of resignation', *Current Anthropology* 51(4):459–86.

Biersack, A. 1999. 'Porgera – whence and whither?' In C. Filer (ed.), *Dilemmas of Development: The Social and Economic Impact of the Porgera Gold Mine 1989–94*, pp. 260–79. Canberra: Asia Pacific Press.

Blowfield, M. and Frynas, J.G. 2005. 'Setting new agendas: critical perspectives on corporate social responsibility in the developing world', *International Affairs* 81(3):499–513.

Brumbaugh, R. 1990. 'Afek sang: the "old woman" myth of the Mountain-Ok'. In B. Craig and D. Hyndman (eds), *Children of Afek: Tradition and Change among the Mountain-Ok of Central New Guinea*, pp. 54–87. Sydney: University of Sydney Press.

Brutti, L. 2000. 'Afek's last son: integrating change in a Papua New Guinean cosmology', *Ethnohistory* 47(1):101–11.

Burton, J. 1997. 'Terra nugax and the discovery paradigm: how Ok Tedi was shaped by the way it was found and how the rise of political process in the North Fly took the company by surprise'. In G. Banks and C. Ballard (eds), *The Ok Tedi Settlement: Issues, Outcomes and Implications*, pp. 27–55. Canberra: Australian National University.

Buttel, F.H. 2000. 'Ecological modernization as social theory', *Geoforum* 31(1):57–65.

Cowell, S.J., Wehrmeyer, W., Argust, P.W., Graha, J. and Robertson, S. 1999. 'Sustainability and the primary extraction industries: theories and practice', *Resources Policy* 25(4):277–86.

Craig, B. and Hyndman, D. (eds). 1991. *Children of Afek: Tradition and Change among the Mountain-Ok of Central New Guinea*. Sydney: University of Sydney Press.

Crook, T. 1999. 'Growing knowledge in Bolivip, Papua New Guinea', *Oceania* 69(4):225–42.

Dolan, C., Gilberthorpe, E. and Rajak, D. 2018. 'Corporate social responsibility'. In H. Callan (ed.), *The International Encyclopedia of Anthropology*. London: Blackwell Wiley.

Ernst, T. 1999. 'Discourse and entification in Onabasulu modernity', *American Anthropologist* 101(1):88–97.

Filer, C. (ed.). 1999. *Dilemmas of Development: The Social and Economic Impact of the Porgera Gold Mine 1989–94*. Canberra: Asia-Pacific Press.

Filer, C., Burton, J. and Banks, G. 2008. 'The fragmentation of responsibilities in the Melanesian mining sector'. In C. O'Faircheallaigh and S. Ali (eds), *Earth Matters: Indigenous Peoples, the Extractive Industry and Corporate Social Responsibility*, pp. 163–79. London: Greenleaf Publishing.

Filer, C. and Macintyre, M. 2006. 'Grass roots and deep holes: community responses to mining in Melanesia', *Contemporary Pacific* 18(2):215–31.

Freund, P.J. 1977. 'Social change among the Kasua, Southern Highlands, Papua New Guinea'. PhD dissertation. Iowa City: University of Iowa.

Frynas, J.G. 2005. 'The false developmental promise of corporate social responsibility: evidence from multinational oil companies', *International Affairs* 81(3):581–98.

Gardner, D. 2004. 'Continuity and identity: mineral development, land tenure and "ownership" among the Mountain Ok'. In J. Weiner and A. Rumsey (eds), *Mining and Indigenous Lifeworlds in Australia and Papua New Guinea*, pp. 101–24. Wantage: Sean Kingston Publishing.

Gelb, A. 1988. *Oil Windfalls: Blessing or Curse?* New York: Oxford University Press.

Gilberthorpe, E. 2004. 'The Fasu, Papua New Guinea: analysing modes of adaptation through cosmological systems'. PhD dissertation. St Lucia: University of Queensland.

——— 2007. 'Fasu solidarity: a case study of kin networks, land tenure and oil extraction in Kutubu, Papua New Guinea', *American Anthropologist* 109(1):101–12.

——— 2009a. 'Pathways to *developmen*: identity, landscape and industry in Papua New Guinea'. In S. Heckler (ed.), *Landscape, Power and Process: Re-Evaluating Traditional Environmental Knowledge*, pp. 202–31. New York: Berghahn Books.

——— 2009b. 'Development and industry: a Papua New Guinea case study'. Canterbury: Centre for Social Anthropology and Computing.

——— 2013. 'In the shadow of industry: a study of culturization in Papua New Guinea', *Journal of the Royal Anthropological Institute* 19(2):261–78.

Gilberthorpe, E. and Banks, G. 2012. 'Development on whose terms: CSR discourse and social realities in Papua New Guinea's extractive industries sector', *Resources Policy* 37:185–93.

Gilberthorpe, E. and Papyrakis, E. 2015. 'The extractive industries and development: the resource curse at the micro, meso and macro levels', *Extractive Industries and Society* 2(2):381–90.

Gilberthorpe, E. and Sillitoe, P. 2009. 'The construction of social capital in the current economic crisis: lessons from Papua New Guinea', *Anthropology News* 50(7):4–5.

Goldman, L. 2000. 'Position paper: ILGs, zones, reforms and rational reform'. Konedobu, NCD: Papua New Guinea Department for Petroleum and Energy.

Golub, A. 2007. 'From agency to agents: forging landowner identities in Porgera'. In J. Weiner and K. Glaskin (eds), *Customary Land Tenure and Registration in Australia and Papua New Guinea: Anthropological Perspectives*, pp. 73–96. Canberra: Australian National University E-Press.

Gylfason, T., Herbertsson, T.T. and Zoega, G. 1999. 'A mixed blessing: natural resources and economic growth', *Macroeconomic Dynamics* 3:204–25.

Hilson, G. 2007. 'Championing the rhetoric? "Corporate social responsibility" in Ghana's mining sector', *Greener Management International* 53:43–56.

Hoben, A. 1997. 'Development'. In T. Barfield (ed.), *The Dictionary of Anthropology*, pp. 113–14. Oxford: Blackwell.

Humphreys, M., Sachs, J.D. and Stiglitz, J.E. 2007. 'Introduction'. In M. Humphreys, J.D. Sachs and J.E. Stiglitz (eds), *Escaping the Resource Curse*, pp. 1–20. New York: Columbia University Press.

Hyndman, D. 1990. 'The Ok Tedi mining project: problems with the pot of gold'. In B. Craig and D. Hyndman (eds), *Children of Afek: Tradition and Change among the Mountain-Ok of Central New Guinea*, pp. 161–97. Sydney: University of Sydney Press.

——— 1994. *Ancestral Rain Forests and the Mountain of Gold: Indigenous Peoples and Mining in New Guinea*. Boulder, CO: Westview Press.

Jacka, J. 2001. 'Coca-Cola and *kolo*', *Anthropology Today* 17(4):3–8.

——— 2018. 'The anthropology of mining: the social and environmental impacts of resource extraction in the mineral age', *Annual Review of Anthropology* 47:61–77.

Jackson, R. and Banks, G. 2002. *In Search of the Serpent's Skin: A History of the Porgera Gold Mine*. Port Moresby: Placer Niugini.

Jike, V.T. 2004. 'Environmental degradation, social disequilaibrium, and the dilemma of sustainable development in the Niger Delta of Nigeria', *Journal of Black Studies* 34(5):686–701.

Jorgensen, D. 1981. 'Life on the fringe: history and society in Telefolmin'. In R. Gordon (ed.), *The Plight of Peripheral People in Papua New Guinea*, pp. 59–79. Cambridge, MA: Cultural Survival.

——— 1996. 'Regional history and ethnic identity in the hub of New Guinea: the emergence of the Min', *Oceania* 66:189–210.

——— 2004. 'Who and what is a landowner? Mythology and marking the ground in a Papua New Guinea mining project'. In A. Rumsey and J. Weiner (eds), *Mining and Indigenous Lifeworlds in Australia and Papua New Guinea*, pp. 68–100. Wantage: Sean Kingston Publishing.

——— 2005. 'Third wave evangelism and the politics of the global in Papua New Guinea: spiritual warfare and the recreation of place in Telefolmin', *Oceania* 75:444–61.

Jorgensen, D. (ed.). 1986. 'Concepts of conception: procreation ideologies of Papua New Guinea', *Mankind*, special issue, 14(1).

Kapelus, P. 2002. 'Mining, corporate social responsibility and the "community": the case of Rio Tinto, Richards Bay Minerals and the Mbonambi', *Journal of Business Ethics* 39(3):279–96.

Karl, T. 1997. *The Paradox of Plenty: Oil Booms and Petro-States*. Berkeley: University of California Press.

Kayaok, T. 2003. 'Revelation of Min secrecy and power'. Unpublished manuscript.

Kepore, K.P. and Imbun, B.Y. 2010. 'Mining and stakeholder engagement discourse in a Papua New Guinea mine', *Corporate Social Responsibility and Environmental Management* 18(4):220–33.

Kirsch, S. 1997. 'Indigenous response to environmental impact along the Ok Tedi'. In S. Toft, (ed.), *Compensation for Resource Development in Papua New Guinea*, pp. 143–55. Canberra: Australian National University Press.

——— 2006. *Reverse Anthropology: Indigenous Analysis of Social and Environmental Relations in New Guinea.* Stanford: Stanford University Press.

——— 2008. 'Social relations and the green critique of capitalism in Melanesia', *American Anthropologist* 110(3):288–98.

Kronenberg, T. 2004. 'The curse of natural resources in the transition economies', *Economics of Transition* 12(3):399–426.

Kurita, H. 1994. 'Blood and semen reconsidered: childbirth and child rearing among the Fasu of Papua New Guinea'. In K. Yamaji (ed.), *Gender and Fertility in Melanesia*, pp. 47–73. Nishinomiya: Kwansei Gakuin University.

Lawrence, P. 1964. *Road Belong Cargo: A Study of the Cargo Movement in the Southern Madang District, New Guinea.* Manchester: Manchester University Press.

Lohmann, R. 2001. 'Introduced writing and Christianity: differential access to knowledge among the Asabano', *Ethnology* 40:93–111.

Macintyre, M. and Foale, S. 2004. 'Politicized ecology: local responses to mining in Papua New Guinea', *Oceania* 74:231–51.

Mehlum, H., Moene, K. and Torvik, R. 2006. 'Cursed by resources or institutions', *World Economy* 29(8):117–31.

Mikesell, R.F. 1997. 'Explaining the resource curse, with special reference to mineral-exporting countries', *Resources Policy* 23(4):191–9.

O'Faircheallaigh, C. and Ali, S. 2007. 'Extractive industries, environmental performance and corporate social responsibility', *Greener Management International* 52:5–16.

——— 2008. *Earth Matters: Indigenous Peoples, the Extractive Industries and Corporate Social Responsibility:* Sheffield: Greenleaf Publishing.

Okoko, E. 1999. 'Women and environmental change in the Niger Delta, Nigeria: evidence from Ibeno', *Gender, Place and Culture* 6(4):373–8.

Ovadia, J. 2016. *The Petro-Developmental State in Africa: Making Oil Work in Angola, Nigeria and the Gulf of Guinea.* London: Hurst.

Owen, J.R., and Kemp, D. 2015. 'Mining-induced displacement and resettlement: a critical appraisal', *Journal of Cleaner Production* 87:478–88.

Papyrakis, E. and Gerlagh, R. 2003. 'The resource curse hypothesis and its transmission channels', *Journal of Comparative Economics* 32:181–93.

Poole, F.J.P. 1982. 'The ritual forging of identity: aspects of person and self in Bimin-Kuskusmin male initiation'. In G. Herdt (ed.), *Rituals of Manhood*, pp. 183–242. Berkeley: University of California Press.

Robbins, J. 1995. 'Dispossessing the spirits: Christian transformations of desire and ecology among the Urapmin in Papua New Guinea', *Ethnology* 34:211–24.

——— 2004. *Becoming Sinners: Moral Torment in a Papua New Guinea Society.* Berkeley: University of California Press.

Ross, M. 1999. 'The political economy of the resource curse', *World Politics* 51(2):297–322.

——— 2001. 'Does oil hinder democracy?', *World Politics* 53(3):325–61.

Sachs J.D. and Warner, A.M. 1995. 'Natural resource abundance and economic growth'. Working Paper No. 5398. Cambridge, MA: National Bureau of Economic Research.

Sahlins, M. 2011. 'What kinship is (part one)', *Journal of the Royal Anthropological Institute* 17(1):2–19.

Torvik, R. 2002. 'Natural resources, rent seeking and welfare', *Journal of Development Economics* 67(2):455–70.

Trebeck, K. 2008. 'Corporate social responsibility and democratisation: opportunities and obstacles'. In C. O'Faircheallaigh and S. Ali (eds), *Earth Matters: Indigenous Peoples, the Extractive Industry and Corporate Social Responsibility*, pp. 8–23. London: Greenleaf Publishing.

Wagner, R. 1981. *The Invention of Culture.* Chicago: University of Chicago Press.

Watts, M. 2008. *The Curse of the Black Gold.* New York: Powerhouse Press.

——— 2010. 'Oil city: petro-landscapes and sustainable future'. In G. Doherty and M. Mostafavi (eds), *Ecological Urbanism*, pp. 420–30. Baden: Lars Muller Publishers.

WCED (World Commission on Environment and Development). 1987. *Our Common Future: The World Commission on Environment and Development.* Oxford: Oxford University Press.

York, R. and Rosa, E.A. 2003. 'Key challenges to ecological modernization theory', *Organization and Environment* 16(3):273–88.

8

Memory and historical narratives among Orthodox Christians in Syria at the start of the twenty-first century

Noriko Sato

The 1915 persecutions of Christians in the Ottoman Empire resulted in them being expelled from their homeland in Anatolia. Syrian Orthodox Christians are one such group, and many of the survivors settled in Syria in the aftermath of the massacre. Their accounts of what occurred in 1915 have served as one of the important symbolic resources that they mobilize to construct the identity of their group. As a minority and a displaced group, Syrian Orthodox Christians have sought to reshape and recast their collective memories in order to secure their political rights within Syrian society. In their recent narratives, they have attempted to conceal their origin as emigrants from Turkey, claiming instead that they belong to one of the indigenous religious groups of Syria. These Christians are involved in a project of transforming their ethnos and its genesis.

It is well documented that the disintegration of the Ottoman Empire resulted in massive population movements, massacres, the re-appropriation of resources, and the creation of fear and hatred between various ethnic and religious groups, phenomena that have lasted to this day. It was not only the Armenians and the Greeks who were expelled from their homeland in present-day Turkey; in fact, there were many others, including the subjects of my research, Syrian Orthodox Christians (*Suriyan qadim* or *Suriyan Orthodoks*) (see e.g. Yonan 1996).[1] During the last quarter of the nineteenth century, the

---

1 Theologically, Syrian Orthodox Christians see themselves as members of a Monophysite church in Syria. In the fifth century, political and religious conflicts divided Byzantine Christians, which Emperor Justinian resolved by enforcing the

Ottoman government promoted policies of Ottomanism that emphasized the common citizenship of all the inhabitants of the empire, whether they were Muslim or non-Muslim. The Syrian Orthodox Christians of Tur 'Abdin, located in the south-eastern part of present-day Turkey, attempted to reinforce their position by exploiting these Ottoman political reforms. However, this only increased the hostility of the Muslim population against them and resulted in massacres and expulsion during the First World War (see e.g. Joseph 1983). The 1915 slaughter of Christians both symbolized and hastened the destruction of the Ottoman *millet* system, under which people of different religions and ethnic groups coexisted, and facilitated its replacement by the modern nation-state. The religious and ethnic persecutions in the eastern provinces of the Ottoman Empire in the early twentieth century forced its Christian population to emigrate to Syria, Lebanon and Iraq.

Although there are few differences between Christians and the rest of the population in terms of social traditions and ways of life, it is their religion which separates them from the Muslim majority of the region. Syrian Orthodox Christians who emigrated from Tur 'Abdin to the Jazira region in north-east Syria have been marginalized and feel threatened. The Syrian regime has attempted to promote the idea of a homogeneous nation-state, and consequently the anxiety of these Christians has increased due to the fact that their religion prevents them from integrating fully into the Syrian nation. The political tension in the region has woven itself into the web of their historical narratives. This chapter is an attempt to explore the collective memories of Syrian Orthodox Christians, and how they articulate them in narrative. Their account of the past, which acts as a touchstone for establishing the current identity of their group, changes in response to their desire to infuse the past with the images they currently have of themselves. This chapter focuses on Syrian Orthodox Christians living in a small town of in the north-eastern part of the Syrian Jazira, who have attempted to reconstruct their political and social identities within the broader perspective of nationalism, ethnicity and their relationships with their Muslim neighbours. As a minority and a displaced group, Syrian Orthodox Christians have sought to reshape and

---

decrees of the Council of Chalcedon (AD 451), which labelled the Monophysites (Nestorians) as heretics. It is difficult to discover when this particular group started using the term 'Syrian Orthodox' to describe themselves, and thus identify themselves with Syria, but it was certainly after their forced migration there. Syrian Orthodox Christians attempted to adjust to the new circumstances, and forge their unity. It is known that the former Syrian Orthodox patriarch Mar Ignatius Yacoub III (1912–1980) adopted such a strategy.

recast their collective memories in order to secure their political rights within Syrian society.

One can present the situation of Syrian Orthodox Christians in Syria in terms of uprootedness, which presupposes that they feel detached both historically and socially from Syria, the land to which they migrated, and which is now their home. Yet they have not grieved over their marginalization within the host society, but rather have struggled for acceptance in their new home. Their narratives of the 1915 massacre serve as one of the important symbolic resources they have mobilized to construct an identity which separates them from their Muslim Kurdish neighbours and yet which asserts their right to be considered as one of the religious groups of Syria. This is one strategy of Syrian Orthodox Christians, who have sought opportunities to integrate themselves into a society where they feel displaced.

The 1915 massacre of Christians in Ottoman Turkey both traumatized the surviving community and compromised their group identity. In their narratives, memories of their lives before migration cannot act as mnemonic devices to recall their past. There is no sense that this diasporic community harks back to a lost homeland. Rather this silence is an uprooted silence, which attempts to erase some historical linkages with the true past, and substitute an imagined one. This past includes memories of life in their Anatolian homeland as well as their relationship with their Syrian Kurdish neighbours. Yet conveniently forgetting the past and breaking off previous associations have not always been paths followed by former Ottoman Christians. The Armenians attempted to maintain their memories of their lives before the 1915 persecution as an idealized past (e.g. Bedoukian 1978; Kherdian 1988; Ohanian 1990), which they have tried to use as a basis for the 'reformation' of their group at critical moments in their displacement as they reconstruct their lives in foreign lands (cf. Benjamin 1970).

For Syrian Orthodox Christians, the past is a vehicle with which to define their present status and identity within the host society. They themselves act as their own agents in negotiating with the host society by using narratives of their past. Articulation of the past is their way of creating a present and acceptable identity whilst they struggle for social empowerment. Syrian Orthodox Christians reconstruct narratives in response to the narrative structure of the host country, thereby framing their identities. It is now accepted in anthropology that nationalism brings about a radical recasting of the past in order to promote people's solidarity and loyalty to the nation (Gellner 1983). Yet state-sponsored nationalism is not the only source by which to establish a unified cultural community. Each group in a state responds to the discourse promoted by the political centre and attempts to reshape its history within the power structure of the state (e.g. Ranger 1993; Shryock 1997). Even in the case where an immigrant group finds a rupture between a dominant discourse of national history and their own group history, they tend to adopt the existing narrative frames given by the state by altering them in such a way that their own history can be accommodated within national history.[2] One of the aims of my research is to show that public remembering and forgetting are not so much state-formed, but are equally a series of collective grassroots acts intended to reshape a group's history by reference to the national history sanctioned by the state.

As a strategy for surviving in Syria, Syrian Orthodox Christians have concentrated on creating communal history, which locates them within the wider framework of national politics whilst at the same time developing their own identity as a Christian group. They articulate their own history to provide a meaning for, and an interpretation of, a particular historical event. The historical account of the 1915 massacre given by the Syrian Orthodox Christians is one such discourse that articulates their position in society. Yet their account of the massacre is not uniform, and they have altered it as the social and political situation has changed. Howarth *et al.* (2000:6–7) assert that the key to understanding and explaining the emergence and logic of discourse lies in discovering the relational systems of meaning and practice that constitute the identities of subject and object. They focus their attention on explanations of the formation of identities, where meanings, interpretations and practices are always inextricably linked. By contrast, my research interest is concentrated on the nature of uncertainty articulated by a historical discourse. Epistemological problems arise when historical accounts express one's identity. The different historical accounts of the 1915 massacre that Syrian Orthodox Christians have produced at different times and in different situations express their ambivalent position within Syrian society and the uncertainties of their future. Here I pay attention to the process of their production, which clearly influences the shapes and contours of such narratives.

One cannot explain the difference between historical accounts dealing with the same historical event merely in terms of a positivist way of examining the validity and the foundation of historical arguments. Rather, one should be attuned to the possibility that 'history' may be produced in different ways. Davis (1989) suggests that even historians sometimes admit the fact that they are not sensitized to the anomalies that appear in their texts. Less well acknowledged, however, is the suggestion that historical depictions are not uniform, and thus different historiographies emerge in the process

---

2   This is the case, for example, of Soviet veterans of the Second World War in Israel.
     See Roberman (2007:467–8).

of retrieving the past. Historical experience, the actual process of recalling past occurrences, is largely affected by the social position of the 'agent' who relates particular events. Syrian Orthodox Christians who until the 1960s had described themselves as powerless victims of the Muslim persecution of Christians in 1915 have transformed their account into one of 'wars' against the Kurds who brutally attacked them. There seems to be no fundamental change in their total memory and each fragment that they recall. Yet the way they articulate the meaning of the 1915 massacre in their earlier account has been transformed. How they have structured the fragments of their memory into a discourse illustrates both their inner fears and their ambivalent position in modern Syrian society.

The present Syrian government acknowledges Syrian Orthodox Christians as Syrian citizens, and these Christians can therefore identify themselves as one of the religious groups in Syria, but contemporary Syrian Orthodox Christians fear that they will become identified as 'Kurds'. Their historical memories suggest that there is no clear difference between them and the Kurds in terms of origin, language and ethnicity. However, the risk posed by this shared identity increases the anxiety of Syrian Orthodox Christians, as the political rights of Kurds are not guaranteed in Syria; should they become identified as Kurds, Syrian Orthodox Christians might well find themselves in a similar political situation.

Syrian Orthodox Christians remember that, after migration to the area of the small town that is the locus of my study, they tried to maintain control over their villages with the help of their own leaders, yet Kurdish tribal power overwhelmed them. Up until this day, agricultural land is the main capital resource of the region. In order for them to survive by farming the land, some Christian peasants paid tribute to the most powerful Muslim Kurdish tribal leader in the area, Hajo. Whatever villages they lived in, Syrian Orthodox Christians shared the fear of losing their land to such tribal leaders. They had to acknowledge the dominance of Hajo's followers, even though they had been hostile to Hajo, who had attacked Christians during the 1915 massacre.

Tribal domination ended when the Ba'ath party introduced agricultural land reform in 1963 and when the former president Hafez al-Assad strengthened central government control. Yet some Kurds maintain still that Syrian Orthodox Christians are ethnically Kurds, even though they believe in Christianity. By the end of the 1990s, the Christian population has dramatically decreased due to emigration abroad, whereas the Kurdish population still dominates many villages in the area. Syrian Orthodox Christians are therefore afraid that Kurds may once again overwhelm them if there is no clear distinction, in terms of ethnicity, between themselves and the Kurds.

Historical accounts of the 1915 massacre

The Jazira region of north-east Syria, which Syrians regard as a frontier both culturally and politically, is where many Syrian Orthodox Christians settled after the Ottoman religious persecution of 1915. They were not the only people who moved into the area in the first half of the twentieth century. Nomadic Arab tribes (*Shawaya*), such as the Tay, used to roam the area between Tur 'Abdin, Mardin and Diyarbakr and the plains of Jazira (Niebuhr 1992:709) before eventually settling on the Syrian side of the border.[3] Moreover, many Kurds who formerly lived in Tur 'Abdin migrated to Jazira due to Turkish persecution of the Kurdish Sufi orders in Turkey, especially in the aftermath of the Sheikh Sa'id rebellion, which erupted in 1925. They hoped for more liberal Islamic and Kurdish policies in Syria under the French Mandate. Although a small number of both Syrian Orthodox Christian and Kurdish peasants had lived in Jazira before large-scale migration to Syria, this region had been under-populated.

I intend to show how the narratives of the 1915 massacre given by contemporary Christians in the district I studied differ from those offered earlier in the twentieth century. It seems to me that what contemporary Syrian Orthodox Christians heard from their elders may not differ much from the accounts recorded a few decades ago. When I started to collect them in 1998, I was able to meet survivors who had experienced the 1915 massacre first-hand as children. Yet by 2008, all of those whom I had interviewed had died. Others whom I have interviewed are those who remembered accounts of other people's experiences and stories after being told them by their parents, relatives and neighbours. When looking at elements that constitute their historical accounts, one could say that they have preserved these memories. Yet the manner in which these people have retained the complete picture of the event is different from that employed by previous generations.

Bloch (1998) maintains that actual narrative does not recall all that is stored as memory; rather, it is a representation of some sort of mental coding which infuses topography with history, and invokes elements that are not included in the text. Topography represents a physical conjunction of different signs, which charts relations between historical referents. In their memories, people do not recall historical events exactly as they occurred because the actual process of recalling the past is largely affected by two factors: first, the social position of those agents who narrate events; second, their relationship to the polity they inhabit. The effect on memory of a social and political milieu is reinforced by specific topographies familiar to narrators. Thus

---

3   The Tay still regard the area of their former pastoral migration route in Turkey as part of their tribal territory.

a historiographical account creates new relationships among the various referents.

The case of the Syrian Orthodox Christians with whom I worked confirms that it is not the historical nature of a place in itself that produces images of the past, but rather its topography. For people, topography represents their own geographical and political position within the state that they inhabit, and makes them recall their past in a particular way. Thus Syrian Orthodox Christians today show little interest in visiting places in Turkey where their ancestors suffered because they themselves share no topographical relationship with these sites. For the descendants of those who suffered, their geographical and political locus is Syria, and it is in Syria where they find their referents.

Earlier accounts

Earlier written accounts of the massacre that were derived from the narratives of survivors portray their loss, their feelings of marginality and their horror at being caught in the maelstrom of communal strife. Records of memories of Syrian Orthodox Christian survivors (Yonan 1996:22), as well as a study of Armenian memories of the 1915 massacre by Miller and Miller (1993:40–1), suggest that there were several reasons why Young Turks plotted to diminish the possibility of Christian resistance.[4] Many young Christians conscripted into the Ottoman army were treated badly, and many died due to hunger and exhaustion, while early in 1915 the government confiscated arms possessed by Christians, and local Christian leaders were imprisoned, tortured or even killed.

Once possibilities for Christian resistance had thus been reduced, the Ottoman army, in collaboration with Kurdish agencies, started to attack Christians. The miserable situation of Syrian Orthodox Christians is recorded by Jastrow (1994:75–9), who interviewed a survivor, Ibrahim Hanna, in a village near Diyarbakr in Turkey. As Jastrow was interested in an Aramaic dialect, Mlaho, which both Christians and Jews spoke in the area of Diyarbakr, he started to interview Mlaho dialect speakers in 1968, including survivors of the massacre of 1915 (Jastrow 1985:265). Ibrahim Hanna lived in al-Qamishly in Jazira, close to the area of my study, in a village surrounded by Muslims. The following is Ibrahim Hanna's narrative describing the attack by Muslims on his village in 1915.

---

4   The Young Turks were a political reform movement of the early twentieth century.
     Though they promoted democracy, they were notorious for perpetrating the
     1915 genocide of the Armenians and Christians that Dr Sato refers to in the text.
     Turkish persecution of Armenians peaked in the massacres of 1894–96 (RL).

They were in vineyards; these were my father, my (future) father-in-law
and one or, two others from the village ... They hid in the vineyards, while
we were in the village ... Muslims came, saw them in the vineyards. They
[Muslims] took them away and killed them ... I fled to Diyarbakr. However,
my mother and some others were still in the village. I did not know that my
father had been killed! ... My mother and her companions fled to Diyarbakr
... We remain[ed] on the street and suffered from hunger. My mother died.
My brother died. I had a six-year-old sister and I had my old grandmother.
Two women came ... My grandmother thought: These must be Christians.
However, they were Muslims. They said to her: 'Give us this small girl, we
will take care of her' ... On the following day, they returned with my sister,
so that she should not be homesick for her family ... My grandmother
said: 'I do not give her to you' ... They [the Muslims] went to the police.
Policemen dragged my sister away [from us]. She disappeared without trace.

(ibid.)

Sultan Abdul Hamid, the absolute ruler of Turkey until deposed by
the Young Turks, used pan-Islamic sentiment to integrate the eastern
provinces that were dominated by Kurdish *agahs* (tribal leaders). Many
Syrian Orthodox Christians lived in the eastern provinces, where Kurdish
agahs completely dominated political power. There was no Ottoman force to
restrain them. Moreover, some Kurdish tribesmen enlisted in the Hamidiye
regiments, which gave them authority legally sanctioned by the government
(Duguid 1973:140–7). Thus those whom Jastrow recorded as Muslims in his
interview must have been Kurds. Other Syrian Orthodox Christians describe
themselves, like Ibrahim, as helpless victims of Ottoman religious persecution.
Many Christians lost family members, and the survivors, forced to leave their
homeland, suffered from hunger and starvation.

These earlier accounts given by Syrian Orthodox Christians repeatedly
state that it was the evil orders of the Ottoman government that sanctioned the
Kurdish attack upon the Christians. In another account of the 1915 massacre
given by Syrian Orthodox Christians, Armalto (1919:465–6) documented the
massacre of Syrian Orthodox Christian villagers who lived in my study area,
which belonged to the Diyarbakr province before the collapse of the Ottoman
Empire. He explains that the Ottoman government organized regiments
under the command of three Kurdish leaders, including Qudr Bek, in order
to attack the Christians. These Kurdish leaders then started to kill the Syrian
Orthodox Christians in villages. They collaborated with other Kurdish *agahs*
who controlled the villages. Armalto seems to have based his accounts of the
1915 events on the experiences of survivors because his writing offers vivid
descriptions of the incidents:

> The government organized a regiment in order to massacre Christians who
> were in the neighbouring villages [of my research area] ... The regiment
> belonged to three [Kurdish] sheikhs [leaders], who were Bun Nizam Din,
> Qudr Bek, and Sleiman Mjur. The message which ordered them to massacre
> Christians was distributed to [other Kurdish] sheikhs. Therefore, Ibrahim
> Agah gathered Christians in his village and slaughtered them. Ahmad Yusef
> who dominated the village of Shiha brought together its Christian villagers
> and then killed them. Ahmad al-Abbas, who was a leader of the village of
> al-Duger, killed Christians in the village with the help of 50 soldiers whom
> Qudr Beg dispatched there. 'Ali al-'Isa who controlled the village of Halwa
> collaborated with Qudr Bek and murdered its Christian inhabitants. Then,
> they stole valuables from the houses of the rich Christian families. Then,
> Ahmad al-Abbas, Ibrahim al-Halil and Umar al-Awshi, who was a leader of
> al-Dukshriya, started to massacre Christians in the villages of al-Maharkah,
> Gurgeshamo, and Khweitla. No Christians were able to escape from there.
>
> (ibid.)

The accounts given by Armalto and Jastrow explain how the brutality
of the Kurds and Turks brought only suffering and displacement for the
Christians. Syrian Orthodox Christians were deprived of their political rights
as Ottoman subjects, because the Ottoman government rejected them. These
events scarred their memories and reinforced their feelings of vulnerability.
These accounts speak of how many Christians mourned the loss of family
members and they felt desolated and isolated due to Ottoman persecution.
The survivors related that their religion separated them from the Muslim
majority, which led to further persecution. In sum, during the period up to
1968, Syrian Orthodox Christians portrayed themselves as powerless, and it
was this powerlessness that led to their persecution in 1915. They felt that
the fate in store for them was the elimination of their communities by the
Ottoman government.

After the Orthodox Christians emigrated to Syria, Syrian Arab nationalists
fought the policies of the French Mandate that promoted division between
different ethnic and religious groups. Many Syrian Orthodox Christians under
the Mandate did not actively participate in the various Syrian nationalist
movements, yet some did support the movement for regional autonomy of
Jazira, whilst others showed sympathy for Syrian nationalism. Consequently,
they often became embroiled in the internal political conflicts attendant upon
the Syrian nationalist struggle, and French diplomatic sources saw a serious
rise in the level of hostilities between Christians and Muslims. The French
concluded that Muslim Kurds and Christians showed mutual antipathy, which
was exacerbated during the course of conflicts. Yet the French also believed

the Christians to be divided into the two political groups: nationalists and autonomists. By the late 1930s, even the French no longer officially supported the autonomists, because a wave of Syrian nationalism demanded Syrian unity and independence. Consequently, the Muslim majority regarded autonomist Christians as traitors, placing them once again in a vulnerable position (Steite 1937a, 1937b).

During this lengthy and agonizing political process, the position of Syrian Orthodox Christians became ambivalent within the context of an emerging Syrian national ethos. Syria had been in political turmoil until Hafez al-Assad seized power in 1970. In order to strengthen their links to Syria, Syrian Orthodox Christians suppressed the memories of their Turkish past in narratives of the 1915 massacre because such recollections emphasized that they were political dissidents and immigrants. Such labels might hinder their claim to be Syrian, because nationalists proclaimed that Syria was the state whose inhabitants, Muslim and non-Muslim, shared a single Syrian culture and a single Syrian history. Being placed in a situation where nationalists propounded the unity of all Syrians, and one where political tension between Muslims and Christians had become magnified, Syrian Orthodox Christians were afraid that they would be labelled traitors who might seek to divide the nation. Earlier accounts of the 1915 massacre were therefore replaced with accounts of successful resistance against Turkish and Kurdish injustice and brutality. Such accounts are a product of the vulnerable situation faced by the group during the surge of nationalism. Syrian Orthodox Christians had to maintain that they were not the enemy of the Arab Muslim majority in Syrian society, but were assaulted by Kurds and Turks who attempted to exploit them. The change in the focus of their historical accounts reflects the feelings of uncertainty and fear held by these Christians.

Recent accounts

When one compares the earlier written accounts of the 1915 massacre extracted from survivors' narratives with modern ones that I collected in my study area during the late 1990s and early 2000s, certain distinctive characteristics emerge. At least since the end of the 1990s, Syrian Orthodox Christians in this district have expressed anger and hatred against the Kurds, although there was no incident in their own immediate past that might have led to further deterioration in their relationship with their Kurdish neighbours. The narratives of the 1915 massacre that I collected show a clear distinction from other accounts recorded earlier; these more recent accounts describe cases of successful resistance. The following is a summary of the narratives of the 1915 incidents given by the Syrian Orthodox Christians in my district. The framework of each person's account is almost identical, although some people remember certain details more than others.

> The Ottoman soldiers marched to the monastery of Mar Malke in Tur
> 'Abdin.[5] Many Kurdish tribesmen followed them. Syrian Orthodox
> Christians retreated from their villages and gathered there when the lighting
> of the beacon in Midyat notified the Christians that the 'war' between the
> Christians and the Kurdish and Turkish forces had started. The villagers
> braced themselves for the attack by the Turks and Kurds. The monastery
> of Mar Malke lay on an isolated hill in the south of Midyat and, therefore,
> it seemed difficult for the Turks and Kurds to attack it. The Christians
> barricaded themselves in the monastery, which was like a fortress. Then the
> Turks and Kurds besieged it. Although the Turks and Kurds besieged the
> monastery for one year, the Christians did not surrender. The government
> tried to negotiate with the Christians in order to end this war. The
> Christians requested the government officials appoint Sheikh Fathallah
> to the peace mission. This Kurdish sheikh of al-Muhallamiya, which was
> located to the north-east of Midyat, was believed to be a descendant of
> a Syrian Orthodox bishop who had converted to Islam. The Christians
> thought that this sheikh might be trustworthy. The sheikh negotiated with
> the government officials and they promised to withdraw their army.

Bell observed the monastery of Mar Malke between 1909 and 1911, and describes its appearance as that of a little fortress that had been recently repaired or rebuilt (Bell 1982:38). The Syrian Orthodox Christians in my district have a propensity to describe these events as a 'war' between Christians and Kurds. It is depicted as a conflict between two different but equal groups rather than one in which Kurds exploited the Syrian Orthodox Christians, which had been the leitmotif of earlier accounts. Today, these Christians describe how their ancestors were socially equal to the Kurds.

The village of 'Ain Ward, where the Christians barricaded themselves in a village church, was also besieged. The following is a narrative of the 1915 incidents in the village of 'Ain Ward, given by Syrian Orthodox Christians in my study area.

> The Ottoman soldiers and Kurdish tribesmen marched to the village of 'Ain
> Ward, which Syrian Orthodox Christians occupied and was located in the
> east of Midyat. A beacon was the signal which notified the Syrian Orthodox

---

5   The monastery of Mar Malke is in south-east Turkey, near the Syrian border (see
     de Courtois 2004).

Christians of the start of the war between themselves and the Muslims. When many Syrian Orthodox Christian villagers whose villages were located in the east and north-east of Midyat received this message, they joined the villagers of 'Ain Ward in order to defend themselves. 'Ain Ward lay on the top of a hill and it was difficult for the Turks and Kurds to attack the village. The Christians barricaded themselves in a village church. When the Kurds broke down the church door and tried to enter the courtyard, they could not find the Christians. The Christians, under the command of their leader, had hidden in the upstairs rooms surrounding the courtyard and started to attack the Kurds. Eighty Kurds were killed there.

There were 150 families living in the village at that time. In all, including people from other villages, 2,000 people had been in 'Ain Ward. No one can tell how they fed such a large number of people. Although the Turks and Kurds had besieged the village for two months, the Syrian Orthodox Christians did not surrender.[6] The government tried to negotiate with the Christians in order to put an end to this war. The Christians requested the government officials to appoint Sheikh Fathallah to the mission. The Christians thought that this Kurdish sheikh might be trustworthy, because he was believed to be a descendant of a Syrian Orthodox bishop who had been converted to Islam. The sheikh and the government officials did a deal and the government officials withdrew their army.

The structure of the account of the 1915 siege of 'Ain Ward is thus almost identical with that of the monastery of Mar Malke. The Christians in 'Ain Ward even tried to protect the honour of their fellow Christians in the church and killed one of the Kurdish leaders, since he had tried to violate the sexual honour of Christian women. The Christians see the church as a sanctuary that only Christians were allowed to enter. The description given by these Christians suggests a fundamental belief in imminent divine justice that protects Christians from falling prey to their 'sinful enemies', who sought to plunder their properties, and therefore attacked them. During this 'war', the Christians cooperated and strove for collective salvation for their community as a whole, rather than for themselves as individuals. The barricaded church, which is used as a framework for encoding the various historical referents, creates a relation between these referents. The symbol of the barricaded church encourages the Christians to enhance their historical consciousness in order to demonstrate that the difference between the two opposed peoples is obvious. Moreover, it enhances their pride in being Syrian Orthodox

---

6   The Turkish policy of oppressing Christians continued for three years after 1915.

Christians by showing that they are not powerless, but have defended themselves successfully against their wicked enemies.

The following account, which Ritter collected from a survivor of the siege of 'Ain Ward (referred to as Ainwarda) in 1961, shows us that there is no fundamental change in memories of the 1915 Christian persecution. Yet the way this survivor articulated the meaning of the 1915 massacre is still different from the ones that I collected in the late 1990s and early 2000s.

> When the Muslims attacked the Christians and killed them, the residents of Ainwarda held on to their defences in [their] village. They also gave people in Midyat information [about the attack]. With this advice, they could flee [from Midyat] to [Ainwarda]. The Muslims attacked the village from all sides. They had gathered from all the surrounding areas. Our village contained many Christians who fled from other villages … Approximately 12,000 soldiers surrounded the village [of Ainwarda] … They then wanted to seize the residents' possessions and kill the people so that they could capture the village. But Ainwarda fought two months and six days until the government became tired of this war and negotiated [with the villagers].
>
> (Yonan 1989:283)[7]

This narrative focuses on the Muslims who took advantage of the persecution and exploited the opportunity to eliminate the Christians in order to steal their land and other property. The person who related the incident of was working in Beirut in Lebanon when Ritter interviewed him. In Lebanese society before the civil war (which began in 1975), sectarian identities and armed militias, which were organized along religious lines, influenced the formation of political alliances (Khuri 1973), although at the same time the patronage of successful strongmen became a centripetal force for consolidating their followers and enlarging class differences in which power was consolidated at the top (Gilsenan 1977). This contemporary Lebanese political structure seems to be reflected in the narrative of the 1915 incident given to Ritter. He depicts the incident as a conflict between the two different religious groups,

---

7   *Als die Muslime die Christen überfallen und getötet hatten, verschanzten sich die Bewohner von Ainwarda in Dorf. Sie geben auch den Leuten aus Midyat Bescheid, damit diese sich hierher retten konnten. Die Muslime griffen das Dorf von allen Seiten an, sie hatten sich aus der ganzen Umgegend gesammelt. In unser Dorf hatten sich viele Christen aus anderen Dörfen geflüchtet … Gegen das Dorf standen ungefähr 12000 Soldaten...Dann wollten sie die Habe der Einwohner an sich bringen und die Leuten töten, so daß das Dorf ihnen zufallen würde. Aber Ainwarda kämpfte zwei Monate und sechs Tage lang, bis die Regierung dieses Krieges müde wurde und verhandelte.*

Christians and Muslims. He pays little attention to ethnic labels such as Kurds and Turks, in contrast to the significance these play for the Syrian Orthodox Christians in my district. In the version that Ritter documented in 1961, the village church is not mentioned, whereas in the version from my district it is a symbol which is used to separate the Christians from the Kurds. The account given by the survivor in 1961 describes the Christian victims being attacked by overwhelming numbers of Muslims. By contrast, the present day Syrian Orthodox Christians in my district depict the 1915 persecution as one of 'war' with the Kurds who brutally attacked them. A comparison of the two accounts demonstrates that it is not a gradual loss of memory, but rather the social position of the Syrian Orthodox Christians that transformed their narratives. In other words, the actual process of recalling past events is largely affected by the social position of the 'agent' who relates the events.

The reasons that Syrian Orthodox Christians today seek to reconstruct their account of the 1915 persecution is not just because of their resentment towards the Kurds, but also because the current political situation requires it. The Syrian constitution guarantees freedom of belief and respect for all religions, but has no provisions for recognizing and guaranteeing the rights of ethnic sub-groups in the country (HRW 1996:27). Syrian society embraces different group identities: Sunni, Isma'ili, 'Alawi, Druze, Armenian, Syrian Orthodox Christian (*Suriyan*) and so on. One can openly acknowledge them as religious groups, because such recognition does not counter government guidelines.

Yet the Kurds cannot identify themselves as a single religious community because there are different groups among them who embrace Islam in different ways and whose beliefs are diverse: some are orthodox Sunnis while others have adopted local religious elements (Van Bruinessen 1999:6–8). In Turkey, Kurdish religious movements are equally complex. Although many are oriented towards Islam, others such as the Alevis shade into heterodoxy, which undoubtedly serves to exacerbate ethnic and national cleavages (ibid.:20–5). For its part, the Syrian government ignores this religious heterogeneity and categorizes Kurdish identity in Syria as ethnic. Thus the Syrian state cannot guarantee their legal rights because the official ideology of the Syrian state identifies Syrian citizens ethnically as Arabs. In fact, the Syrian government treats much of the Kurdish population in Syria as either foreigners or illegal inhabitants, *makutumeen* (HRW 1996; Vanly 1992). By contrast, the Syrian government acknowledges Syrian Orthodox Christians as Syrian citizens, and they can identify themselves as one of the religious groups in Syria. Since 1962, the Ba'athist regime has threatened the position of the Kurds. In that year, the regime launched an anti-Kurdish campaign embodied in the slogan, 'saving

Arabism in Jazira', and 120,000 Kurds in Jazira were categorized as 'foreigners'.[8] This regional situation has affected Syrian Orthodox Christians, and their account of the 1915 massacres. Thus their historiographical account is not only an attempt to explain what occurred in the past, for it also provides the Syrian Orthodox Christians with a tool to explore future possibilities.

Syrian Orthodox Christians must therefore portray Kurds as 'others' in order to secure their own position in society. Yet a relatively large number of the Kurds who emigrated from the area of Tur 'Abdin to Syria are, in fact, descendants of former Syrian Orthodox Christians who converted to Islam. The memories of the Syrian Orthodox Christians imply that their elders used to speak Kurdish as well as a western Syriac dialect, Toroyo, and that many of those who converted to Islam at the time of the 1915 religious persecutions in Turkey became identified as Kurds. The historical memories of Syrian Orthodox Christians suggest that, in terms of ethnicity, there is no clear difference between them and the Kurds. This certainly increases the anxiety of the surviving Syrian Orthodox Christians about not being identified as Kurds. If they were to become identified as Kurds they might well find themselves in a similar political situation. It is this ambivalent position that leads Syrian Orthodox Christians to describe the 1915 persecution as the 'war' between the Kurds and themselves, and thus to try to distinguish themselves from this maligned group.

Ironically, the historical account given by Syrian Orthodox Christians in my district reveals their ambivalent position. One of the key figures in their accounts is Sheikh Fathallah of Muhallamiya in Tur 'Abdin. A powerful Kurdish leader in the region and a descendant of a former Syrian Orthodox Christian bishop, he undertook the role of peacemaker during the conflicts of 1915. The Syrian Orthodox Christians in my district describe the ancestor of this sheikh, who was both a religious and communal leader in the mid seventeenth century, as being responsible for saving his congregation at a time when they suffered from famine. The community was fasting in hopes that by performing this act of piety, God would intercede and break the famine. Yet the fast was a failure because the famine persisted. In order to end the famine and save his flock, the Syrian Orthodox bishop, the ancestor of Sheikh Fathallah, therefore converted to Islam. The ancestors of the Syrian Orthodox Christians of my district attributed a firm commitment to honour his descendants to the now 'apostate' bishop. Due to the action of the former bishop, his descendant, Sheikh Fathallah, was regarded symbolically as a person who was able to cross

---

8   The motive behind this policy was to control the recently discovered oilfields of Rumilan and Qarachok in Jazira, and to track down Syrian Kurds associated with autonomy movements in Iraqi Kurdistan (Vanly 1992:151–2).

the boundary between the Syrian Orthodox Christians and the Kurds and negotiate with both sides. It was essential to create a putative link between Syrian Orthodox Christians and the sheikh in order for them to accept him as a mediator in peace talks at the time of the massacre.

The positivist approach of the Syrian Orthodox Church authorities does not and cannot accept the story that the conversion undergone by Sheikh Fathallah's ancestor relieved the famine because to do so would be to accept that in the sight of God, Islam is better than Syrian Orthodox Christianity. Their historical approach focuses on the evolution of the Syrian Orthodox Church itself, but is less concerned with power struggles between Kurds and Syrian Orthodox Christians. Barsoum, one-time patriarch of the Syrian Orthodox Church, claims that the story of the famine, which brought about the conversion, is a 'legend' (Barsoum 2000:353–4), but it is accepted as fact by the Syrian Orthodox Christians in Tur 'Abdin. Barsoum maintains that Patriarch Isma'il excommunicated those Christians who rejected his reprimand for breaking the fast. This made the situation more serious for it then became a social problem causing the dispute to spread.

The contemporary population in the district where I worked are constructivists and attempt to justify the decision of their ancestors to ask Sheikh Fathallah to negotiate with Ottoman government officials. The Syrian Orthodox Christians of my district cannot accept the fact that their ancestors had simply asked a Kurdish sheikh to become a mediator for the ceasefire because Syrian Orthodox Christians today attempt to separate themselves from the Kurds.

Syrian Orthodox Christians also pay attention to the way in which their religious affiliation defines their political position, and how the boundary between the Kurds and themselves can disappear when a Syrian Orthodox Christian converts to Islam and is assimilated into the Kurds. Their narrative of Sheikh Fathallah, the descendant of a former Syrian Orthodox bishop who now sees himself and is regarded by others as a Muslim Kurd, suggests that one's identity as Syrian Orthodox Christian evaporates when one abandons one's faith. For Syrian Orthodox Christians, conversion to Islam means assimilation into another ethnic group, such as Kurds or Arabs (*Shawaya*), composed of Muslims. In fact there were some women and children who were obliged to convert to Islam at the time of the 1915 massacre because they were incorporated into Muslim families through marriage and adoption. Thus the historical account of Sheikh Fathallah exacerbates the anxiety of contemporary Syrian Orthodox Christians who fear that, as a small ethnic group, they might disappear and be absorbed into a larger one.

State-sponsored national identity, which defines Syria as a religiously multicultural nation, provides Syrian Orthodox Christians with a framework within which they can assert themselves as a religious group. Their particular religious identification camouflages their ethnic one, and provides them with a distinctive identity that is different from the Kurdish one. The oral accounts given by Syrian Orthodox Christians in my district stress that military operations by the Turks and Kurds provoked a reaction by the Christians, and that those who fought back were just as powerful as the Kurds. By contrast, older written accounts of the 1915 massacre describe the Syrian Orthodox Christians as victims of Ottoman power and Christian weakness. The difference between the two accounts dealing with the same historical event is largely affected by the transformation of the social and political position of Syrian Orthodox Christians in their relationship with Syrian state authorities. The version given by contemporary residents of my district is silent about how their ancestors perished. Their anxiety not to be identified with the Kurds is a stimulus to their creativity, and the result is that they have provided themselves with symbolic meaning with which to claim an identity distinct from the Kurds.

Conclusion

Despite their attempts to secure their social and political position in Syrian society, Syrian Orthodox Christians feel threatened and have not been successful in achieving their goal. The problem is not so much their failure to establish a secure identity, but rather their social antagonism toward others, which arises from their feelings of uncertainty. Syrian Orthodox Christians fear that the state may threaten their rights in society due to their 'otherness'. Their historical accounts are therefore an attempt to define their identity in relation to other groups in a way that the state can acknowledge, while at the same time militating against their identification with a larger Kurdish community, whose loyalty to the state is suspect. If their future dislocation within society disrupts their present identity, a new historical account might well emerge in order to establish a more secure identity. Thus, when the political situation changes, new relationships between historical referents are created in order to infuse them with collective significance and to illustrate, explain and legitimize power relations with other groups (see e.g. Santos-Granero 1998).

The historiographical account of the 1915 persecution of Christians has been a means of re-ethnicizing Syrian Orthodox Christians by emphasizing the distinction between them and the Kurds. This account also enhances the imagery of the past, in which the church is a consecrated place as well as a landmark of desecration, terror and retreat. The imagery of the barricaded church overlaps with the topographic image of contemporary village churches in my district, which stand alone in localities where they are surrounded by Kurds. Both their current hopes of securing an assured position in society, and their anxiety that Syrian Orthodox Christians as a group might become extinct, influence the process of reconstructing the history of the 1915 atrocities. The Syrian Orthodox Christian population in the area of my research has dramatically decreased over the past ten years. In 1998 there were 280 families, whilst in 2008 their number had declined to 120. Many had emigrated from Jazira to Europe and Australia. There was no physical threat to these Christians, who deemed themselves persecuted due to their religious identity. It is important to understand why they feel insecure living in this area and believe that the future holds few prospects for them.

Political subjectivity emerges when social identity is in crisis (Howarth *et al.* 2000:14). In order to strengthen their identity within the Syrian polity, Syrian Orthodox Christians must clarify it by participating in certain national political projects. The account of the 1915 persecution infuses them with an image of the modern topography of my district. This topography is a conjunction of different signs that crafts relations between the past and the future. When Syrian Orthodox Christians envisage an image of their perilous situation in the past, they become emotional and anxious about their place in the future.

This chapter has explored how the social position of Syrian Orthodox Christians influences both the processes of their own historical production and the constellation of referents articulated in their narratives. The 'creativity', which is present in the process of reconstructing the 1915 persecution of Christians in Ottoman Anatolia, demonstrates that they have followed a new direction in presenting their historical experience. This is affected principally by the nature of their social and political insecurity, particularly their relationship to Syrian state authority.

The case of the Syrian Orthodox Christians suggests that people do not relate to historical events in a uniform way. When the position of a particular group within society changes, its history mutates into a new form appropriate to its current identity. Thus, when it retrieves its past, different historiographies emerge at different times. During the upsurge of Arab nationalism, Syrian Orthodox Christians identified themselves as powerless victims of religious persecution by Kurds and Turks. This particular self-identification derived from their own dislocation within Syria. Even though there had been a small number of Syrian Orthodox Christians in Syria before the 1915 massacre, the majority of them were refugees from Turkey. After expulsion from their homeland and the loss of their place in the Ottoman political system, they were obliged to construct for themselves a new position in Syrian society. Their religious identity camouflaged the fact that, as émigrés from Anatolia, they were ethnically alien to Syrian society and had difficulty in asserting Arabness within a newly created community that proclaimed itself as the embodiment of Arabism.

When Syrian statist ideology shifted from its exclusive focus on Arabism to one which accepted religious multiculturalism and the acknowledgement of the existence of plural religious groups within society, Syrian Orthodox Christians found it difficult to articulate their identity vis-à-vis Muslims. In order to assert their right to a place within Syrian society, they therefore started to articulate a new account of the 1915 massacre as a way to show that Kurds, who are a politically marginalized group within Syria, were their enemies, but that they themselves were as powerful as the Kurds. There is no 'loss of memory', but rather the creation of new relationships between historical referents within a framework of changing political ideologies. A common thread runs through their narratives of the 1915 persecution – a thread that enflames their hostility and resentment towards the Kurds. The image of barricaded churches, besieged in 1915 by both Turks and Kurds, overlaps with the image of contemporary village churches in Jazira, which are enclaves surrounded by Kurds. The endeavour to articulate their historical experience, in order to assert their rights as one of the religious groups in Syria, reflects both their position in society and apprehension for their future.

References

Armalto, I. 1919. *Al-Qusara fi Nakbat al-Nasara*. Beirut: al-Tab'a al-Awwal.

Barsoum, I.A. 2000 [1963]. *History of Syriac Literature and Sciences* (ed. and trans. M. Moosa). Pueblo, CO: Passeggiata Press.

Bedoukian, K. 1978. *The Urchin: An Armenian Escape*. London: John Murray.

Bell, G. 1982. *The Churches and Monasteries of the Tur 'Abdin*. London: Pindar Press.

Benjamin, W. 1970. *Illuminations*. London: Jonathan Cape.

Bloch, M. 1998. 'Autobiographical memory and the historical memory of the more distant past'. In M. Bloch, *How We Think They Think: Anthropological Approaches to Cognition, Memory, and Literacy*, pp. 114–30. Boulder, CO: Westview Press.

Davis, J. 1989. 'The social relations of the production of history'. In E. Tonkin, M. McDonald and M. Chapman (eds), *History and Ethnicity*, pp. 104–20. London: Routledge.

De Courtois, S. 2004. *The Forgotten Genocide: Eastern Christians, the Last Arameans*. Piscataway, NJ: Georgias Press.

Duguid, S. 1973. 'The policy of unity: Hamidian policy in eastern Anatolia', *Middle Eastern Studies* 9(2):139–55.

Gellner, E. 1983. *Nations and Nationalism*. Oxford: Blackwell.

Gilsenan, M. 1977. 'Against patron–client relations'. In E. Gellner and J. Waterbury (eds), *Patrons and Clients in Mediterranean Societies*, pp. 167–83. London: Duckworth.

Howarth, D.R., Norval, A.J. and Stavrakakis, Y. 2000. *Discourse Theory and Political Analysis: Identities, Hegemonies and Social Change*. Manchester: Manchester University Press.

HRW (Human Rights Watch). 1996. 'Syria: the silenced Kurds': www.hrw.org/legacy/reports/1996/Syria.htm (accessed 31 October 2018).

Jastrow, O. 1985. 'Mlahso: an unknown neo-Aramaic language of Turkey', *Journal of Semitic Studies* 30(2):265–70.

——— 1994. *Der Neuaramaishe Dialekt von Malhso*. Wiesbaden: Harrassowitz.

Joseph, J. 1983. *Muslim–Christian Relations and Inter-Christian Rivalries in the Middle East*. Albany: State University of New York Press.

Kherdian, D. 1988. *The Road from Home: The Story of an Armenian Girl*. New York: Puffin.

Khuri, F.I. 1973. *From Village to Suburb: Order and Change in Greater Beirut*. Chicago: University of Chicago Press.

Miller, D.E. and Miller, L.T. 1993. *Survivors: An Oral History of the Armenian Genocide*. London: University of California Press.

Niebuhr, C. 1992 [1879]. *Reisebeschreibung nach Arabien und Andern Umliegenden Landen*. Zurich: Manesse Verlag.

Ohanian, M. 1990. *Un Armmenien Parmi les Autres* (trans. E. Kitayama). Tokyo: Akashi Shoten.

Ranger, T. 1993. 'The invention of tradition revised: the case of colonial Africa'. In T.O. Ranger and O. Vaughan (eds), *Legitimacy and the State in Twentieth Century Africa*, pp. 62–111. London: Macmillan.

Roberman, S. 2007. 'Fighting to belong: Soviet WWII veterans in Israel', *Ethnos* 35(4):447–77.

Santos-Granero, F. 1998. 'Writing history into the landscape: space, myth, and ritual in contemporary Amazonia', *American Ethnologist* 25(2):128–48.

Shryock, A.J. 1997. *Nationalism and the Genealogical Imagination: Oral History and Textual Authority in Tribal Jordan*. Berkeley: University of California Press.

Steite. 1937a. 'Déclarations de Mgr. Steite, archevêque syriaque catholique de Damas, fait au correspondant de l'Agence Havas, le 22 Décembre 1937'. Fonds Beyrouth, Cabinet Politique 1926–1941, Syrie-Liban, Box 504.

——— 1937b. 'Le Colonel Sarrade délégué-adjoint du haut-commissaire à Monsieur le haut-commissaire de la République Française en Syrie et au Liban, Septembre 1937'. Fonds Beyrouth, Cabinet Politique 1926–1941, Syrie-Liban, Box 504.

Van Bruinessen, M. 1999. 'The Kurds and Islam'. Islamic Area Studies Working Paper Series No.13. Tokyo: Islamic Area Studies Project, University of Tokyo.

Vanly, I.C. 1992. 'The Kurds in Syria and Lebanon'. In P.G. Kreyenbeowk and S. Sperl (eds), *The Kurds: Contemporary Overview*, pp. 143–70. London: Routledge.

Yonan, G. 1989. *Einvergessener Holocaust: Die Vernichtung der Christlichen Assyrer in der Türkei.* Göttingen: Gesellschaft für bedrohte Völker.

——— 1996. 'Lest we perish in a forgotten holocaust: the extermination of the Christian Assyrians in Turkey and Persia', Unpublished paper.

9

Nations with/out borders

Neoliberalism and the problem of belonging in Africa, and beyond

Jean Comaroff and John L. Comaroff

Anthropologists are fond of stories and riddles. The stranger, the more puzzling, the better. So let us first pose a riddle, then tell a story.

The riddle: what might the Nuer, a remote Nilotic people in the southern Sudan, have to do with Carl Schmitt, the noted German philosopher, notorious apologist for Nazism, and, of late, one of the most quoted social theorists in the English-speaking world? For their part, the Nuer are famous among anthropologists, not least because, in the 1940s, they were held to pose an epistemic challenge to received Western political theory (Fortes and Evans-Pritchard 1940:4). This was largely due to the fact that they had a political system without government. According to Evans-Pritchard (1940a, 1940b), their storied ethnographer, they lived in 'ordered anarchy': a state of being without a state to rule over them. In this respect, they were the archetype of so-called 'acephalous' African political systems, systems that were later to be evoked, by Michael Barkun (1968) and others, in efforts to account for the segmentary oppositions on which the fragile coherence of the Cold War world system sustained itself. *Contra* Hobbes, order here did not congeal in offices or institutions, in courts or constabularies, in finite territories or fixed geographical borders. It inhered, rather, in a virtual logic of action encoded in the idiom of kinship: in an immanent socio-logic of fission and fusion, of relative social distance, that brought people together or forced them apart in situations of conflict. Thus, if a homicide occurred within the 'tribe', it was dealt with by established means of self-help and retribution; if it occurred beyond its margins, what followed was warfare between polities. Practically speaking, though, those boundaries between inside and out were renegotiated, dialectically – they were objectified and made real – in the process of dealing with the very transgressions that breached them. The Nuer polity, in sum, was a field of potential action, conjured by the need to distinguish between allies and antagonists, law and war.

Which is where Carl Schmitt comes in. In his study of the nature of the political, Schmitt (1966) portrays politics, Nuer-like, as a pragmatic matter of the will to make life-or-death distinctions between friend and enemy. In other words, as a matter of making order by drawing lines: of inscribing the political in collective identities, at once physical and metaphysical, carved as much out of the logic of who we are *not* as who we are; indeed, of entailing the one in the other and both in the sublime act of arriving at unequivocal oppositions when they count. Like those, for example, of radically different theologico-civilizations caught up in an apocalyptic clash between the good and the bad in the ugly days after 9/11; days in which the planet was terrified by uncertainty because it was so uncertain about terror, specifically, by the capacity of violence without sovereign signature to ambiguate formerly clear axes of global geopolitics; days in which US came to spell not just the United States but 'us'. As Nuer might have put it, in an orderly world, a world of absolutes, everything is relative since all things are relatives. Except those who are not, who fall beyond the law, beyond the ethical margin and who, therefore, are to be excised, outlawed or, *in extremis*, unsacrificially disposed of (cf. Agamben 1998). Order, in short, is wrought from disorder, political existence from anarchy, by virtue of drawing the line. It is at that line that the riddle is resolved: that line where the Nuer and Schmitt meet, there to agree on the inscription of the normative in a grammar of difference, made manifest by enacting boundaries at once existential, ethical and legal – and, as we shall see, immanently violent.

Fire, last time

So much for the riddle, to which we shall return. Now for the story. It is about a fire, about aliens, about a nation-in-the-making and about its borders, both internal and external. It is also about a world in which borders, *sui generis*, are becoming ever more enigmatic, ever more troublesome. We have recounted this story before, but think it worth revisiting in light of recent global events. It raises a host of questions: What might natural disasters tell us about the architecture of twenty-first-century nation-states? How might the sudden flash of catastrophe illuminate the meaning of borders and the politics of belonging? And to what extent are those two things, borders and belonging, morphing – along with the substance of citizenship, sovereignty and national integrity – in this, the neoliberal age, an age frequently associated with states of emergency? These questions have a number of deeper historical implications hidden in them. But we are running ahead of ourselves. Let us title our tale ...

Apocalypse, African style

The millennium passed in South Africa without incident; this despite public fears, before the event, of murderous violence and mass destruction. Then, two weeks later, Cape Town caught fire. On a hot, dry Saturday, the veldt flared up in a number of places across the greater metropolitan area. High winds carried walls of flame up its mountain spine, threatening historic homes and squatter settlements alike. As those in its path were evacuated, the TV projected disjunctive images of civic cooperation: of the poor helping each other their carry paltry possessions from doomed shacks; of the wealthy, having dropped their silverware into their swimming pools, lining up to pass water buckets to those dousing the flames.[1] As the bush continued to burn, helicopters dumped ton after ton of water on it. Round-the-clock reports told horrific tales of beasts grilled alive, of churches incinerated, of vineyards razed. The city sweltered beneath a blanket of smoke as ash rained down on its boulevards and beaches.

In total, 9,000 hectares burned. The mountains smouldered sullenly for weeks. So did the tempers of the populace. Blame flew in many directions, none of them politically random. Fire is endemic to the region. But, being of calamitous proportions, this one raised fears about the very survival of the natural kingdom at the Cape. Its livid scars evoked elemental anxieties, saturating public discourse as it called forth an almost obsessive desire to construe it as an apocalyptic omen, an indictment, a call to arms. The divinations that ensued – in the streets, the media, the halls of government – laid bare the complex social ecology whence the conflagration itself had sprung, casting a sharp light on the state of a nation then barely six years old.

Apocalypse, of course, eventually dissolves into history. Therein, to borrow Mike Davis's phrase, lies the 'dialectic of ordinary disaster' (Davis 1995). Thus, while early discussion of the fire was wild and contested, it reduced, in time, to a dominant interpretation, one that, while not universal, drew enough consensus to authorize strong state action and broad civic collaboration. Here, clearly, was an 'ideology in the making'. As such, it played upon an implicit landscape of affect and anxiety, inclusion and intrusion, prosperity and loss. Via a clutch of charged references, it linked the fire to

---

1   M. Merten, 'A chronology of destruction', *Mail and Guardian*, 21–27 January 2000, p. 7; V. Foxcroft, 'Flames past, present – and future?' *Cape Times*, 3 February 2000, p. 11; 'Kaap lek sy wonde: Weskus veg met hulp uit noorde', *Die Burger*, 21 January 2000, p. 1; 'Bokkie se trane', *Die Burger*, 22 January 2000, p. 8.

other public concerns – concerns about being and identity, about organic society and common humanity, about boundaries and their violation – at the heart of contemporary nationhood. But its efficacy in this respect rested, first, on producing a plausible explanation for the extent of the blaze.

Initially, cigarette ends and cooking fires were held responsible. But this soon gave way to talk of arson, pointing, specifically, to a campaign of urban terror attributed to Muslim fundamentalism that had gripped the Cape long before 9/11.[2] Then the discourse abruptly changed direction, alighting on an aetiology that took hold with unusual force: whatever sparked it, the catastrophic scale of the fire was blamed on alien plants, plants that burn more readily and fiercely than does native vegetation. Outrage against those plants grew quickly. Landowners who had allowed them to spread were denounced for putting the population, and its 'natural heritage', at risk.[3]

Note: 'natural heritage'. Heritage has become a construct to conjure with as global markets and mass migration erode the distinctive wealth of nations, forcing them to redefine their sense of patrimony. And its material worth. A past mayor of Cape Town, for example, was wont to describe Table Mountain as a 'national asset' whose value is 'measured by every visitor it attracts'.[4] Not coincidentally, South Africa was then engaged in a bid to have the Cape Peninsula declared a World Heritage Site in recognition of its unparalleled biodiversity. This heritage is embodied, above all, in *fynbos* (Afrikaans, 'fine bush').[5] These small-leaved evergreens that cover the mountainous uplands and coastal forelands of the region have come to epitomize its organic integrity and its fragile, wealth-producing beauties. And, as they have, local people have voiced ever more anxiety that their riches are endangered by alien vegetation, whose colonizing effect is to reduce it to 'impenetrable monotony' (Hall 1979:134). Ours, to be sure, is an age in which value and profit reside, perhaps more than anything else, in the creation of variety, difference, distinctiveness.

The blaze brought this to a head. 'Wake up Cape Town', screamed a newspaper headline set against the image of a lone red fire lily poking, phoenix-like, from a bed of ashes. Efforts by botanists to cool the hysteria – to insist that fire in *fynbos* is not abnormal – had no effect. A cartoonist, casting

2   B. Jordan, 'Ash city: why the fires were so bad', *Sunday Times*, 23 January 2000, p. 7.

3   J. Yeld, 'Force landowners to clear invading alien plants', *Sunday Argus*, 22–23 January 2000, p. 7; also L. de Villiers (chair of Peninsula Mountain Forum), 'Take decisive steps to avoid future fire disaster', letter, *Cape Times*, 28 January 2000, p. 11.

4   '*Ukuvuka* the biggest ever', editorial, *Cape Times*, 7 February 2000, p. 10.

5   For early technical accounts of *fynbos* and its ecology, see e.g. Kruger (1978) and Day *et al.* (1979).

his ironic eye on the mood of millennial anxiety, drew a flying saucer above Cape Town. Peering down on the city as it sinks into a globally-warmed sea, its mountain covered by foreign flora, a diminutive space traveller exclaims '*Glork plik zoot urgle*': 'They seem to have a problem with aliens'.[6]

The satirist touched a raw nerve: the obsession with alien plants gestured toward a scarcely submerged sense of civic terror and moral panic. Significantly, when the fire was followed two weeks later by floods to the north, another headline asked: 'First fires, now floods – next frogs?'.[7] By then, it was not surprising to read that vast forests of alien trees, owned by logging corporations, were held to have 'caused all the trouble'.[8]

What exactly was at stake in this mass-mediated chain of consciousness, this litany of alien nature? What does it tell us about perceived threats to the nation and its patrimony? To the conception of social cohesion, ethical citizenship and shared humanity at its core? Observers elsewhere have noted that an impassioned sense of autochthony, of birthright – to which alienness is the negative counterpoint – has edged aside other images of belonging at the end of the twentieth century; also, that a fetishism of origins seems to be growing up the world over in opposition to the effects of neoliberal laissez-faire.[9] But why? Why, at this juncture in the history of the modernist polity have boundaries and their transgression become so incendiary an issue? Could it be that the public anxiety here over invasive plant species speaks to an existential conundrum presently making itself felt at the very heart of nationhood everywhere: In what does national integrity consist, what might polity and society mean, what moral and material entitlements might it entail, at a time when global capitalism appears almost everywhere to be dissolving sovereign borders, almost everywhere to be displacing politics-as-usual?

In order to address these questions – in order to make sense both of our narrative of catastrophe and of the more general matter of why it is that aliens of all kinds have become such a widespread preoccupation – we must take a brief detour into the interiors of 'the' late-modernist nation-state.

---

6   Chip, 'They seem to have a problem with aliens', *Cape Argus*, 27 January 2000, p. 23.

7   I. Powell and H. Hogan, 'First fires, now floods – next frogs?' *Mail and Guardian*, 11–17 February 2000, p. 9.

8   F. Macleod, 'The trees that caused all the trouble', *Mail and Guardian*, 11–17 February 2000, p. 8.

9   For a thoughtful, Africa-centric reflection on this tendency, see Geschiere and Nyamnjoh (2000).

The nation-state in perspective, retrospectively

Euro-nations – as Benedict Anderson (1983) has emphasized – were founded on the fiction of cultural homogeneity: on an imagined, often violently effected sense of fraternity. Much has been said about that imagining: that Euro-nationhood was always more diverse than its historiography allows, always a work in progress. But that is another story. Since the late twentieth century, those polities have had increasingly to come to terms with difference. Historical circumstance has pushed them, often unwillingly, toward ever greater heterodoxy. Hence the growing concern, scholarly and lay alike, with citizenship, sovereignty, multiculturalism, minority rights and the limits of liberalism. Hence, too, the xenophobia that haunts contemporary nationhood almost everywhere, of which more later.

The move toward heterodoxy is itself part of a more embracing world-historical process, one in which 1989 figures centrally. That year, symbolically if not substantively, heralded the political coming of age, across the planet, of neoliberal capitalism. While its economic roots lie much deeper, this, retrospectively, is typically taken to have been the juncture at which the old international order gave way to a more fluid, market-driven, electronically articulated universe: a universe in which *supra*national institutions burgeon; in which space and time are recalibrated; in which geography is rewritten in four dimensions; in which a new global jurisprudence displaces its internationalist predecessor, overlaying the sovereignty of national legal systems; in which transnational identities, diasporic connections and the mobility of human populations transgress old frontiers; in which 'society' is declared dead, to be replaced by 'the network' and 'the community' as dominant metaphors of social connectedness; in which governance is reduced to a promiscuous combination of service delivery, security provision and the fiduciary; in which liberty is distilled to its postmodern essence, the right to choose identities, subjectivities, commodities, sexualities, localities and almost everything else. A universe, also, in which older institutional and instrumental forms of power – refigured, now, primarily as biopower – depart most states as never before, dispersing themselves everywhere and anywhere and nowhere tangible at all: into transnational corporations and NGOs, into shadowy, privatized parastatal cabals, into syndicated crime and organized religion, and into unholy fusions of all of these things.

In the upshot, 'the' state, an entity ever more polymorphous *and* amorphous, is held, increasingly, to be in constant crisis: its legitimacy is tested by debt, disease, poverty and corruption; its executive control is perpetually pushed to the limit; and, most of all, its hyphen-nation – the articulation, that is, of state to nation, nation to state – is everywhere under challenge. This is especially so in post-colonial nation-states, whose ruling regimes often rely on theatrical means to produce state power, to conjure national unity, and to persuade citizens of the reality of both (Mbembe 1992; Worby 1998). They are not alone in this, of course. Resort to mass-mediated ritual excess – not least ritual orchestrated in the name of security – features prominently right now in the politics of states in many places.

This broad historical transformation – the move, that is, from an imagined homogeneity to the inescapable realities of heterodoxy – has any number of corollaries. For present purposes, we raise just three.

The first is the refiguration of the modernist subject-citizen. One corollary of the changing face of nationhood, of its growing diversity, has been an explosion of identity politics. Not just of ethnic and cultural politics, but also of the politics of, among other things, gender, sexuality, age, race, religiosity and style. While most human beings still live as citizens *in* nation-states, they tend only to be conditionally citizens *of* nation-states. Which, in turn, puts ever more stress on their hyphen-nation. The more diverse nation-states become, the higher the level of abstraction at which '*the* nation-state' exists, the more dire appear threats against it. And, at least for those affectively attached to it, the more urgent becomes the need to divine and negate whatever endangers it. States, notes David Harvey (1990:108), have always had to sustain a definition of the commonweal over and above sectarian concerns. One solution that has presented itself in the face of ever more assertive claims made against it in the name of identity is an appeal to the primacy of national autochthony: to the ineffable loyalties, the interests and affect, that flow from rootedness in a place of birth (see above). Nor is this just a tactic, one that appeals to those in the business of government. It resonates with deeply felt populist fears – and with the proclivity of citizens of all stripes to deflect shared anxieties onto outsiders.

Autochthony is implicit in many forms of identity of course; it also attaches to places within places, parts within wholes. But, as a specifically national claim against aliens, its mobilization appears to be growing in direct proportion to the sundered hyphenation of the sovereign polity, to its popularly perceived porousness and impotence in the face of exogenous forces. Citizens *in* many contemporary states, whether or not they are primarily citizens *of* those states, seem able to reimagine nationhood in such a way as to embrace the ineluctability of internal difference: 'multiculturalism', 'rainbow nation' and terms like them provide a ready argot of accommodation, even amidst political conflict. However, when it comes to the limits of that difference, autochthony constitutes an ultimate line, the *fons et origo* of fealty, affect, attachment. Whatever other identities the citizen-subject of the twenty-first century may bear, s/he is unavoidably either an autochthon or an alien. Nor only s/he; it too. Non-humans, also – flora, fauna, commodities, cultural practices – may be autochthons or aliens.

The second transformation of the modernist polity concerns the regulation of borders – and, hence, the limits of sovereignty. Much of the debate over the 'crisis' of the nation-state hinges upon the contention that governments no longer control the mobility of currencies and commercial instruments, of labour and goods, of information, illegal substances and unwanted aliens. What is more, goes the same argument, they tend to enjoy limited or no dominion over enclaved zones, the frontiers within their realms, under the sway of organized crime, religious movements, corporations and the like; all of which has led many contemporary nation-states to resemble patchworks of sovereignties, laterally arranged in space, with tenuous corridors between them, surrounded by terrains of ungovernability (Comaroff and Comaroff 2006). National frontiers have always been more-or-less porous, of course. But technologies of space-time compression do appear to have effected a sea change in patterns and rates of global flow – of the concrete and the virtual, of humans, objects, signs, currencies, communications. Which is why so many states, most maybe, act as if they were constantly subject both to invasion from the outside and to the seeping away of what ought properly to remain within. South Africa, for instance, laments the pull of the market on its human capital,[10] while anguishing, xenophobically, over the inflow of migrants. And the global North, despite its so-called 'demographic winter', agonizes over the ubiquitous presence of racially marked, criminally inflected 'others' of various provenances, not to mention the spectre of a future Muslim Europe.

Our object, though, is not just to remark the heightened concern with borders and their transgression. It is also to observe that this concern is the product of a paradox. Under current global conditions, given the logic of the neoliberal capitalist economy, states find themselves in a double bind. In order to garner the value spun off by that economy, they are required at once both to open up their frontiers and secure them: on the one hand to deregulate the movement of currencies, goods, people and services, thus to facilitate the inflow of wealth; on the other, to establish enclaved zones of competitive advantage so as to attract transnational manufacture and media, investment, information technology and the 'right' kind of migrants – tourists, corporate personnel, NGOs and the sorts of labourer who will work cheaply and tractably without the entitlements of citizenship. In this way, the nation-state is made, in aspiration if not always in reality, into a meta-management enterprise: a business both in itself and in the business of attracting business. In sum, part franchise, part licencing authority. This in the interest of its

---

10   See e.g. 'Official figures for brain drain released', *The Star*, 14 March 2000, p. 2.

'stakeholders', who desire simultaneously to be global citizens and yet also to be corporate national subjects with all the benefits that accrue to membership of a sovereign nation. The corollary is plain. The border is a double bind – 'schismogenic', to recall Gregory Bateson's (1972) term – because the commonweal appears to demand, but is threatened by, both openness and closure. No wonder the angst, the avid public debate in so many places, about what should or should not be allowed entry, what is or is not in the collective interest. And who ought to share it. Hence the arguments, also, between those who would globalize capital by erasing all barriers and those protective of the national patrimony.

The third salient feature of the predicament of the nation-state is the decentring of politics into other domains: into the law, religion, the media, the non-governmental sector and, above all, the economy.[11] The conventional argument goes like this: neoliberal capitalism, in its triumphal, global phase, appears to offer no alternative to laissez-faire; nothing else seems even thinkable. The primary question left to public policy is how to succeed materially in the 'new' world order. Why? Because this order hides its ideological scaffolding in the dictates of the 'free' market, of capital growth and the accumulation of wealth, in the exigencies of technology, in the imperatives of national security, in drawing sharp lines between friend and foe. Older axes of ideological commitment seem ever more anachronistic as public action tends to be articulated around urgent questions of the moment, often sparked by catastrophe, be it ecological, terrorist or whatever. Each takes the limelight as it flares into public awareness, becomes 'hot' for a while, and then burns down, its embers consigned to the recesses of collective consciousness – only to flame up again if kindled by contingent conditions or vocal coalitions, or both.

Our evocation of the imagery of fire returns us to South Africa, but to a South Africa now situated, if all too summarily, in the contemporary history of capitalism, governance and the nation-state: a history that implicates altered forms of citizenship, an obsession with boundaries, aliens and autochthony, and various displacements of the terms of modernist politics as we have come to know it.

---

11   On South Africa, in this respect, see Xolela Mangcu's comment: 'Political choices are depoliticized and given the aura of technical truth. Public policies that get implemented are those backed by "growth coalitions" which span government, business, the media and other interest groups ... [These] shape national consensus on priorities' (X. Mangcu, 'The score so far: poverty alleviation 0, soccer World Cup 10', *Sunday Independent*, 12 March 2000, p. 8).

Naturing the nation
A lesson from fynbos
The full impact of the fire in January 2000 flowed from the capacity of the burning bush, of the flowers and flames, to signify. To signify charged political anxieties, many of them unnameable in everyday discourse. To signify the aspiration that, from the ashes, might arise a distinctly local, new South African sense of community, nationality, civil society. The question, patently, is how: How *did* those flowers and flames come to mean so much?

First, the flora. Flowers have long served as national emblems. The giant protea (*Protea cynaroides*) which typifies *fynbos*, has been South Africa's for many years. It stands in a totemic relationship to the nation; a relationship, that is, of people to nature, place to species, in which the latter enriches the former – so long as it is venerated and not wantonly consumed. But it is also a fetish, a natural displacement of emotively charged identities rooted in acts of ethno-racial exclusion.

It was not always so.

For a start, the use of the term *fynbos* for the indigenous plants of the southern Cape is recent. It was only at the end of the 1960s that the word, and the category to which it now refers, became established in either popular or botanical parlance.[12] This was precisely the time when international demand for local flora took off, and a national association was formed to market it; *fynbos* export is now a huge industry. It was also the point at which statesmen began to dub these flora a 'natural asset' – and at which botanists first asserted that they were a fragile species worthy of conservation as a 'unique biome type' (Kruger 1977). Not long before then, in 1953, an authority on the subject actually described *fynbos* as an invader that threatened the local grassveld (Acocks 1953:14, 17). What is now said of aliens was being said, a half-century ago, of this 'South Africa treasure', this passionately protected icon of national, natural rootedness.

But it is not just as fragile natural heritage that *fynbos* has captured the imagination of the South African public. It is also as a protagonist locked in mortal struggle with invasive aliens that threaten to take over its habitat and choke off its means of survival. A parenthetic note here: similar anxieties

---

12   This was confirmed by botanists working on the Fynbos Biome. While *'fynbos'* seems first to have been used in a publication in 1916, it only entered the academic lexicon in the early 1970s (Dave Richardson, personal communication). The term appears on a list of summer school lectures at the University of Cape Town in 1972, for example, and in the title of a paper read at the South African Wild Life Management Association's Second International Symposium (Kruger 1977). We do not recall it being in circulation while we were growing up in the Cape.

about plant invaders have manifested themselves in other Western nations as well: nations, tellingly, where human in-migration is a mass concern – in the USA for example, and in Australia, where, ironically, South African flora are demonized (Carr *et al.* 1986; Wace 1988); also Britain, where huge expanses of alien rhododendrons, once very popular, are to be removed at great cost from National Trust properties.[13]

Time was when there was great enthusiasm for non-indigenous vegetation. In the high colonial age, British expatriate rulers encouraged the import of exotics for what seemed, at the time, like good, 'modern' ecological reasons (Hall 1979). It took a long while for desirable imports to become 'invasive aliens', 'pests', 'colonizers', even 'green cancers'.[14] It was only in the 1950s that the Botanical Society of South Africa started to promote awareness of the problem; only in the 1960s that the first volunteers took to the veldt to cut down the interlopers; only in the 1970s that the Department of Nature and Environment Conservation at the Cape published its popular sourcebook, entitled, like a pornographic work of science fiction, *Plant Invaders, Beautiful but Dangerous* (Stirton 1978); only in the 1980s that 'hack groups' spread in upper-middle-class rural white areas. And it was only in the 1990s that aliens came to be held largely accountable for the fragility of Cape flora. This is abundantly clear from the way in which attitudes to fire in the *fynbos* have shifted over the past decade, culminating in the catastrophe of January 2000.

Playing with fire

Which takes us to the matter of fire: as we have said, fires are endemic to the Cape. While the media usually speak of them as 'devastating' (Fraser and McMahon 1988:140), expert opinion acknowledges that the conservation of biodiversity actually depends on natural conflagration (van Rensberg 1986:41). Such caveats, however, were muted in the debate that raged after the millennial blaze in Cape Town. Most salient to us here is the changing place accorded to aliens in this argument, and in the politics and the perceptions that informed it. In the past, foreign plants were only one of many factors held to produce fires of distinct kinds; in fact, an authoritative report on the topic published as late as 1979 does not even list them as a concern (see Kruger

---

13   See, for example, 'Why have we removed the rhododendron?', National Trust: www.nationaltrust.org.uk/features/why-have-we-removed-the-rhododendron-

14   The term 'green cancer' appears in the title of a volume whose given publication details are somewhat ambiguous: we have attributed it to the Control of Alien Vegetation Committee, Kirstenbosch (see CAVC 1959). Note that Kirstenbosch, situated in Cape Town, is the national botanical garden of South Africa.

1979). Neither, remember, did public blame in 2000 alight immediately upon them – although when it did, they became a burning preoccupation. Literally.

As we said earlier, not everybody held alien flora to account (see Comaroff and Comaroff 2001). One view attributed the inferno to global climatic change.[15] It was paid no heed. This was a calamity that seemed to demand a local explanation. Another argument came from the Afrikaans press, which glossed the event as an indictment of the African National Congress, of its inefficiency in government.[16] For yet others, excluded altogether from the public debate, foreign plants have a totally different value. Many of the jobless poor who reside in informal settlements around the city, a large number of them recent migrants, depend on those plants for their survival.[17] Their unelectrified communities in the bush comprise row upon row of square shacks built mainly of thin slats of Australian wattle (*Acacia cyclops*; Afrikaans, *rooikrans*). This 'imported' kindling is their chief fuel (van Wyk and Gericke 2000:284). It is also a vital source of income for them: they sell it at roadsides to white commuters for whom alien trees, like *rooikrans*, are an important component of the *braaivleis* (barbecue), a key ritual of commensal sociality in South Africa. Non-indigenous vegetation, in short, has long been a critical part of the local economy – the underclass part, which only tangentially touches the lives of those for whom aliens are held as anathema, and those by whom they are seen to jeopardize civic order and national heritage. Not unexpectedly, the material salience of foreign flora to the poor did not divert the drama of alien nature as it became a public passion play.

But how, precisely, did that passion play take shape? To what anxieties, interests and emotions did it – does it – respond? Which brings us to …

Aliens and the African renaissance

Until the fall of apartheid, the term 'alien' had archaic connotations in South Africa, being enshrined in laws aimed primarily at barring Jewish entry in the 1930s. These laws remained in place until amended in the mid 1990s (when they were replaced by the Aliens Control Act 96 of 1991 and subsequent amendments), when immigrants became a fraught issue in a society seething with a surplus of the unemployed, the unwaged and the unruly. It was at the same time that foreign plants became both the subject of ecological emergency

---

15   M.-A. Feris, 'Scientists pour cold water on global-warming claim', *The Star*, 17 February 2000, p. 3.

16   'Totaalplan teen brande', *Die Burger*, 21 January 2000, p. 8; 'Regering en dienste moet beter koördineer – minister', *Die Burger*, 22 January 2000, p. 3; 'Bokkie se trane', *Die Burger*, 22 January 2000, p. 8.

17   B. Jordan 'Ash city', *Sunday Times*, 23 January 2000, p. 7.

and an object of national renewal (Hall 1979:138). The most striking symptom of this was the Working for Water Programme, launched in 1995. Part of the post-apartheid Reconstruction and Development Plan, the scheme, a flagship project to create jobs and combat poverty, centred on routing out alien vegetation. Its tone was urgent: alien plants are like 'a health epidemic, spreading widely out of control', said the programme's home page.[18] Out-of-work women and youth, ex-offenders, the disabled, even the homeless would be rehabilitated by joining eradication teams – and by toiling in industries that turned the invaders into commodities. Meanwhile, the public was exhorted not to buy foreign plants. Alien nature, in other words, was to be the raw material of communal rebirth.

The blaze in Cape Town gave yet further impetus to this. As popular feeling focused on the foreign 'scourge', the African National Congress seemed intent on coaxing 'a spirit of community' from the ashes. Ever more overt connections were made, in official discourse, between the war against aliens and the prosperity of the nation. A much-publicized symposium was held to discuss international cooperation in dealing with invasive species, drawing four ministers of state and several high-level representatives from other nations – notably Australia, Germany, the United States and the United Kingdom – all of which evinced similar anxieties.[19] Global trade and tourism, the participants noted, had created a new class of 'unwanted traveler' in foreign flora and disease-bearing insects.[20] But the most portentous words were those of President Mbeki: alien plants, he said, 'stand in the way of the African renaissance'.[21]

---

18 This homepage (www-dwaf.pwv.gov.za/idwaf/projects/WFW/Default.htm, accessed 27 February 2000) has since been replaced. While the text has changed, both its essential substance and its urgent tone remains. So does the promise that the programme will continue to create jobs and take a lead in the national 'fight against poverty' (see: http://www.dwaf.gov.za/wfw/, accessed 4 July 2007).

19 International Symposium on Best Management Practices for Preventing and Controlling Invasive Alien Species, Kirstenbosch (Cape Town), 22–24 February 2000.

20 M. Merten, 'Eradicating invasive aliens', *Mail and Guardian*, 3–9 March 2000, p. 33.

21 Message from President Thabo Mbeki, read by Valli Moosa, minister for environmental affairs and tourism, at the International Symposium on Best Management Practices for Preventing and Controlling Invasive Alien Species, Kirstenbosch (Cape Town), 22–24 February 2000; see also K. Bliksem, 'Only the truly patriotic can be trusted to smell the roses, and weed them out', *Sunday Independent*, 22 February 2000, p. 8.

Foreign objects: the politics of estrangement in the post-colony

And so invading plants became embroiled in the state of the nation. But this does not yet answer our key question. To what precise anxieties, interests and historical conditions did the allegory of alien nature speak? An answer is to be found in the public discourses of the time: in a cluster of implicit associations, indirect allusions and organic intuitions that, together, give insight into the infrastructure of popular consciousness under construction – specifically, into the way in which processes of naturalization made it possible to voice the unspeakable, thus to address the challenge of constructing a nation under neoliberal conditions. Conditions, that is, that involve precisely the transformations of which we spoke earlier: the changing meaning of citizenship and belonging, borders at once open and closed, people unavoidably on the move, irreducible social and cultural heterodoxy, the displacement of politics and a shrinking commonweal. Take this satirical comment by a well-known South African journalist:

> **Only the truly patriotic can be trusted to smell the roses**
> Doubtless there are gardening writers who would not think twice about
> sounding off in blissful praise of something as innocent … as the jacaranda
> tree … But … you may be nothing more than … a racist. Subliminally that
> is[22] … Behind its blossoms and its splendid boughs, the jacaranda is nothing
> but a water-hogging … weed-spreading alien.
> (Bliksem 2000:8)

In times past, the jacaranda was regarded as 'almost South Africa's national tree' (Moll and Moll 1994:49). Now, in a bizarre drama in which flora signify what politics struggles to name, it has become an object of estrangement, even racialization. It is not happenstance, then, that, in the heat of the millennial moment, public discourse went as far as to bespeak the 'ethnic cleansing' of the countryside.[23] This in a land obsessed with who is or is not a citizen, with constitutional rights and wrongs, with routing out all vestiges of racism. But it was a wry letter from a West African scholar to the *Mail and Guardian*, the nation's most serious weekly newspaper, that made the political subtext most brutally plain.

---

22 A controversial investigation of racism in the mainstream press, both overt and
    'subliminal', was being conducted by the South African Human Rights Commission
    at the time. See e.g. E. Rapiti, 'Journalists must do their jobs without interference',
    letter, *Mail and Guardian*, 10–16 March 2000, p. 28.
23 C. Lazar, 'Forget alien plants, what about guns?' *The Star*, 7 March 2000, p. 8.

It is alien-bashing time again. As an alien … I am particularly prickly about criticisms of aliens even if they are plants … Alien plants cannot of course respond to these accusations. But before the Department of Home Affairs is dragooned into investigating the residence permits of these plants I, as a concerned fellow alien, wish to remind one and all that plants such as maize … soybean, sunflower … originated outside of the continent of Africa. In any case, did the fire-and-flood-causing alien plants cross the borders and establish plantations … by themselves?[24]

For this human alien, ecology had become the site of a distressingly familiar crusade: the demonization of migrants by the state and its citizenry alike.

It has been noted that the migrant is the spectre on whose wretched fate the triumphal neoliberal politics of the 'new' Europe has been founded.[25] In South Africa too, a phobia about foreigners – above all foreigners from elsewhere in Africa – has been the offspring of the fledgling democracy, waxing, paradoxically, alongside appeals to *ubuntu*, a common African humanity. Over the past decade that phobia has congealed into an active antipathy to what is perceived as a shadowy alien nation of 'illegal immigrants'. The qualifier ('illegal') has become inseparable from the sign ('immigrant'), just as, in the plant world, 'invasive' has become locked, adjectivally, to 'alien'. Popularly held to be 'economic vultures' who usurp jobs and resources,[26] and who bring crime and disease, these anti-citizens are accused – in uncanny analogy with non-indigenous flora – of spreading uncontrollably, and of siphoning off the wealth of the nation.[27] This is in spite of the fact that their role in its economy, especially in the 'informal' market sector, is wealth-*producing*, and often remarkably innovative.

Aliens, then, are a distinctive species in the popular imagination. In a parodic perversion of the past, they are 'profiled' by colour and culture, thence to be excluded from the moral community. Once singled out, 'illegals' are seldom differentiated from bona fide immigrants.[28] All are dubbed *makwerekwere*, a disparaging term for incompetent speech. Not surprisingly, they live in terror that their accents will be detected.

---

24 M.E. Aken'Ova, 'Loving the alien', *Mail and Guardian*, 18–24 February 2000, p. 29.

25 J. Seabrook, 'Racists and hypocrites', *Mail and Guardian*, 18–24 February 2000, p. 22.

26 H. Radebe, 'Time we became a bit more neighbourly', *The Star*, 16 March 2000, p. 13.

27 M.R. Sinclair, 'Unwilling aliens: forced migrants in the new South Africa', *Indicator* 13/3 (1996), pp. 14–18; M. Reitzes, 'Alien issues', *Indicator* 12/1 (1994), p. 7.

28 L. Madywabe, 'My four hours as an illegal immigrant', *Mail and Guardian*, 3–9 March 2000, p. 16.

The fear is well founded. With the relaxation of controls over immigrant labour, South Africa – Africa's 'America' – has become the destination of choice for many people from the north; a decade ago, estimates already ran as high as 8 million.[29] This influx has occurred amidst transformations in the domestic economy that have altered relations of production, leading to a radically downsized job market in which over 80 per cent of employers opt for 'non-standard', casualized work (Adam *et al.* 1998:209), much of it done by low-paid, non-unionized 'illegals', whom farmers and industrialists claim are essential to their survival in competitive global markets.[30] These transformations have also placed a strong emphasis on entrepreneurial initiative and small business ventures, a domain in which many migrants from elsewhere in Africa have prospered. Small wonder, then, that routing 'the' alien – who has come to embody the threat to local work, wealth and welfare – presents itself as a persuasive mode of confronting economic dispossession and regaining a sense of organic community.

Thus it is that dark strangers have become objects of hatred, of hostility, even of homicidal violence across the nation,[31] a process in which the state is an ambiguous actor. On the one hand, it insists volubly on upholding universal human rights and has supported a 'Roll-back Xenophobia Campaign'.[32] On the other, it contributes to that xenophobia: its law enforcement agencies, their capacity to deal with rampant crime and lawlessness deeply in question, have taken to 'waging war' on the foreign spectre. Every now and again, official announcements are made of 'US-style bid[s] to rid SA of illegal aliens'.[33] So-called 'gentlemen's clubs' said to traffic in undocumented sex workers have been subject to high profile raids.[34] So, periodically, have immigrant

---

29   See the findings of the South African Migration Project, summarized in C. Carter and F. Haffajee, 'Immigrants are creating work – not taking your jobs', *Mail and Guardian*, 11–17 September 1998, p. 3; also J. Matisonn, 'Aliens have many years' respite in SA', *Sunday Independent*, 19 March 2000, p. 3.

30   M. Reitzes, 'Alien Issues', *Indicator* 12/1 (1994), p. 7.

31   T. Amupadhi, 'African foreigners terrorized', *Mail and Guardian*, 18–23 December 1998, p. 3.

32   This campaign was a joint initiative of the Human Rights Commission, the National Consortium on Refugee Affairs and the United Nations High Commission on Refugees; see M. Kebede, 'Don't let this be a curse', *Cape Argus*, 12 January 2001, p. 11. An exhibition entitled Kwere Kwere: Journeys into Strangeness, held at the Castle of Good Hope in Cape Town in March/April 2000, was supported by the Arts and Culture Trust of the President and the National Arts Council of South Africa.

33   R. Brand, 'US-style bid to rid SA of illegal aliens', *The Star*, 14 February 2000, p. 1.

34   'Brothel raided', *Pretoria News*, 3 March 2000, p. 1; P. Molwedi, 'Brothel owner granted bail of R10,000', *The Star*, 7 March 2000, p. 2.

businesses, all in the name of removing 'criminal elements and illegal[s]'.[35] At the Lindela Repatriation Centre, a privately owned deportation facility, foreign nationals – and some South Africans mistaken for aliens – have been harshly beaten, their human rights seriously violated, their property looted.[36] The state has taken no steps to put a stop to this. And public outrage has been, at best, muted.

Reference here to the 'US style' of alien management is telling. In the United States, too, shows of decisive action in the face of the 'immigrant problem' exist alongside an almost farcical legal paralysis on the issue at a national level. A long history of official double-speak makes plain how acutely that 'problem' underscores the paradox of borders at once porous and assiduously policed, highlighting the contradiction between sovereignty and deregulation, neo-conservatism and neoliberalism, national protectionism and a globalized division of labour. In the United States, too, spectacles of enforcement serve as futile attempts to redress the anomaly of strangers who have become essential to domestic reproduction; who mix intimate local knowledge and foreign loyalties, real or imagined, raising spectres of crime and terror; who are simultaneously indispensable and disposable, visible and invisible, human and abject; who reside ambiguously inside and yet beyond the law. In December 2006, for example, 'dozens of armed immigration agents, supported by local police in riot gear' stormed a meat-packing factory in Greeley, Colorado, one of five simultaneous, well-publicized raids on similar facilities across the nation.[37] Termed Operation Wagon Train, these raids were hailed by US Homeland Security and Immigration and Customs Enforcement – ICE by name and nature – as a 'major blow' in its 'war against illegal immigration'. Many of those deported were back within a week. Their

---

35   '121 illegal immigrants held in swoop east of city', *Pretoria News*, 3 March 2000, p. 3; 'Police raid sex club', *Sunday Times*, 19 March 2000, p. 4.

36   Reports of violence at the centre, owned by a consortium that includes members of the 'struggle elite', are not new. In one case, the Cameroonian embassy lodged a formal protest to the South African government; see C. Banda and G. Clifford, 'Cameroon to lodge protest over repatriation center beating', *The Star*, 17 March 2000, p. 1; see also M. Tsedu, 'Illegals deserve better than this', *The Star*, 20 March 2000, p. 12. In January 2003, the South African Human Rights Commission reported, in a media release entitled 'Lindela repatriation centre under scrutiny', that it was to establish 'a permanent monitoring presence' at the facility, this in response to the fact that the mistreatment of alleged 'aliens' was 'continu[ing] unabated' (www.sahrc.org.za/sahrc_cms/publish/article_38.shtml, accessed 5 July 2007).

37   Details of the Greeley case in this paragraph are taken from G. Younge, 'The US is clamping down on illegal migrants, but it relies on their labour', *Guardian*, 11 June 2007, p. 29.

labour, like that of an estimated 12 million other undocumented workers, is essential to American industry, agriculture and the service sector; this being evidence of just the kind of late modern boundary-making impasse we witnessed in South Africa – although in the United States it is exacerbated by the conflict between transnational agreements like NAFTA, which liberate capital, and local politicians, who seek to criminalize foreign labour and keep it imprisoned within the 'developing world'. Here, observes Gary Younge, the political border is no longer coterminous with the physical borders of the nation-state. The former, the de facto frontier, is now more a matter of 'economic expediency and political opportunism than either law or order'. And it criss-crosses the country, mobilizing ethnic profiles and securing the homeland by dividing citizens from aliens wherever they might be, which is how, on that December day, 'the border came to Greeley', a town more than 700 miles from the nearest national boundary line.

Shades, here, of the kind of contingency we identified at the outset as characteristic of the Nuer polity and Schmittian philosophy. In Nuer politics, recall, in the absence of fixed geographical borders, the objectification of boundaries between inside and out occurred in the process of dealing with the very transgressions that breached them. For Schmitt, the essential political gesture lay in drawing the line, making life-and-death distinctions, between friend and enemy. This is exactly what happens when aliens in South Africa are flushed out by the police, with little attention to their rights, legal or 'human' – or worse yet, summarily killed by vigilante mobs of unemployed locals. It is also what happens in the United States, where would-be illegal migrants may be apprehended not only at points of entry into the country, but anywhere that their difference from nationals comes to light, anywhere that lines are crossed, anywhere that they may be espied and reported by citizens. Operation Wagon Train is no arbitrary turn of phrase. Its cavalier reference to the conquest of the Wild West frontier – a historical process, incidentally, that made America's first autochthons into aliens – reveals a deeper truth. It returns the United States to a language of state-making as a species of colonial heroics, in which, as one anti-immigrant group put it, 'citizen control' is to be re-established.[38] Seen in this light, armed raids on migrant enclaves might not seal the border, but they *do* create an 'impression of effectiveness' on the part of the state in a political context in which illusion has become, perforce, 'as important as reality'.[39] Here, in short, is an instance of the sort of symbolic

---

38 G. Younge, 'The US is clamping down on illegal migrants, but it relies on their labour', *Guardian*, 11 June 2007, p. 29.

39 S. Friedman, 'Action with too little discussion', *Mail and Guardian*, 24–30 March 2000, p. 25.

activity of which we spoke earlier: the mass-mediated ritual excess, directed at producing state power and the hyphen-nation that features so prominently in efforts to secure sovereignty in a neoliberal age.

Ends and meanings

Geschiere and Nyamnjoh (2000) have noted the growing stress, in Africa, on the exclusion of the stranger, not least in reaction to the kinds of social and economic uncertainties, and the destabilization of borders, set in motion by 'global flows'. This is true of post-apartheid South Africa, where outrage against aliens has provided a versatile call to arms, forcing a new line of separation that unifies a home-grown population otherwise divided by class, colour, culture and other things; not fully or finally, of course, but nonetheless visibly and volubly. Nor, as we have intimated, is South Africa alone in this. Similar processes are evident more or less everywhere that the nation-state is perceived to be plagued by conditions that threaten to dissolve it borders, opening them up to unwanted aliens of all sorts, undermining the coordinates of moral and material community – and making them seem more like contested colonial frontiers than the secure boundaries of the Euro-modernist polity, at least as conventionally imagined.

The effect of making these boundaries ambiguous arises, we have noted, from the absorption of contemporary nationhood into a global economy whose neoliberal ways and means have altered received patterns of production and consumption, the articulation of labour to capital, the movement of persons and commodities, the nature of sovereignty and civic identity, geographies of space and time, normative expectations of order and security, and much else besides. Because of their particular histories, post-colonies like South Africa manifest these transformations in especially acute form. But, in many respects, they are merely condensed, hyper-extended prefigurations of what is becoming increasingly visible elsewhere. Indeed, almost everywhere. As Western states resort more audibly to the language of 'wagon trains' and frontiers, as journalists talk of an 'apartheid planet',[40] as the post-Cold War seems ever more to be giving way to a state of 'ordered anarchy', we may be forgiven for thinking that the colonial societies of the global South were less historical inversions of the metropole than foreshadowings of what, in a postmodern world, the global North might become.

This speculation is not idle. European colonial regimes managed the political and economic contradictions inherent in early capitalist modernity by means of a politics of spatial separation. The segregation of metropole from colony, their distantiation, not only obscured their material and cultural

---

40 N. Klein, 'How war was turned into a brand', *Guardian*, 16 June 2007, p. 34.

interdependence. It also served to keep well apart the humanitarian, rule-governed, rationalizing, freedom-seeking *geist* of liberal democracy from the exclusionary, divisive, violently secured forms of subjection and extraction on which it was erected. Colonial societies were zones of occupation, sites in which the civilizing mission was counterposed against the immediate dictates of command, control and profit – and against the need to secure the contested frontiers seen to insulate order from chaos. Defending those boundaries in the name of 'progress' often warranted the suspension of enlightened ways and means, even in the face of humanitarian outrage and righteous resistance.

The long process of decolonization that set the stage for a new, twenty-first-century Age of Empire has disrupted this spatial logic. The Cold War era might have marked time between two imperial epochs, but it came undone when economies were deregulated and capital moved offshore, escaping state control, globalizing its day-to-day operations, deterritorializing sovereignty and jurisdiction, trafficking in ever more abstract, virtual species of wealth and scrambling received relations between politics and production. As neoliberalized enterprise relocated its polluting factories to distant sites of cheap labour and low or no taxation, new forms of enclaved colonial extraction were invented, extraction with minimal costs, *sans* state apparatuses, safety restrictions, legal liability or civilizing missions. At the same time, workers who could move from devastated post-colonies sought access in exponentially greater numbers to the underclass reaches of cleaner, post-Fordist, Northern economies. In the process, the structural and geographical segregation of metropole and colony has been deeply eroded. And as it has, camps for illegal aliens and asylum seekers, inner-city wastelands, zones of occupation and burning *banlieus* project colonial conditions and modes of governance into the heart of First World polities – there to draw the line, once again, between friend and enemy, law and war. Reciprocally, states in the South and East take on many of the features of Euro-America, from the growing preoccupation with democracy and the law to an inventive engagement with modern urbanism, electronic communications, global finance and the like.

In the face of all this, liberal democratic models of society and politics have undergone drastic revision in the North – among scholars and statesmen alike. The image is fading of an organic society, *suivant* Comte and Durkheim, in which divisions of class, race, religion and culture were contained, ideally at least, within national boundaries; in which, also, criminals and other pathogenic fractions of the population were believed, through welfare and reform, to be recoverable 'citizens in waiting'. On the rise is a rather different archetype, that of the polity as citadel: of national territory as embattled homeland; of prisons as sites not of recuperation but of the warehousing of those deemed disposable; of borders as elusive lines to be drawn and redrawn within the nation-state and beyond against the endless onslaught of enemies who threaten its moral and corporeal integrity – enemies who take the form of aliens, migrants, terrorists, home-grown saboteurs, felons, criminals, deviants, the indigent poor. This, once more, is the world of Carl Schmitt, in which politics is less about national participation and redistribution than about securing the frontier between autochthon and intruder, good and evil, citizenship and subjection. It is also the world of the Nuer, with their constantly shifting lines between inside and out, law and war. Is it any wonder, then, that conditions that nurture phobias of alien nature and campaigns of ethnic cleansing should also have generated a newly animated, newly designated industry, the so-called 'homeland security sector'? Or that the signature products of this industry, which is rapidly gaining ground on a global scale, are 'high-tech fences, unmanned drones, biometric ID's, video and audio surveillance gear, air passenger profiling and prisoner interrogation systems', many of them originating in Israel, recently described as 'a living example of how to enjoy relative safety amid constant war'?[41] All this may seem a world away from allegories of alien plants and natural autochthony. But the link between them is patent. Both speak of efforts to bring to order the anarchy of our late modern age. Or, to be more precise, to make sense of, and act upon, some of the contradictions and contingencies, the uncertainties and insecurities, the ambiguities and ambivalences, that come with a world-historical disjuncture: the disjuncture, that is, between the modernist universe as we once knew it and the neoliberal universe now rapidly taking shape around us.

Acknowledgments

As we note in the text, this chapter revisits another piece, published a few years back, parts of which are reprised here. This earlier work, 'Naturing the Nation', was published in *Hagar: International Social Sciences Review* 1/1 (2000), pp. 7–40. It was later republished, in very similar form, in *Social Identities* (2001) and in the *Journal of Southern African Studies* (2001), the latter in a special issue dedicated to Shula Marks, in whose honour it was originally written. We should like to acknowledge, again, the debt owed to our son, Joshua Comaroff, an architect and geographer whose specialist knowledge of landscape has drawn us into many discussions on the topic; he was with us in Cape Town during the events described here and participated in the formulation of our analysis of them. The present version returns to those events with longer hindsight, placing them in a different conceptual frame, one more in tune with contemporary concerns in the social sciences.

----

41   Ibid.

References

Acocks, J.P.H. 1953. *Veld Types of South Africa*. Pretoria: Division of Botany, Department of Agriculture.

Adam, H., van Zyl Slabbert, F., and Moodley, K. 1998. *Comrades in Business: Post-Liberation Politics in South Africa*. Cape Town: Tafelberg.

Agamben, G. 1998. *Homo Sacer: Sovereign Power and Bare Life* (trans. D. Heller-Roazen). Stanford: Stanford University Press.

Anderson, B. 1983. *Imagined Communities: Reflections on the Origin and Spread of Nationalism*. London: Verso.

Barkun, M. 1968. *Law without Sanctions: Order in Primitive Societies and the World Community*. New Haven: Yale University Press.

Bateson, G. 1972. *Steps to an Ecology of Mind*. New York: Ballantine Books.

Carr, G.W., Robin, J.M. and Robinson, R.W. 1986. 'Environmental weed invasion of natural ecosystems: Australia's greatest conservation problem'. In R.H. Groves and J.J. Burdon (eds), *Ecology of Biological Invasions: An Australian Perspective*, p. 150. Canberra: Australian Academy of Science.

Comaroff, J. and Comaroff, J.L. 2001. 'Naturing the nation: aliens, apocalypse and the postcolonial state', *Social Identities* 7(2):233–65.

Comaroff, J.L. and J. Comaroff. 2006. 'Law and disorder in the postcolony: an introduction'. In J. Comaroff and J.L. Comaroff (eds), *Law and Disorder in the Postcolony*, pp. 1–56. Chicago: University of Chicago Press.

CAVC (Control of Alien Vegetation Committee, Kirstenbosch [National Botanical Gardens]). 1959. *The Green Cancers in South Africa*. Kirstenbosch: Control of Alien Vegetation Committee.

Davis, M. 1995. 'Los Angeles after the storm: the dialectic of ordinary disaster', *Antipode* 27:221–41.

Day, J.A., Siegfried, W., Louw, G.N. and Jarman, M.L. (eds). 1979. *Fynbos Ecology: A Preliminary Synthesis*. Pretoria: Cooperative Scientific Programme, Council for Scientific and Industrial Research.

Evans-Pritchard, E.E. 1940a. 'The Nuer of the southern Sudan'. In M. Fortes and E.E. Evans-Pritchard (eds), *African Political Systems*, pp. 272–96. London: Oxford University Press.

——— 1940b. *The Nuer*. Oxford: Clarendon Press.

Fortes, M., and Evans-Pritchard, E.E. 1940. 'Introduction'. In M. Fortes and E.E. Evans-Pritchard (eds), *African Political Systems*, pp. 1–23. London: Oxford University Press.

Fraser, M., and McMahon, L. 1988. *A Fynbos Year*. Cape Town: David Philip.

Geschiere, P. and Nyamnjoh, F. 2000. 'Capitalism and autochthony: the seesaw of mobility and belonging'. In J.Comaroff and J.L. Comaroff (eds), 'Millennial capitalism and the culture of neoliberalism', *Public Culture*, special issue, 12(2):423–52.

Hall, A.V. 1979. 'Invasive weeds'. In J.A. Day, W. Siegfried, G.N. Louw and M.L. Jarman (eds), *Fynbos Ecology: A Preliminary Synthesis*, pp. 133–47. Pretoria: Cooperative Scientific Programme, Council for Scientific and Industrial Research.

Harvey, D. 1990. *The Condition of Postmodernity: An Enquiry into the Origins of Cultural Change*. Oxford: Blackwell.

Kruger, F.J. 1977. 'Ecology and management of Cape fynbos: towards conservation of a unique biome type'. Paper read at the South African Wild Life Management Association's Second International Symposium, Pretoria, 7 July.

——— 1978. 'A description of the fynbos biome project'. Committee for Terrestrial Ecosystems, National Programme for Environmental Sciences, Report. Pretoria: Cooperative Scientific Programmes, Council for Scientific and Industrial Research.

——— 1979. 'Fire'. In J.A. Day, W. Siegfried, G.N. Louw and M.L. Jarman (eds), *Fynbos Ecology: A Preliminary Synthesis*, pp. 43–57. Pretoria: Cooperative Scientific Programme, Council for Scientific and Industrial Research.

Mbembe, A. 1992. 'Provisional notes on the postcolony'. *Africa* 62(1):3–37.

Moll, E. and Moll, G. 1994. *Common Trees of South Africa*. Cape Town: Struik.

Schmitt, C. 1996. *The Concept of the Political* (trans. G. Schwab). Chicago: University of Chicago Press.

Stirton, C.H. (ed.). 1978. *Plant Invaders, Beautiful but Dangerous: A Guide to the Identification and Control of Twenty-Six Plant Invaders of the Province of the Cape of Good Hope*. Cape Town: Department of Nature and Environmental Conservation, Cape Provincial Administration.

Van Rensberg, T.F.J. 1986. 'An introduction to fynbos'. Bulletin No.61. Pretoria: Department of Environment Affairs.

Van Wyk, B.-E., and Gericke, N. 2000. *People's Plants: A Guide to Useful Plants of Southern Africa*. Pretoria: BRIZA Publications.

Wace, N. 1988. 'Naturalized plants in the Australian landscape'. In R.L. Heathcote (ed.), *The Australian Experience: Essays in Australian Land Settlement and Resource Management*, pp. 139–50. Melbourne: Longman Chesire.

Worby, E. 1998. 'Tyranny, parody, and ethnic polarity: ritual engagements with the state in northwestern Zambia', *Journal of Southern African Studies* 24(3):560–78.

Cultural concentration camps

Resettlement in Borneo, and other insults to the social order of indigenous peoples

George N. Appell

The powerful outboard motor drove the longboat across the bay and up the estuary. The blazing heat in this section of Indonesian Borneo was somewhat relieved by the wind from the longboat's journey to the interior. It was 1980. We entered the major river flowing down from the distant interior highlands. Shortly, we arrived at a landing platform leading to a resettlement village. I looked up. What I saw were newly constructed houses, painted white and laid out in rows duplicating what I had seen on many reservations in Canada. My astonishment grew as I discovered further aspects of this resettlement of interior peoples of Borneo that were similar to what I had found in Canada. The resettlement site we had arrived at had been created by the Indonesian government along the lower reaches of a river system that was inhabited by people who called themselves Bulusu'.

The parallels between my experiences in Canada and Indonesia led me to consider two related questions. First, do resettlements, reservations or similar attempts at forcing indigenous peoples into government-controlled areas form a particular social type? Are there certain universal social elements that are found in all variations of this social type? Should we consider reservations and other control centres to be an almost universal type similar to other social types that the anthropologists study, such as the village or the family?

Second, how is the stress of social change manifested in the relocated population? Such stress can manifest itself in dysfunctions in three critical systems: the physiological, the psychological and the behavioural. To understand the full health consequences of social change, all three systems have to be carefully monitored for growing impairments arising from psychosocial stress.

To deal with these questions, I will present what we discovered among an ethnic group identified as Bulusu', who lived in East Kalimantan, Indonesian Borneo, and among whom we conducted research in 1980/81.[1] I will first describe traditional Bulusu' society, then the socio-cultural changes caused by the Indonesian government herding the Bulusu' into a resettlement area. The organization of the resettlement by government representatives will be analysed next. Following this I will discuss the deliberate ethnocide involved in forcing the Bulusu' into a resettlement area and its social and health consequences. This will finally lead us on to a discussion of the characteristic social elements that are found in all forms of resettlement or reservation systems.

The traditional order of the Bulusu'

The Bulusu' are a self-conscious ethnic group of East Kalimantan, a province of Indonesian Borneo. Traditionally, the Bulusu' were longhouse-dwelling, swidden agriculturalists. At the time of our research in 1980/81, the Bulusu' lived in the middle reaches of several rivers that flowed into the Celebes Sea. At the upper reaches of these rivers lived groups of hunters and gathers referred to as Punan, while on the lower reaches of the rivers and along the coast lived the Tidong and Bulungan, Islamic ethnic groups who concentrated on fishing and trading. At the mouths of these rivers lies the large island of Tarakan, on which oil production occurs, and its commercial centre is the city of Tarakan. A few Chinese shops are found around the mouth of the rivers and in Tarakan.

The Bulusu' village

The major social entities of the Bulusu' were the village and the domestic family. There were no overall social linkages between villages except by kinship ties. The domestic family and its members were the sole economic production and consumption units. The domestic family subsisted on swidden agriculture and relied on a variety of crops (Appell 1983a, 1985c).

Village organization was not complex. The inhabitants of a village lived in one or two longhouses, composed of the various apartments of domestic

---

1   The members of the family who were involved in research on the Bulusu' were my wife Laura W.R. Appell and our daughters Laura P. Appell (now Appell-Warren, Edu. D.), Amity P. Appell (now Doolittle, PhD) and Charity R. Appell (now Appell McNabb). Support for the research was from the National Science Foundation (grant no. BNS-7915343) and the Ford Foundation.

families. A village headman was appointed by the government, and more recently the government had instituted the position of a village head of *adat*, customary law. There were no hereditary social classes. A number of female and male shamans were employed in curing illness. The village controlled an area for farming by its inhabitants, which we have termed the village reserve (Appell 1985c).

The boundaries of village territories were marked by natural phenomena along a river, such as rapids, mouths of tributaries or a large tree, and by the watershed between two river systems. Originally, if a stranger came into a village territory and took any produce from the forest or from the swiddens, he was liable to be killed. Therefore, it was customary when travelling to stop at each longhouse village and ask permission of the village headman to proceed. It was still considered to be good form and a wise precaution against trouble to do so. Population pressure on the land had not yet developed. Land was not scarce, and as a result it never became necessary to define more precisely village rights over specified tracts of land.

There had thus been little pressure on the resources of the village reserve to produce a further development of the jural personality of the village with regard to its assets. The defining feature of the jural personality of the village was not so much its relation to land as to the services of the headman in resolving disputes. One headman said that boundaries between villages represented the division between the authority and power of headmen, and that the actual boundaries had been very rough until the Dutch came. Rather than an explicit, well-defined territorial entity, the village was in fact both a nexus of kin relations and a centre of the power of an individual leader who, with the coming of the government, became the official village headman.

The domestic family cycle

The developmental cycle of the domestic family was initiated by marriage, which involved bride price. Before marriage a young man would 'go to [visit] a girl' (*moi dandu'*) in her family's longhouse apartment. If the relationship progressed, the boy could join the girl in her sleeping sarong. Sexual foreplay was possible. If it led to intercourse, the father received a payment of several jars and a small pig from the boy's family. If the two married, there was still a fine of property and a pig, but the fine was smaller. Marriage was usually monogamous.

Following marriage the husband and wife would reside in the longhouse apartment of the bride's family for a year or so, then they would move to the longhouse apartment of the husband's family. Virilocal residence was justified by the bride price paid, which consisted of gongs, cannon, brassware and jars. The Bulusu' bride price is of the redistributive type (see Appell 1983a, 1985c).

A man putting together a bride price for the wife of his son got help from his network of kin, each of whom was repaid by the father at a later point when those who helped him needed help for a similar prestation. The father of the bride redistributed the items of the bride price among his network of kin according to the help that they had given him in the past and the help that they had provided in the form of provisions for the wedding feast. As a result, Bulusu' society was composed of a vast, intricate network of debts and credits.

There were two forms of domestic family. In the patrilocal extended form, the couple resided in the longhouse apartment (*lamin*) of the groom's father. They may have stayed there until they had several children. This patrilocal longhouse domestic unit may have included two or more nuclear families consisting of the parental generation and one or more married siblings with children. On the other hand, some couples wanted to build their own longhouse apartment shortly after marriage, forming a domestic family of the nuclear type.

Land tenure

Residents of a village have had the right to plant their swiddens in any part of the village reserve. The Bulusu' system of swiddening is 'circulating usufruct' (Appell 1983a, 1985c, 1986b, 1997). That is, once a swidden area has had all of its crops removed and it begins to revert to forest, anyone else in the village may reuse that area again for a swidden as it reverts back to the village reserve. Thus, no permanent usufruct rights are established by clearing the forest. However, if the swidden area is planted with fruit trees at the end of the swidden cycle, this removes that area from circulating usufruct. Villages are interlinked by a network of kin, and as a result an individual may have rights to fruit trees in a number of closely related villages.

A man and his new wife, as members of the longhouse apartment of the husband's father, still made their own swidden and swidden field house. Families also raised chickens for sale, for use in ceremonies and for eggs. Pigs were kept by families in some villages for sale at the regional centre, Tarakan, and sale to the Chinese, but not for their own consumption. People in these villages would eat pig meat if killed and cooked by some other ethnic group, and they would still kill and eat wild pig. This prohibition on the killing of pigs appeared to be confined to the river system where we did our fieldwork. The explanation for this is that the blood of pigs would bring malevolent spirits. In another, smaller river system which was close by, Bulusu' still killed pigs for sacrifice in cases of adultery and incest.

Fruit was a major foodstuff for the Bulusu' families and an important source of income. It was regularly taken by longboat and sold at the oil and port town on the island of Tarakan. When there was a major fruiting season, once every four or five years or more, everyone gorged themselves on fruit. Swiddening activities may have ceased while the fruit was enjoyed. Rights to fruit trees and their yield devolved to the children of the original planter. This set of kin was in essence a cognatic descent isolate (see Appell 1983a, 1983b, 1985c), but it was not a corporate unit, as the rights were held by the individual members. The eldest son, as in all matters, tended to organize affairs with regard to the grove of trees. Because of this, his rights were considered to be more firm and somewhat more extensive, particularly if it were he who cultivated the grove and trees. Each year the brush around the trees should be cleared. The individual who cleared around the trees got the right to enjoy the first fruits. He was then responsible for calling all other members of the cognatic descent isolate to participate. Members living in far away villages may not have been called, unless it were a heavy fruiting year. The right to clear could be shared between the male members, so that each had a chance to enjoy the first fruits. Women's rights were somewhat less strong than men's, and they might not have received a similar share to men if the fruit or grove were sold.

The agricultural surpluses of the nuclear family and returns from the sale of forest products were invested in a variety of items including beads, beaded headbands and ankle bracelets (all of which were women's jewellery) as well as brassware, gongs, cannon, old swords and so forth. There was a tendency for women's jewellery to be given to daughters and swords to sons, but this was not absolute. Rights to a very expensive item of property, such as an old jar, were usually split among all children. Each child then gave his rights to his own children until there existed a large set of kinsmen each of whom owned rights to the jar. As with fruit trees, this process eventually became a source of dispute so that the jar was sold and the proceeds split among the rights holders, with the person who had been taking care of the jar receiving a larger portion than the others. Alternatively, the person who had been taking care of the jar would buy out the other rights holders.

Religion and the propitiation of spirits
The Bulusu' had a complex religion with a creator god, a variety of spirits (usually of place) and a complex afterworld consisting of a number of layers. Illness was the result of soul loss, and spirit mediums went into trance to negotiate the return of souls lost to those spirits who had been offended. Traditionally, the Bulusu' raised pigs and chickens to sacrifice to these spirits, to cleanse a village after incest and for rituals associated with headhunting.

When an individual died, his body was placed in a coffin carved out of a tree trunk and then stored in the longhouse until the final ceremony for his entombment was organized. It frequently took several years for the family to gather all the necessary supplies of food and drink for this large gathering and ritual following a death. This ritual included cleansing the village of all ghosts and spirits and sending the soul of the dead to the afterworld with the proper accoutrements. During the final part of this ceremony the coffin was moved to the entombment house, the *baloi-patoi*.

Sometime, either right before or after the Japanese occupation, a number of people living in scattered villages – headmen and spirit mediums primarily – had a dream that the blood of sacrificed pigs would attract the malevolent spirits to Bulusu' dwellings and a number of people would die. At that time the sacrifice of pigs ceased and the killing of chickens in these ceremonies may have declined. Thereafter, chickens were presented to the spirits at ceremonies, but were released afterwards. Where pigs had once been sacrificed, an effigy of a pig was made of rice paste flavoured with sesame, which was consumed during the ceremony (Appell and Appell 1993).

The resettlement of the Bulusu'

In the Indonesian language, resettlement villages are called *respen*, an acronym for *resetelmen penduduk*, 'resettlement of inhabitants'. For simplicity we will use *respen* to refer to resettlement sites.

A theatre of the absurd

Any attempt to portray or comprehend what went on at resettlement sites in Indonesia in a logical, coherent and rational way fails. Instead you are led into a theatre of the absurd. Policies and plans of government agents were based on gross stereotypes and caricatures of the indigenous peoples and their way of life. Confusion was rampant in communication between government personnel and the *respen* inhabitants. Different government personnel gave contradictory orders. While the Bulusu' were the major inhabitants of the *respen* we resided in, there was a small number of representatives of other ethnic groups, speaking seven or eight different languages. To overcome this Babel, Indonesian became the lingua franca but it was only slightly understood by most. The river flowing alongside the *respen* was used for drinking water, bathing and as a latrine. One of the reasons given for bringing in the Bulusu' was to provide health services, but the dresser for the *respen* was ill-trained, did not understand causes of illness and was thus spreading illness himself.

The Bulusu' were also brought in to 'give them religion'. This meant enrolling them in any of the world religions, preferably Islam. One of the primary principles of the Indonesian state is that all ethnic groups, and all religions, should believe in one supreme god. Those belief systems that did not include the concept of one supreme god were not considered to be religions, and individuals without religion were feared to be communists. As it was thought that the Bulusu' as other Dayak peoples were primarily animists without belief in a supreme being, it was critical that these peoples be enrolled in one of the approved world religions. Thus, the Bulusu' were gathered together and were told to choose a religion. But, as one government officer in the religion department later conceded, the Bulusu' traditionally had a high god (see Appell-Warren 1985; Conley 1973).

There were two major themes that ran through the whole play in the theatre of the absurd. The first was that government personnel and the various members of the two coastal Muslim ethnic groups were superior to the Bulusu', knew more, and that the Bulusu' were stupid and inferior beings. The Bulusu' were to be instructed, used and ordered around for the benefit of those who were superior. The second theme was the complete ignorance of the directors of this play regarding the consequences of that major theme: the psychological, physiological and behavioural impairments that their actions caused to the Bulusu' people.

The irony of this play was that those who claimed to be the most educated and knowledgeable of all were in fact the least informed. It is absurd to be half-modern but to claim to be modern. It courts disaster to then impose the values of the half-modern way of life on an ecosystem in which it has never been tested by trial and error.

A government policy of ethnocide

There was an explicit government-organized policy of ethnocide – the destruction of the socio-cultural system of the Bulusu'. Directed attempts were made to eradicate the cultural ecology and other major contours of Bulusu' culture. Ethnocide was not an unexpected consequence of other policies or actions. All levels of the Indonesian government were intimately engaged in ethnocide by policy, actions and sanctions. One of the unexpected consequences, however, was the shadow of genocide, as the physiological and psychological reaction to this form of cultural concentration camp was expected by our research team to lead to increased and unnecessary deaths, as we will now discuss.

Management of the respen

The liaison officer was notorious for threatening the Bulusu', commanding them to do what he wanted them to and for skimming off funds designated for the *respen* and villages in it. Each village was allotted so much per year for development purposes. One year the villages used the funds to buy chainsaws, the purchase of which the liaison officer arranged. We were able to check the price at the store where they were bought and compare it with the price he had said he had paid. He told the village headmen that each saw had cost 400,000 rupiah (approximately $667 at that time) when he was able to purchase them at roughly 300,000 rupiah (approximately US$500).

The liaison officer organized night guards for the *respen*. The head night guard was a Bulusu', who was promised a salary for his work. He quit when he had received no salary for seven years. There were two unsalaried night guards, a Bulusu' (or Punan) and a coastal Muslim, each pair held the duty for three nights before being replaced. All male *respen* members were eligible for this duty. When an individual was on the duty roster, he had to come in from wherever he was living or working – for example, one man had to come up from the mouth of the river where he had established a camp for fishing, several hours away by longboat and outboard motor. Guarding the *respen* tended to fall into abeyance when things were quiet and the liaison officer was not present, as those who had the duty found it burdensome.

The liaison officer ran the *respen* in an unnecessarily authoritarian manner. Bulusu' were periodically ordered to clear all the grass from around their houses so that the ground was bare. Everyone was supposed to do it at the same time, and a bell was rung to call the *respen* residents to work. No explanation was given, and the Bulusu' did not know the reason for it, though a coastal Muslim told me it was for mosquito control. In one instance a Bulusu' who had become Muslim was planning a traditional Bulusu' wedding. The liaison officer called the couple to his office and required them to have an Islamic ceremony first.

The commandant of police for the regency was not someone you could report to on embezzlement or bribes. He visited the *respen* during one celebration and saw an old cannon that a coastal Muslim trader had in his house. He demanded it, and said that if it was delivered to him at his home he would look out for the trader's affairs in the future. The trader seemed to feel that he had no choice.

Bulusu' economics: provisioning domestic families

How were the Bulusu' to make a living? Instructions and orders from government and local Muslim representatives varied and were frequently contradictory. They were based on stereotypes of the Bulusu' and their culture. As a result they were in many cases illusionary.

When the government began the resettlement of the Bulusu' in 1968, the Bulusu' heard that they were no longer permitted to cut the primary forest for swiddens. But, like a lot of government regulations, it was reported that the ruling had little effect. The instructions given to the Bulusu' were bafflingly contradictory. One of my informants was the *kepala adat* (Indonesian, 'head of the customary law') of his village, a newly appointed government position introduced about two years previously. The *kepala adat* is the authority on customary law, and his role includes settling disputes. He summarized his understanding of the *respen* situation as follows: if a Bulusu' had finished his house in the *respen*, he could go upcountry to his traditional village to cut his swidden. He himself planned to make the traditional swidden longhouse (a small longhouse of a few doors) used when cultivating far from one's home base. If the government would not permit that form of housing, he would make a field house and live in that. However, at one celebration and feast organized by the liaison officer and attended by many government officials, the liaison officer gave a long speech and told the Bulusu' that they were no longer to make their swiddens in their old village territories. How could they get medicine if they lived far away, he argued. Then a military man in uniform stood up and also told them that they were not allowed to make their swiddens away from the *respen*.

About a month later the liaison officer told the headmen that they were supposed to cut primary forest that year to plant cloves. He may have referred only to primary forest within the *respen* boundary. The district officer during a visit made this explicit, yet there was no primary forest in the *respen*. The liaison officer informed the Bulusu' that they were to be given clove trees to plant at a small cost, and that this was why the government had told each village to buy a chainsaw. Thereafter, if anyone cut primary forest, there would be a fine of 100,000 rupiah per hectare, as the government wanted the trees. They would, however, be permitted to cut secondary forest, presumably in their old village sites. The problem was, some Bulusu' said, that most of the secondary forest had already been planted with fruit tree groves. And since the clove trees would not start bearing for six years and would not be fully mature for ten, how would they make a living?

There was insufficient land in the *respen* area to support the agricultural activities of the Bulusu' population. Furthermore, as the soil was much less fertile, yields have been considerably less than in the traditional Bulusu' areas. One informant said that the soil was bad for all crops, including fruit trees, and that rice yields were one-third to one-quarter of what they were upcountry. Most of the trees in the *respen* had been felled about ten years previously. The use of heavy equipment to remove the trees had caused considerable disturbance of the surface soil, bringing up the infertile layer below. After ten years one could still see deep tractor tyre marks, and most of the soil still supported no vegetation. The Bulusu' say that timber operations were ruining the soil, making it infertile and causing it to 'dissolve'. Even before this new ruling, there was a great deal of concern among the Bulusu' as to how they were going to make a living in their own traditional areas. One informant said that they had already lost half of their land to the timber companies, and without any consultation.

Mengajar: 'teaching' the Bulusu'

The government personnel and the coastal Muslims took the position that the Bulusu' had to be 'taught' (*mengajar*, Indonesian). And so at various times the Bulusu' were brought together to be lectured to, usually at times of celebrations, but also sometimes more informally when only a few were present.

When the *respen* was opened and the Bulusu' had been given religion, they were told that the men could not wear their hair long and they had to wear clothes. In other words, the men had to stop wearing loincloths and the women had to wear blouses. Bare breasts encouraged fornication. If Westerners and Japanese saw the Bulusu' in loincloths they would think that there was not enough cloth in the country. We will revisit this attack on loincloths in a subsequent section.

The burial customs of the Bulusu' conflicted with Islamic law. Bodies were not to be kept in coffins, as in the past, until sufficient supplies for a funeral feast had been collected, nor were they to be put in the raised entombment houses. The Muslims found these customs disgusting. It was argued that the government wanted them stopped because they would spread disease. The Bulusu' were to put bodies in the ground immediately. This caused considerable conflict with the Bulusu' as, in their religion, if the dead are not properly cared for, their souls will not reach the afterworld but will wander among the living and cause disease and disaster. The liaison officer forced one Bulusu' family who had lost a young child to bury her in the *respen* burial ground, which had not yet been fully opened up. The area contained a Punan grave. According to Bulusu' tradition, burying a body with those from another village puts the villages in ritual jeopardy. As a result, the Bulusu' family was unable to carry out its own funeral ritual and complete their mourning. They were very distressed. They quickly departed to their old village as soon as their daughter was buried.

The Bulusu' were absolutely convinced that any discussion of headhunting was forbidden by the government and, if they knew that we were being told about the customary law of headhunting and how it occurred in the old days, the government would be angry and arrest them. Visiting girlfriends (*moi dandu'*, Bulusu') was also forbidden. The liaison officer reasoned that you never knew what someone would want when he came visiting after dark. He might be coming to steal, to rob you, to take your head or to simply kill you.

The liaison officer instructed the Bulusu' that they were no longer allowed to purchase jars, brassware, gongs and the other items of traditional property in which the Bulusu' invested their agricultural surpluses. They were to purchase mosquito nets, beds, mattresses, dressers for clothing, modern kitchen supplies, plates and bowls. (They already had plates, bowls, mosquito nets and storage trunks for clothes!) Contradicting previous instructions, the liaison officer said that they were now not to make large swiddens any longer but to make small gardens for food only and to look for wage labour. Where that employment would be found was not explained. They were also instructed to make plantations and sell the yield to Tarakan, although they had been doing this all along with their fruit plantations! The Bulusu' were told not to make their alcoholic beverage, except when they were ordered to do so for visiting government personnel. But then one member of the local parliament who was visiting during a celebration said that the government would not tell this generation to stop drinking; rather, it would tell their children not to drink.

In the beginning the Bulusu' were forbidden to build longhouses in the *respen*. Then, about two years prior to our research, it was reported that they were told they could. In one *respen*, a longhouse was built behind the row of separate houses, and the entrance to the longhouse was through the back doors of the various houses. The Bulusu' did not like the individual housing that they were required to build because it was both too small to hold any of their traditional ceremonies and feasts and, as result of using metal roofing, too hot.

Shops, traders and entrepreneurs

There were two shops in the *respen*. One had been organized by a Bulusu', but the owner had closed it down because he was unable to get the Bulusu' who bought on credit to repay him. The other store was owned by the eldest son of a prominent coastal Muslim family. I will call him Kasim. It might be concluded that he represented a unique character except that his personality type and his behaviour are in fact common to most resettlement situations. The opportunities presented by the structure of resettlement villages permit such a personality type to thrive (see Appell 1985a,1985b, 1985c 1985d, 1985e). Kasim had taken on the additional responsibility of seeing that the government's wishes, as translated through the liaison officer, were carried out when there were no government officers in residence. He was constantly telling the Bulusu' what to do and ordering them about. At times he used a loudhailer to communicate to the *respen* inhabitants. For example, when the liaison officer was returning for a visit, he called out the Bulusu' with his loudhailer to help unload the officer's boat and carry his belongings to the *respen* office.

Kasim solved the problem of debt repayment by going to the house of a Bulusu' who owed him money and seizing the personal property of the Bulusu' individual. He intruded in any dispute in the *respen* and took over mediation. At the same time, he entered into various disputes himself, losing his temper frequently. He became so angered with his younger brother that he would throw stones at him whenever he saw him. In dealing with cases such as stealing, it was said that he kept the fines for himself. He was able to intrude in such cases because the Bulusu' were more afraid that he would report them to the government. The fact that he was the assistant head of *adat* (customary law) for the nearby coastal Muslim village also lent him some authority.

Kasim started an enterprise to sell rock to Tarakan for road building. He hired Bulusu' to gather rock along the banks of the river in their boats, and he transported this cargo to Tarakan by boat. The Bulusu' who worked for him were never paid, and the enterprise itself went bankrupt. He was obsequious to us, and arrogant and authoritarian to the Bulusu'. While criticizing the Bulusu' custom of visiting girlfriends and trying to stop it, he availed himself of the services of certain mixed Bulusu'-Punan women who appeared to be prostitutes (see below).

Health services

The dispensary was never open while we were at the *respen*. It contained a lot of different medicines that were out of date and which, in any event, the dresser did not know how to use. One of the arguments for bringing the Bulusu' into the *respen* was to make medical facilities available. However, the medical facilities were at best inadequate and in fact were dangerous in that the procedures being used could spread disease. The dresser never boiled the needles he used. He was treating several people for tuberculosis, but he used only one drug rather than the two required to cure and prevent the development of resistant strains. He maintained that he did not have any other medicine for tuberculosis, although he had INH, the second drug, in his medicine cabinet. His eldest son would brush his teeth in the river, which was loaded with faeces.

In sum, the general knowledge of medicine and hygiene was limited and in fact dangerous, even among those who were supposed to know better. I raised the question of inoculations for childhood diseases that were particularly virulent among the Bulusu with a member of the region's parliament. Shortly before our fieldwork, the Bulusu had lost almost a third of their children in one river system, as a result of a measles epidemic brought to the area by oil workers. But the member of parliament was either completely uninterested in the situation or was ignorant of the health value of inoculations.

Schooling

It was presumed that those who went to school would be working for the government or with the timber or oil companies. They would not be following their fathers in farming. 'What use is it going to school if you end up working in the forest', one informant said. Several Punan and Bulusu' families had sent their children out to Tarakan or the region's capital to obtain schooling, but some had returned to work in the swiddens.

Antisocial or unusual behaviour was frequently explained on the basis that the individuals had not had enough schooling, which would have taught them 'to think'. With regard to a case where some Bugis carpenters beat up a youth, I asked whether that was permissible under customary law, and was told that the Bugis had not had enough schooling. However, they had had more schooling than the Bulusu'. The Bulusu' perceived that when they had had schooling they would not be cheated by the storekeepers in Tarakan, the commercial trading centre; and they would not have to take abuse from or follow the orders of government personnel.

The teacher, a Javanese Muslim, complained about how backward it was in the *respen*. We were unable to see the schooling in progress, as the rebuilding of the school was not completed until just before we left the field. At that time few Bulusu' were in attendance. Some felt that they needed their children at home for work, and others were afraid to let their children that far out of their sight to attend school. As a result, and as it was Ramadan, the teacher turned the school into an Islamic religion class.

Religious conversion

Government officials told the Bulusu' that if they did not convert to a world religion they had no 'brains'. Furthermore, it was argued, the Indonesian communists had no religion. Catholic and fundamentalist Protestant missionaries had visited the Bulusu' region long before resettlement. Visiting Catholic missionaries from the Italian-staffed mission in Tarakan had established a small Catholic church just below the *respen*, but it had fallen into disuse sometime before our fieldwork. It was reported that one village had converted to Christianity prior to resettlement, and that the spirit mediums there 'threw away' their guardian spirits. Two years afterwards there was a serious illness and many people, both adults and children, had died. The spirit mediums called back their guardian spirits, and it was said that those who were sick recovered.

Some Bulusu' women had slowly been acculturating, in terms of dress, to Tidung society, a Muslim group. There had also been some intermarriage between Bulusu' women and Tidung men. It therefore appeared less difficult for them to choose Islam as a religion. Also, the government urged the Bulusu' to become Muslim. It was reported that the government did not like Christianity. To enter Islam they merely had to learn the profession of faith and tell the imam that they wanted to convert. However, in the government census of the *respen* all those not listed as having a religion were simply entered as Muslim.

Many Bulusu' became Christian because there were no food taboos and they could drink alcohol. However, if you became a Christian you were not supposed to use spirit mediums. Muslims, on the other hand, did employ their own spirit mediums for illness. A visiting native minister told the Bulusu' that now that they were Christian they did not have to follow any of their omens that kept them from their work in the fields; they could now really get down to work. The Catholic missionaries appeared to be somewhat more tolerant of native customs than their Muslim and Protestant counterparts, and they allowed a mingling of traditions with Catholic ritual. One convert to Catholicism said that if you genuflected before meals and before you went to bed you would not get sick. A native minister would be asked to participate in a Bulusu' wedding if the couple were really strong in their belief. This involved a Christian marriage and a blessing.

There was some changing of religion back and forth between the Christian denominations. But Christianity, like Islam, seemed to rest lightly on the Bulusu'. At one celebration, a very drunk Bulusu' kept telling me over and over that he had got 'religion'. He became bothersome, and so I asked him, 'What religion?' 'Don't know', he replied. On the other hand, the *kepala adat* ('head of customary law') in his village told me that you cannot throw away your *adat* if you enter Islam or become a Christian, and said, 'Our religion is our *adat*'. In sum, as a result of all these changes in their way of life, the Bulusu' found resettlement to be a very threatening, confusing situation, and one which they tried to find the means to avoid.

Socio-cultural changes and their consequences
Prior to resettlement, Bulusu' society was in a state of moving equilibrium with its ecosystem. This equilibrium was rent asunder by the Indonesian government resettlement programme and attempts to integrate the Bulusu' closely into national culture. These social changes were revolutionary.

Health consequences of social change
Before we analyse how the policy of ethnocide has impacted the Bulusu', I review how, in general, social change impacts on the health of a population (see Appell 1986a). What do we mean by the health consequences, or health impairment, resulting from social change?

The health of a population is a continuing property, potentially measurable by its ability to rally from insults (in the medical sense), whether chemical, physical, infectious, psychological or social (see Audy 1971).[2] Engel writes that the understanding of health requires 'consideration of psychological, social, and cultural factors, not to mention other concurrent or complicating biological factors' (Engel 1977:132). He argues that the biomedical model thus fails adequately to diagnose and manage disease and calls his approach a 'biopsychosocial' model. I refer to Engel's model here as the sociobiological model.

Each population has its own endogenous levels of health impairment. When social change is introduced, changes in levels of health provide a measure of the degree of impairment, but it is critical to measure all health domains for impairment, all sociobiological systems: the physical, psychological and behavioural (see Appell 1986a).[3] The sociobiological stress as experienced by the Bulusu' in dealing with imposed social change could manifest itself in any of these major systems – physiological, psychological and behavioural – depending on the culture and endogenous forms of stress (see Audy 1971, 1973; Brenner 1977; Dohrenwend and Dohrenwend 1974; Gunderson and Rahe 1974; Menninger 1963; Rabkin and Struening 1976; Vaillant 1977).

This approach involves a broad view of health, including dysfunction in behaviour. If accidents and/or rates of divorce rise, if stealing or vandalism rise, these are indicators of a rising level of psychosocial stress in the population as it attempts to cope with the demands of social change (see e.g. Mazer 1965, 1976). If psychosocial stress reaches too high a level, the adaptive capacities of the population may be overwhelmed (see Appell 1986a). The population is not able to rally against insults. These measures can thus indicate the rise of maladaptation as traditional adaptive responses are overwhelmed.[4]

---

2   Audy's original statement was focused on the individual (Audy 1973:102). I have substituted 'population's ability' for 'individual's ability'. Populations similarly have a property of health. Health impairment is never solely that of an individual. There is always the problem of contagion from diseases. When an individual falls ill, the social support mechanisms of a population are initiated to alleviate the distress of the individual. Each culture of a population also has its vulnerabilities, its endogenous load of stress, a direction in which Audy's work moves (see Audy 1973; Audy and Dunn 1974).

3   Menninger states with regard to those systems involved in health impairment: 'Genetic, constitutional, and psychodynamic factors contribute to determining the particular form and organ of somatic involvement ... They serve as expensive means to an end, but to a very important end – that of preserving the whole through sacrifice of a part' (Menninger 1963:187). Menninger does not also consider how the culture of a population may also play a part in focusing stress on a particular organ or behavioural system.

4   Brenner (1977) has been studying the health impact of economic change in the United States and in European countries. He considers the physical and mental

It is critical in this approach to determine how the cultural lens of any society under stress modifies or directs the force of stress. Each society has its own level of stress prior to change and has its own favoured health systems through which stress is expressed. The leading indicators of growing health impairment are the erosion of self-esteem, confusion over social identity, and role conflicts and ambiguity (see ibid.). These indicators are themselves a form of psychosocial stress and contribute to dysfunction in other realms. We will now briefly review the literature on these before discussing the impacts on the Bulusu' population of ethnocide, the most pernicious form of social change.

Depreciation in self-esteem has been found with major health impairments (Engel 1968; Schmale and Engel 1967). Engel (1968) found an association between loss of status or self-esteem and sudden death. Aberle (1962) views the loss of self-esteem as one factor contributing to a variety of behavioural impairments that lead to millenarian movements. Gurr (1970) identifies political violence as one reaction to the depreciation of self-esteem.

Wintrob (1968, 1969, 1970), Chance (1965) and De Vos (1976:354–9) all report psychiatric disorder associated with disturbances of social identity. Wallace (1968:44) argues that people's propensity for hostility may be a consequence of their extreme vulnerability to fear induced by threats to the identity processes.

Role conflict and ambiguity have been found to be associated with health impairment in other societies (see e.g. Kahn *et al.* 1964:149). Abramson writes, 'Cultural changes may have far reaching health implications' (Abramson 1961:156). In a South African Indian community undergoing social change, he found greater psychiatric disorder with increased role conflict and ambiguity among adolescent girls.[5] Colson gives an ethnographic account of how changes in cultural ecology among the Gwembe Tonga of Southern Africa, as a result of resettlement, led to changes in family roles, 'straining family relationships to ... breaking point ... [R]esettlement altered the context within

---

impairments from psychosocial stress related to the rise in unemployment rates. A 1 per cent rise in the unemployment level was associated with an increase in the suicide rate, a rise in stroke, heart, and kidney disease deaths, and a rise in number of admissions to state mental hospital facilities. In the United States this 1 per cent rise was responsible for 57,000 to 58,000 deaths.

5   Davis writes: 'Extremely rapid social change ... tends to increase parent–youth conflict, for within a fast-changing social order the time-interval between generations, ordinarily but a mere moment in the life of a social system, becomes historically significant, thereby creating a hiatus between one generation and the next. Inevitably, under such conditions, youth is reared in a milieu different from that of the parents; hence the parents become old-fashioned, youth rebellious, and clashes occur' (Davis 1940:523).

which family members were accustomed to interact ... [disrupting] the old reciprocal arrangements which had made the family system seem equitable to its members' (Colson 1971:101).[6]

Behaviour impairments also arise from the destruction of a social system that controlled the expression of aggression. This can result in a striking increase in behaviours such as setting fire to houses, as was found in Newfoundland when the outport people were relocated into centres. Loss of one's life ways can result in grieving for that lost life, part of the social separation syndrome (see Appell 1980, 1986a), which is similar to grief experienced after a personal loss. This can cause health deterioration (Fried 1969; Marris 1974). Parkes (1972), for example, found that bereavement is associated with an increase in psychological impairment involving apathy and depression, as well as an increase in mortality rates.

Responses to change

Ethnocide, as in this case, destroys a population's exchanges with its environment. This can lead to exposure to new pathogens and create an inability to produce sufficient food, impoverishing the population (see Appell 1992; Dunn 1972). It can also have deleterious consequences on the total sociobiological system of the population involved. Among the Bulusu', impairments began to arise at every level of the population: the culture, the psychology of individuals, the social system, the physiological system, the child-rearing system and the population structure. One of the defects of the social sciences is that social scientists only take slices out of a total sociobiological system for purposes of analysis, focusing on such things as social organization, cultural ecology, the family system or the cultural system. But when psychosocial stress is added to this complete sociobiological system, the 'slice' approach does not take into account the complex series of feedback loops that impact other aspects of this sociobiological system (see Appell 1986a). Because the soil was poor, when the Bulusu' were ordered to cultivate their swiddens in the *respen*, pressure was put on the individual psychological system through anxiety over food, and on the physiological system due to an inadequate diet. This led to conflict in the family system and had implications for the enculturation of children. As the adults and children became thinner for lack of food, the children became more prone to disease.

---

6   Colson's long-term study of social change among the Gwembe Tonga as a result of resettlement is an important study but nevertheless flawed. I tried but failed to convince her assistant, Thayer Scudder, that all fields of potential impairment for that study needed to be covered to really understand the full impact on the population.

Once health impairments appear, they have an amplifying impact on a population. But it will be difficult to analyse these as we are accustomed to a linear system of analysis that does not easily facilitate the consideration of these complex feedback loops, which contribute to adaptation overloads at various social levels. If, for example, the head of a family is incapacitated or dies as a result of psychosocial stress, his parents, at level one, are faced with grief from losing a son. The son's wife is now in great stress, at level two. And the children, in losing a father, are now under great psychosocial stress at level three. Health impairments from psychosocial stress cascade through various social levels and add to psychosocial stress and additional health impairments throughout the community. This is generally ignored.

Changes in cultural ecology

We have discussed how traditional Bulusu' society was enmeshed in a complex series of exchanges with its environment. The Indonesian government representatives, as part of their efforts at ethnocide, set out to destroy this cultural ecology. Simplifying the trophic web of the Bulusu' eliminated the various ecological baffles and adaptive resources that insulated the Bulusu' against perturbations in the physical and social environment. The new cultural ecology prescribed by the government brought the Bulusu' into closer exchanges with the world system and its perturbations without any support to cope with such pressures (see Appell 1985c, 1992; Eder 1985).

Moving to resettlement centres meant that the Bulusu' were far removed from their fruit tree groves, their fields, their grave sites and their cultural symbols. The move involved a drastic redesign of their economic life. Eventually many Bulusu' built houses at the *respen*, but their permanent relocation there was not complete at the time of our fieldwork. It was in the *respen* that the Bulusu' were most vulnerable to the government's efforts to control them and inflict ethnocide. The Bulusu' found the living conditions to be much more crowded than they were used to in their own villages. Fights broke out between ethnic groups. The resettlement compound was hot as all the trees were removed when preparing the site.

As the Bulusu' could not make a living in the *respen*, they had to go back to their village areas to cut swiddens, but they were constantly being called back to the *respen* when government officers came for a visit. It was thus difficult to continue farming, particularly since much of their labour was needed in the *respen* to build the required housing and to keep the *respen* well groomed.

It was obvious that those who had moved permanently to the *respen* did not have as good a standard of nutrition as those who were still living upcountry in their traditional villages and only visited the *respen* when the government called them in. One day a group of Bulusu' men, women and children came into the *respen* from way up country, where they had been living. I was shocked at the plump, healthy-looking women of that group in comparison to the Bulusu' women living in the *respen*, who were thin and anxious. Young girls from traditional villages in particular appeared to be better fed and to have more subcutaneous fat. I was told that the people in the *respen* were thin because they did not get enough meat, while those living upcountry had lots of meat: wild pig, deer, mouse deer and domesticated pigs for those who still ate them. One informant said it was hard to find food in the *respen*. Another informant said that his brother got beriberi from the food at a timber camp while working there, but this would not have happened if he had been living in the forest because of the variety of foods available.

Relocation to the *respen* had further health consequences other than nutrition that no one considered. The methods of handling excreta and the defences against waterborne diseases in the traditional village areas, while not perfect, were nevertheless adequate and the population thrived. Not many deaths were attributable to such diseases. However, with the increased population density at the *respen*, the traditional methods were no longer adequate. Latrines had been build on rafts on the river with the result that the river was in effect an open sewer, and a disastrous epidemic will eventually occur. An epidemic disease struck the chickens raised in the *respen* during 1977 and most of them died. This had never been experienced in the traditional villages, and it was still difficult to raise chickens in the *respen*.

The destruction of self-esteem and social identity

The government agents and the various coastal Muslims made a concerted effort to attack and destroy the self-esteem and social identity of the Bulusu'. But when an individual's self-esteem is eroded and his social identity threatened, there is clear evidence of health impairment following (see Appell 1986a and above). Erode these leading indicators and they in turn add to stress in other socio-cultural realms. We will start with an analysis of threats to social identity.

The term 'Dayak' has been traditionally used to refer to the indigenous peoples of Kalimantan who were not Muslim. In the district of the *respen*, the population was divided into two major status groups: Muslims, along with a few Christianized Dayak who had an education, and then those Dayak who were perceived to have no religion. Dayak had not gone to school and could not read and write. They were perceived in highly pejorative terms by Muslims and also by Christianized Dayak. When resettlement started, the term 'Dayak' was viewed as inappropriately retrograde. It indicated a people without religion and without the benefits of 'village' life organized according to a Javanese model. We were told not to use the term 'Dayak' and that the preferred term for indigenous peoples was now *orang pedalaman* (Indonesian), 'people of the interior'. Even Bulusu' informants said they were no longer 'Dayak' as they had converted to a religion.

This resulted in probably the most significant change in Bulusu' psychological organization, in the way the Bulusu' perceived themselves. Several generations ago they were independent headhunters who maintained their own against their enemies. Now they were being perceived as 'ignorant' and their culture as 'backward'. They were ridiculed and ordered about. In the process of integrating the Bulusu' into the economic mainstream of Indonesia, effort was thus made to destroy their self-esteem and social identity, forcing the Bulusu' into an acceptance of the lowest social position in the new organization of periphery and centre. Their opportunity to develop and participate in the economy was impeded so that they always presented as a social and economic problem. In sum, the Bulusu' had been moved into the category of the 'rural poor', when before they were not. Worst of all, the Bulusu' had been made to perceive of themselves as such. Further, the *respen* brought the Bulusu' into daily contact with ethnic groups with whom they previously had had only limited contact, one or two of which the Bulusu' considered to be traditionally unfriendly. These groups included Timorese, Javanese, Bulungan, Tidung and various Punan subgroups (see Appell 1983a, 1985c; Appell-Warren 1985).

The attacks on self-esteem and identity were both horrendous and continual. In some cases they included physical attacks on clothing and the body. The coastal Muslims of Borneo have a long history of treating the indigenous population such as the Bulusu' in dehumanized terms.[7] Thus, coastal Muslims in the region of the *respen* would ridicule the Bulusu' to their faces as to their demeanour, their intelligence and their way of life. The government officials used the same phrases. They would refer to the Bulusu' as 'dumb' (*bodoh*, Indonesian), which sometimes meant they had not had any schooling and at other times meant that they even lacked the normal capacities for thinking. They were said to be 'dirty' (*kotor*, Indonesian), that they smelled 'like pigs'. It was claimed that they did not have soap. Their food was disgusting, as was their alcoholic beverage made with rice and/or cassava. They ridiculed the Bulusu' traditional clothing and their burial customs. It was believed that they suffered a lot of sickness and a high mortality rate. Coastal Muslims would laugh uproariously at the thought that the Bulusu' might have a religion. In sum, the Bulusu' were not *maju* (Indonesian), which meant that they were not 'progressive', 'forward looking', 'developed'. Yet exactly what *maju* consisted of was impossible to elicit. One coastal Muslim, when asked

---

7   For a discussion of dehumanization and its consequences, see Appell (1991).

what would make the *respen* population *maju*, replied that a brass marching band would do it.

While the majority of the government personnel were Muslim and therefore shared these values, there were a few Christian personnel. However, they also adopted the attitude that traditional Dayak people were objectionable and objects for derision. For example, several Christian government officials who were originally Dayak said, with a bit of scorn in their tone, that Dayak longhouses were unhealthy. The airy longhouses of the Bulusu', with their carved portals, were considered 'dirty' while, within sight of the *respen*, the government-approved housing for employees of a forest company consisted of a line of squalid, cramped apartments. Nothing was said about these being unhealthy. One of the Christianized government officials said, while decorating his Christmas tree, that the Dayak worshipped trees.

In the past, prior to resettlement and the loss of their traditional clothing, when the Bulusu' had gone to Tarakan in their loincloths they were harassed by the police. I was told that the police would grab their testicles. In the resettlement area one Bulusu' was put to 'dry out' in the sun, that is stand in the midday sun, for wearing a loincloth. At an earlier point in the building of the *respen*, the Javanese workers there lined the Bulusu' men up to remove their loincloths. The loincloths were thrown into a barrel to be burned and the Bulusu' were issued the equivalent of Jockey underpants. These were perceived as being an acceptable substitute for loincloths, even though they were more revealing. Some government personnel told the Bulusu' that foreigners would be 'ashamed' and 'embarrassed' (*malu*, Indonesian) if they saw them in loincloths. Even we were asked if we were not embarrassed to see the 'unclothed' Bulusu'.

Government personnel frequently stated that the Bulusu' only ate cassava, not rice, indicating just how backward they were. For example, the commandant of police of the regency said, after the government had shown a film on birth control, 'All the Bulusu' do is work a few hours in their gardens, come back and eat cassava, and make children'. This attitude ignores the fact that not only did the Bulusu' eat rice but, before resettlement, produced enough to sell their surplus in Tarakan.

It is impossible to give the full flavour of the attitudes held about the Bulusu' and the treatment that they received by recounting only the statements of coastal Muslims and government officials. There was a pervasive feeling of dehumanization and intimidation that was communicated in various ways. This appeared in kinesics, tone of voice and the manner by which Bulusu' people were frequently treated. They were barely tolerated and often ignored, as if they were second-rate citizens. The coastal Muslims and the government would, at every chance, intimidate the Bulusu'. They were ordered about as if they were indentured servants. They were constantly bullied, threatened, hectored and harassed. Miller (2001) argues that one of the entitlements due to individuals by virtue of their humanity is the right to respect. Disrespect, on the other hand, leads to anger and various forms of retaliation including apathy, theft, sabotage and violence.

The impact of resettlement on child-rearing

The mixing together of different ethnic groups, including former enemies of the Bulusu', created considerable anxiety and fear. This resulted in Bulusu' child-rearing becoming more constrained.[8] In her study of children's play in the *respen*, Appell-Warren (1987) found that there was less play there than in the traditional villages. The *respen* was hot, there were not the resources of forest and swidden, houses were separated so that families were more distant from each other than in the traditional longhouse, and the anxieties and fears of both parents and children were heightened because they perceived the *respen* environment as hostile due both to the juxtaposition of individuals from other ethnic groups and the frequent arrival of strangers. Appell-Warren also concluded that parents may have been reacting to the normless situation of the *respen* by being harsher on their children due to their own doubts and fears. There was little work in the *respen* for the children to do or to copy in their play activities, and so parents perceived their children to be naughtier and more lazy, and not developing character (*kakada'*, Bulusu') as they should have been.

Role conflict and ambiguity

There were growing tensions between parents and children over roles in the *respen* and how to live one's life under the new imposed forms of culture. Changes in child-rearing practices also contributed to this role conflict and ambiguity. There were disputes over the choice of religion, and of traditional values versus the new values. Sons were now more interested in purchasing flashy consumables and consumer products – radio-cassette players, wrist watches and so forth – and young men showed less interest in working hard in the swiddens.

The Bulusu' also were unsure of themselves in their role vis-à-vis government representatives. This was an area of great conflict and ambiguity. There was conflict between the Bulusu' and employers over selling labour.

---

8   Ploeg writes: 'It can be argued that, especially in larger settlements, the mixing of
     settlers introduces a greater risk of conflicts and consequently makes the success
     of the settlements more precarious, and that little is gained by bringing together
     settlers with different cultural backgrounds' (Ploeg 1971:123).

The Bulusu' did not seem to understand the responsibilities that go with employment. Many did not stay long in a job.

The loss of meaning, motivation and belief

A society's beliefs and rituals provide meaning and motivation to work. The Bulusu' world of meaning and motivation was on the verge of serious impairment. Their burial rites were forbidden. Weddings were beginning to include other rituals. Their religion was treated as if it did not exist. The Bulusu' were perceived as empty vessels to be given new religions, new beliefs, new values that conflict with what they had. This period of loss of the old religion, before a full understanding of the new, was a time of confusion. Loss of meaning results in psychological impairment (see Frankl 1973) leading to other health impairments.

Engel and his collaborators asked why people fall ill or die at the time they do. They identified a psychological pattern that appears to be associated with disease onset and which they call the 'giving up–given up complex'. Five characteristics have been identified with this complex: (1) the effects of helplessness or hopelessness; (2) a depreciated image of the self; (3) a loss of gratification from relationships or roles in life; (4) a disruption of the sense of continuity between past, present and future; and (5) a reactivation of memories of earlier periods of giving up (see Engel 1968).

The loss of belief in one's world reduces the ability of a population to adapt. This includes the loss of belief in the efficacy of traditional cures for disease and disability. Even if traditional methods of curing disease are materially ineffective, there is evidence that placebos commonly relieve symptoms by between 20 and 70 per cent (see Appell 1986a). Therefore, with the loss of belief in traditional cures, and with inadequate medical care being offered in its place, health impairment should increase due to a loss of ability to respond to health insults.

The erosion of social support mechanisms

Social support mechanisms are those social networks of kin and friends, the members of which provide scarce social and material resources to a focal member when an individual needs help as the result of unexpected demands or when they are ill (see Appell 1986a). The traditional method of curing illness involving a priest or priestess and a sacrifice was being eroded. The breakup of longhouses fractured the support networks based on curing that helped in caring for children, the sick and the elderly. The anomie of the *respen* made it difficult to organize additional help in the swiddens during weeding and harvesting. Consequently there were heavier demands on the individual, making it harder to cope. Individuals who have adequate support mechanisms are found to be healthier and to recover more quickly from a variety of illnesses (Cobb 1976).[9]

Behavioural impairments

Under 'behavioural impairment' we include the more obvious forms of sociopathic behaviour that involve injury to others or their property, and forms of behaviour that result in injury to oneself. Disorders of affect and affiliation with others that produce impaired social relationships are also included (see e.g. Mazer 1965, 1976; Menninger 1963; Vaillant 1977). In his study of adaptation in an island community, Mazer develops the concept of 'parapsychiatric predicaments', defined as human events presumed to be the behavioural, socially visible manifestations of interpersonal or individual societal maladaptation (Mazer 1965:163). In this class of impairments Mazer includes chronic alcoholism, non-marital pregnancy, suicide and suicide attempts, marital desertion and divorce, criminal convictions, juvenile delinquency, single-vehicle car accidents and school disciplinary problems.

The destruction of the Bulusu' traditional cultural ecology, the breakdown of their traditional social organization, the attacks on self-esteem and social identity, the loss of support mechanisms – all are psychosocial stress factors that can contribute to the growth of deviance, antisocial acts and various forms of maladaptive behaviour. As noted above, in the *respen* the Bulusu' were more anxious, more defensive and more irritable than they were when we visited them in their own villages upriver. In these villages everyone was known, and when a stranger visited their purposes were shortly discovered. In the *respen* there was the constant wondering and worrying as to what this or that stranger was up to. Once a child was taken by a Timorese to his lumber camp, and another time there was an alert that a stranger had tried to kidnap two children.

Fights broke out frequently in the *respen* between children and between adults, usually but not always from different ethnic groups. In 1976 one substantial fight between the Bulusu' and coastal Muslims resulted in the *respen* being deserted by the Bulusu' for some time. The theft of chickens,

---

9   The lack of social support mechanisms has been found associated with increased rates of psychiatric disorders, coronary disease, accidents, suicide, respiratory diseases and tuberculosis (Cobb 1976; Henderson 1977; Kaplan et al. 1977; Lynch 1977). Cobb (1976) argues that adequate social support mechanisms are protective against the health consequences of life stresses. Cobb concludes: 'adequate social support can protect people in crisis from a wide variety of pathological states: from low birth weight to death, from arthritis through tuberculosis to depression, alcoholism, and other psychiatric illness. Furthermore, social support can reduce the amount of medication required and accelerate recovery' (ibid.:310).

personal property, parts of outboard motors and canoe paddles was rampant, causing serious social problems. Informants generally assessed there to be more fighting, stealing, fornication and unmarried pregnancies than in the traditional villages. One informant thought there were also more divorces.

Sexual promiscuity was believed by all to have increased and was a major source of disputes. Bulusu' customary law regulating 'visiting girls' (*moi dandu*') appeared to have broken down. Informants said that there was much more fornication taking place now during these visits than in the traditional villages. The Bulusu' were under the influence of new religions at the *respen*, and therefore the fear of ritual jeopardy from fornication may have lessened. They were no longer permitted to raise the pigs that were used for the ritual necessary to cleanse the village after fornication. Older informants said that boys visiting girls had become much more noisy and disruptive than in the past. This was partially related to the loud use of radio-cassette players by young men when visiting their girlfriends.

Two women of mixed Bulusu'-Punan ancestry were apparently prostitutes. They had spent some time in the cities, and then returned to the *respen* for a while. They were visited not only by the Bugis and various workers from the timber companies, but also by Kasim, the trader. The Bugis carpenters, there to rebuild the school, were enjoying the sexual services of certain girls. Once, when the *respen* guard caught a carpenter in this, the carpenter tried to knife the guard. Workers from various parts of Indonesia employed at the two timber camps nearby also came to take advantage of the Bulusu' custom of visiting girls. They brought brandy, beer and other forms of enticement to encourage the girls to fornicate with them. This is why the liaison officer prohibited all forms of visiting girls, even among the Bulusu', and had the night guards on the alert for such activities. One Bulusu' found engaged in visiting was taken bodily and thrown into the river. In another instance, a boy was visiting his fiancée when discovered by the night guards. This was permitted, but nevertheless they confiscated his radio-cassette player as punishment and threatened to whip him with a skate's tail. The search by night guards, particularly Muslim guards, for men visiting girls at night became a major source of friction. They would burst into a house where they thought something was going on without permission, which was against the customary law of the Bulusu'.

It was clear that both adults and young people did not have as much to keep them busy in the *respen* as they would have had upcountry. Gangs of young boys without adult supervision hung around getting into trouble. One section of the *respen*, composed of individuals of mixed Punan-Bulusu' ancestry, was perceived as being a particular source of trouble, yet they were regarded as having changed the most and were the most modern. This was the village that produced the two supposed prostitutes. It was also the prime source of fights and theft. The boys and girls had had more schooling. A few of the women wore trousers occasionally, dresses frequently, and one time a woman appeared in running clothes. The use of lipstick and nail polish was common. There was considerable drunkenness. There was also a lot of divorce among the younger generation. One of the younger generation committed suicide, which is unheard of among the Bulusu'. It was said of them 'their behaviour is uncertain' (*tidak buatan tentu*, Indonesian).

This illustrates the point that it is not only psychosocial stress that precipitates the growth of deviance. With the previous system of reward and punishment of the traditional social system no longer operating, one could now do things that were previously forbidden without the imposition of negative sanctions. The destruction of the previous social system dissolved the network of interpersonal ties and informal exchanges that constrained behaviour. As a result, all sorts of new opportunities opened up for choosing alternative forms of behaviour. For example, one informant stated that nowadays people were no longer concerned about paying off their bride price obligations in full. The problem was that there were no reliable guides to the choices in behaviour to be made. The primary guide provided for both *respen* inhabitants and the government officers making policy was whether a choice was modern, progressive (*maju*, Indonesian) or not. Choices were no longer based on whether they were appropriate to the local ecosystem and local social conditions. Thus, as long as you had a religion, you could not be a communist; as long as you had medical facilities, no matter how bad, you were modern.

Abuses of power and the social construction of a subordinate role

The major feature of the social organization of the *respen* that raises concern was the lack of control over the abuse of power by administrators, the police and the military. There were no explicit mechanisms whereby the Bulusu' could appeal to higher authorities for protection when they were abused. This, among other things, gave the *respen* the aspect of a concentration camp. Psychosocial stress from devaluation and deprivation coupled with abuse, particularly when those in control believe that it represents the attitudes and interests of their superiors, can lead to violence, physical and psychological disability, and death. It can even sanction massacres (see Kelman 1973). Perhaps the Bulusu' did not commit more violence in response because it was still early in the game.

The most difficult aspect of living in the resettlement area was the way that it put the Bulusu' at the mercy of government representatives and their surrogates. Their authoritarian behaviour was a major factor making the *respen* a place to avoid.[10] Burbank reviews how such hierarchical behaviour is a major factor leading to ill health among subordinate groups. She illustrates this with a study of an Australian Aboriginal community, writing:

> Loss of autonomy and control is associated with high blood pressure, obesity, diabetes, coronary heart disease, kidney failure and depression ... Pregnancy punctuated by episodes of hunger, social disruption, anger and fear results in less adequate nourishment for the fetus. Stress interferes with gestation and can generate fragility in generations to come.
>
> (Burbank 2011:156)

Structural changes in the centre–periphery relationship

Over the years following Indonesian independence in 1945, the Bulusu' had been developing as independent agricultural entrepreneurs, selling their surplus fruit, vegetables, rice, pigs, chickens and forest products in Tarakan. Originally, this trade had been largely in the hands of coastal Muslim traders but, as the market grew in Tarakan, so the Bulusu' became more accustomed to dealing with the outside world and, as communication and safety of transportation grew in the region, they moved into this niche. With the growth of agricultural exports to Tarakan, larger fruit groves were planted.

After resettlement, however, the amount of agricultural and forest products sold in Tarakan dropped by about 40 to 50 per cent, according to several informants. Resettlement therefore cut off the development of an independent farming class, economically viable and equivalent in income and assets to the urban lower middle class. Instead, the government had taken control of their land and had sold the rights to harvest trees from their forest to timber companies, many of them foreign. It had forced the

---

10 It was sometimes difficult for us to manage the cognitive discontinuity that occurred when asked about America by those administrators and coastal Muslims in the *respen* who maintained such righteous superiority over the Bulusu', since of course they themselves were on the road to modernity and were educated. They would ask us: Do you eat rice in America? Do you have streams? Do you have mountains? One member of the provincial parliament asked me if there were still wild Indians in America. In a sense this type of social understanding and that which lay behind the institution and management of the *respen* might be viewed as more primitive than the Bulusu'. The Bulusu' world view was appropriate to their environment, to their social economy, to their situation. The world view of the government driving the development and modernization policies was in fact less appropriate to the environment and the social economy of the region and contained many delusional aspects.

proletarianization of the Bulusu' by converting their labour into a commodity, labour that formerly had been used in their own agricultural enterprises or in exchange for similar labour within the Bulusu' community. Certainly, the Bulusu' could not make a living from the *respen*. But wage labour was only occasionally available, as in the timber camps or when oil companies were exploring in the area and workers were needed to cut lines, build walkways through swamps and so on. Worse, we were told that the wages obtained were only sufficient to sustain an individual. There was nothing left over, unlike the previous situation where surpluses could have been invested in old jars, gongs, brassware and so on. In some instances, Bulusu' undertook wage labour and were never paid. But one of the worst disadvantages of wage labour is that when one is sick and cannot work one receives no income, whereas, when a farmer is sick (unless it is for an extended period), he can still make a living as the crops continue to grow and the fruit trees continue to bear, and he can always rely on help from his family.

It is ironic that the government officials who exhorted the Bulusu' to take up wage labour nevertheless appropriated Bulusu' labour for their own personal use or for the advantage of the government in the upkeep and management of the *respen*. Their time, which was valuable to those who have to do manual work for their food or wages, was now being captured by government officials for a variety of duties, and without compensation.

As few would be able to make their living from wage labour in the foreseeable future, farming and developing fruit, clove and coconut plantations would have to be the major source of their economic survival, but they were receiving no instruction on this in school. School graduates with expectations raised would find few opportunities, and they would have to return to farming without practical knowledge or resources. Furthermore, now the government had ordered them to stop investing their surplus in their traditional method of banking in jars, gongs and brassware, and as there were no banking services in the *respen*, there was no substitute place or form in which to save their cash. On the other hand, the availability of consumer goods is growing.

In addition to the loss of their traditional lands and the growing commoditization of labour, the society has been undergoing monetization. This process had begun when the Dutch organized the economy of the region, and forest products could be sold for cash, but this probably had a minor effect on the Bulusu' economy, as trading forest products for gongs, jars and brassware still continued until the development of the *respen*. Monetization expanded when the Bulusu' started managing their own trading with Tarakan rather than going through the coastal Muslims. There was nonetheless a quantum leap in monetization with resettlement. It became necessary to undertake wage labour when it was available, and it was usually performed by young, unmarried men. Clothing must now be purchased from the shops. Only cloth had been purchased previously, and before that cloth was made from bark or woven from various local fibres. Rice had to be purchased. Inoculations by the nurse required cash. The nurse was organizing a football team and asked each member to contribute 4,000 rupiah for team kits. With the advent of outboard motors cash was needed to purchase them, for repairs and for fuel. There was also a greater number and variety of consumer goods to attract the Bulusu', from radio-cassette players to sunglasses, cosmetics, sugar, soft drinks and so on. The feasts at weddings and funerals have became more expensive as a proper feast requires the use of consumer products purchased at stores, such as sugar, brandy, beer, cigarettes, coffee and rice, rather than being based on swidden products as before. The growing monetization of economic relations was typified in the statement by one informant that when all the children had been to school, bride prices would be made up of money rather than old property (*gama'*, Bulusu').

As they needed to purchase supplies to finish their *respen* houses, as the demand for consumer goods had risen and as their agricultural profits had dropped and they had to buy food, the Bulusu' began to sell their inherited property, their *gama'*. Old jars in particular were sought out by traders to sell to Java and Europe. The jars are valuable, but the Bulusu' did not receive their true value in the market place as they did not have access to this information. And yet from time to time in Tarakan we heard the Bulusu' ridiculed for investing in jars.

With growing monetization there has also been a growing individualization. People said that from now on everyone would be going their own way. They would not farm as a group, with each family's swiddens beside other families from their village. Each would look for their own economic opportunity separately from their village mates, their kin. In response to this breakdown of social ties, some had already moved into niches that have been considered characteristic of the lumpenproletariat, such as prostitution. The Bulusu' were ordered to build separate houses. They were told to engage in wage labour. They were told by the liaison officer that when they killed a wild pig they were not to divide it up but sell it. The informant who told me this was astounded, for, he said, if you are poor and cannot buy meat, you will not have any to eat. The whole system of traditional redistribution of the Bulusu' was being attacked and destroyed, and exchanges monetized.

It is common in situations of imposed social change for the agents of change to believe that the traditional redistributive system is wasteful. They attempt to supplant it by greater individualism (e.g. Tibbles 1957). However, one of the purposes of a redistributive system is to ensure that the less fortunate and disabled are taken care of, as in the example of the distribution

of pig meat. Where a more individualistic social economy can be found, the
less fortunate or the disabled located at the centre are cared for through
a variety of social support services that the centre maintains by various
forms of taxation and charitable giving. But when the imposition of a more
individualistic social economy occurs in the periphery, institutionalized social
support services are not in place. The disabled and less fortunate therefore
carry a disproportionate load and suffer more in the growing linkage of the
periphery to the centre. This may put them in a position where they are never
able to respond to demands for adaptation.

With growing individualization and monetization, one can expect growing
conflict over property in which there had once been equal rights of access held
by individual members of a group of kin, descendants of the original purchaser
of the property or planter of a grove of fruit trees. Thus, conflict will probably
grow over the distribution of yields from groves held jointly, as the moral
order that should pertain between kin dissolves in favour of a morality of
individualism.

Rampant individualism is a product of social breakdown. For the Bulusu'
this societal breakdown may follow the model presented to the Bulusu' by
government officials, traders and businessmen, in which the interests of the
individual are paramount over the interests of the group for which they work,
and over the responsibilities of their position. Here corruption and bribery are
not only common but expected, so that the public good is sacrificed for private
greed. Under such conditions, genuine development will be hard to achieve.

The future for the Bulusu'

The future for the Bulusu' was highly questionable. Unfortunately, further
research has been discouraged by the government. They may have been put in
a situation similar to Aboriginal communities in Australia (see Burbank 2011).
They may have become peripheral people, poor and sick derelicts in a society
of elites who are increasingly addicted to property. Unfortunately, we can only
extrapolate on the health of the Bulusu' as a result of their *respen* experience
from what we witnessed. One might expect that a few very resilient Bulusu'
will have survived quite well, but that the rest of the population may have
become discouraged, disoriented and apathetic rural slum dwellers with little
chance of ever moving out of that category, being at the very end of the line,
lacking opportunities, lacking information by which to grasp opportunities
and lacking in resources to create opportunities.

We were not able to put systems in place to monitor the growing health
impairments of that form of directed social change termed ethnocide. I
personally was so shocked and appalled by the human rights violations and
brutality inflicted on the Bulusu', some of whom were our friends, that I was

never able to return. I was never entirely sure whether or not the brutality of the government agents was in part because we were there. There is a similar case in western New Guinea, where the government representative had to show an American anthropologist that he was the person in charge, so he beat up the anthropologist's friend and informant (see Appell 1978).

Conclusion: resettlement and reservations as a social type

Having done research on the Dogrib First Nation resettlement site in the Northwest Territories of Canada in 1957, having studied development projects for the Rungus people in Sabah, Malaysia (Appell 1985b), having experienced the Bulusu' resettlement programme and having visited a number of reservations in the United States and Canada, I have concluded that the idea of a reservation or a resettlement area as a method of dealing with ethnic minorities seems to arise in all parts of the world at various times without any common historical, geographical or cultural roots. It is the process by which governments take possession of the natural resources of peripheral peoples. But the features of this social form appear to be the product of universal structures of modern administration, including bureaucratization and the need to simplify people's organizational world (see Scott 1998). This particular social form appears under various names, such as re-education centres and certain types of development. It appears wherever a minority or indigenous population controls resources that the central government wants to appropriate. Such resources includes the labour of the population itself. To gain access, the government forces the population to move into a centralized residential area that is administered by the government, leaving behind an environment and cultural ecology that supported them. For simplicity I will refer to all these institutions as relocation centres.

While this enduring social form continues to be used, we know little about its defining features, processes and functioning, or how they are joined to the larger society. There are several reasons why it is important to reach some generalizations and theories about these relocation centres as social systems. First, from the view of expanding anthropological knowledge, we have an opportunity to witness first-hand the processes which lead to the development of relocation centres and their consequences. Both processes have formed a major part of the expansion of Western culture and the industrial economy for the past two centuries. It is important that they be fully recorded and analysed, not only for their intrinsic interest but also so that we have the data and insight to reinterpret historical accounts where such processes were, as was often the case, not witnessed by trained social scientists. Second, by understanding these processes and the management of administered peoples we can perhaps develop better approaches to the problem so that the impact of resettlement on minority ethnic groups is minimized.

At this point I therefore put forward some of what I perceive to be the constant features and some of the questions that relate to all relocation centres.

The fundamental reason for bringing a minority population into a relocation centre is to enable the government to gain access to their resources: land, minerals, oil, forest and labour power. But the standard, explicit justification for this is given as the need to provide governmental services such as health, education and other welfare services, or to protect a population from predatory exploitation by other groups. The implicit justification is to bring a population under the bureaucratic control of the government and modify or destroy those aspects of the population's culture which the government does not understand and therefore feels threatened by. A juxtaposition of symbols from the dominant society and the indigenous society, in terms of dress, housing and so forth, is frequently found in such centres. In paintings and pictures of early reservations for the American Indian there appear Indians in traditional clothing but with a top hat. In the Bulusu' resettlement centre a Punan in a loincloth wore a double breasted, worsted, brown suit coat with blue pencil lines.

In view of the parallels between the Bulusu' resettlement centre and the situations described by Colson (1971), Mazer (1965) and Scott (1998), I ask whether all relocation centres fall into a bounded essentialist category of social phenomena, or whether they form a set of family resemblances that can be better understood using prototype theory (see Saler 1993, 1999), in which some members of a category are more central than others. Of particular importance is the incidence of conditions that lead a relocation centre to become a total institution analogous to a prison, as argued by Robertson (1970). Only further research can answer this question, but there are four areas of enquiry that particularly need comparative research.

Ethnocide

Does every relocation centre involve an explicit policy of ethnocide of the target population, or is ethnocide an unintended consequence of other policies for social change? Does the dehumanization of the ethnic minority by the dominant society always precede the creation of a relocation centre (Bernard *et al.* 1971:102)? Are terms such as 'dirty', 'drunken', 'sexually unlicensed', 'ignorant', 'stupid', 'lazy' and 'savage' used to characterize the target population? These are psychological projections of the fears of dominant societies about themselves, but they serve to put the subject population beyond the dominant population's own moral community and justify actions taken against a controlled or subservient community that may violate its own moral code (see Appell 2002).

Are those in charge of relocation centres always ignorant of the traditional culture of the confined population and the functions of its features? What are the consequences of this ignorance? Do all relocation centres provide education that ignores the beauty, history and knowledge of the confined population? Is expenditure on the traditional rituals of the controlled population ridiculed as wasteful, while expenditure on the rituals of the dominant population considered justified (see e.g. Tibbles 1957)? Is there a policy to inculcate the idea of individual ownership of productive resources rather than maintain traditional forms of multiple ownership, and do administrators ignore the various forms of ownership in modern economies where there are multiple owners of a resource, or perceive they are inappropriate for the controlled population?

Social control

The methods used to obtain control over an administered population and the maintenance of social control in a relocation centre are powerful indicators of the prison-like character of such centres. This can be investigated by establishing whether the population has any formal control over its situation in order to limit the abuse of power by administrators, or to right injustices and wrongs, or whether it has to resort to informal methods (see Scott 1985). Are traditional methods of conflict resolution appropriate to the new social situation or are conflicts and conflicts of a type not previously dealt with experienced for the first time? If this is the case, are indigenous conflict resolution mechanisms overwhelmed and, if so, what new mechanisms emerge or are instituted in their place?

Do relocation centres always result in a change in distributive justice and, if so, what are the consequences? Do such centres, for example, change the organization of gender roles and the distributive justice between these roles?

Measuring the health of populations confined in a relocation centre

Health and well-being are also powerful indicators of the conditions prevailing in a relocation centre. Is it inevitable that, as often seems to be the case, the nutritional level of the population in a relocation centre declines precipitously during the early stages of confinement? Does the experience of relocation produce common psychological symptoms of dysfunction and adjustment problems?

When this is the case, do all such centres provide health services that ignore the methods of healing of the confined population and destroy indigenous social support mechanisms? Does the relocation experience facilitate or hinder the adaptation of the minority group to the dominant society and its economic system?

The development of relocation centre policy

Comparative studies suggest that newly established relocation centres are frequently characterized by the presence of predatory traders, corrupt administrators and police that use unnecessary physical force.[11] Are these pernicious characteristics permanent features, or do such forms of exploitation cease at more mature levels of development?

If the answers to these research questions do show that relocation centres have a common tendency to become total institutions analogous to prisons, there would be a powerful case for the greater involvement of human rights organizations in monitoring the policies applied, and the conditions created, in such centres.

References

Aberle, D.F. 1962. 'A note on relative deprivation theory as applied to millenarian and other cult movements'. In S.L. Thrupp (ed.), *Millennial Dreams in Action: Essays in Comparative Study*, pp. 209–14. The Hague: Mouton.

Abramson, J.H. 1961. 'Observations on the health of adolescent girls in relation to culture change', *Psychosomatic Medicine* 2(3):156–65.

Appell, G.N. 1978. *Dilemmas and Ethical Conflicts in Anthropological Inquiry: A Case Book*. Waltham, MA: Crossroads Press.

——— 1980. 'The social separation syndrome', *Survival International Review* 5(1):13–15.

——— 1983a. 'Ethnic groups in the northeast region of Indonesian Borneo and their social organizations', *Borneo Research Bulletin* 15:38–45.

——— 1983b. 'Methodological problems with the concept of corporation, corporate social grouping, and cognatic descent group'. *American Ethnologist* 10:302–11.

——— 1985a. 'Integration of the Periphery to the Centre: Processes and Consequences. In G.N. Appell (ed.), *Modernization and the Emergence of a Landless Peasantry: Essays on the Integration of Peripheries to Socioeconomic Centres*, pp. 3–50. Williamsburg, VA: Studies in Third World Societies.

---

11   A former vice president of Indonesia's National Audit Board estimates that corruption siphons off between 30 and 40 per cent of the country's annual budget (Mayer 1986:36).

——— 1985b. 'Land tenure and development among the Rungus of Sabah, Malaysia'.
  In G.N. Appell (ed.), *Modernization and the Emergence of a Landless
  Peasantry: Essays on the Integration of Peripheries to Socioeconomic Centres*,
  pp. 111–55. Williamsburg, VA: Studies in Third World Societies.

——— 1985c. 'The Bulusu' of East Kalimantan: the consequences of resettlement'.
  In G.N. Appell (ed.), *Modernization and the Emergence of a Landless
  Peasantry: Essays on the Integration of Peripheries to Socioeconomic Centres*,
  pp. 184–240. Williamsburg, VA: Studies in Third World Societies.

——— 1985d. 'Resettlement of the Bulusu' in Indonesian Borneo: social
  consequences', *Borneo Research Bulletin* 17:21–31.

——— 1985e. 'Introduction: theoretical issues in the study of reservations and
  resettlement', *Borneo Research Bulletin* 17:5–9.

——— 1986a. 'The health consequences of development', *Sarawak Museum Journal*
  36:43–74.

——— 1986b. 'Kayan land tenure and the distribution of devolvable usufruct in
  Borneo'. *Borneo Research Bulletin* 18:119–30.

——— 1991. 'Dehumanization in fact and theory: processes of modernization and the
  social sciences'. In J.A. Lent (ed.), *Social Science Models and Their Impact
  on the Third World*, pp. 23–44. Williamsburg, VA: Studies in Third World
  Societies.

——— 1992. 'Ecological approaches to rural development'. In G. Ismail, M. Mohamed
  and S. Omar (eds), *Proceedings of the International Conference on Forest
  Biology and Conservation in Borneo, July 30–August 3, 1990*, pp. 375–90.
  Kota Kinabalu: Yayasan Sabah.

——— 1997. 'The history of research on traditional land tenure and tree ownership in
  Borneo'. *Borneo Research Bulletin* 28:82–98.

——— 2002. 'Our vision of human rights is too small! Anthropological perspective
  on fundamental human rights'. In M.N. Alam (ed.), *Contemporary
  Anthropology: Theory and Practice*, pp.419–47. Dhaka: Dhaka University
  Press.

Appell, L.W.R., and Appell, G.N. 1993. 'To do battle with the spirits: Bulusu' spirit
  mediums'. In R. Winzeler (ed.), *The Seen and the Unseen: Shamanism,
  Mediumship and Possession in Borneo*, pp. 55–99. Williamsburg, VA:
  Borneo Research Council.

Appell-Warren, L.P. 1985. 'Resettlement of the Bulusu' and Punan in Indonesian
  Borneo: policy and history', *Borneo Research Bulletin* 17(1):10–20.

——— 1987. 'Play, the development of *kakada'* and social change among the Bulusu'
  of East Kalimantan'. In G.A. Fine (ed.), *Meaningful Play, Playful Meaning*,
  pp. 155–71. Champaign, IL: Human Kinetics Publishers.

Audy, J.R. 1971. 'Measurement and diagnosis of health'. In P. Shepard and D. McKinley (eds), *Environ/Mental: Essays on the Planet as a Home*, pp. 140–62. New York: Houghton Mifflin.

——— 1973. 'Health as a quantifiable property', *British Medical Journal* 4:486–7

Audy, J.R. and Dunn, F.L. 1974. 'Community health'. In F. Sargent II (ed.), *Human Ecology* 4:486–7. Amsterdam: North-Holland Publishing.

Bernard, V.W., Ottenberg, P. and Redl, F. 1971. 'Dehumanization'. In N. Sanford and C. Comstock (eds), *Sanctions for Evil: Sources of Social Destructiveness*, pp. 102–24. San Francisco: Jossey-Bass.

Brenner, M.H. 1977. 'Personal stability and economic security', *Social Policy* 8:2–4.

Burbank, V.K. 2011. *An Ethnography of Stress: The Social Determinants of Health in Aboriginal Australia*. New York: Palgrave Macmillan.

Chance, N.A. 1965. 'Acculturation, self-identification, and personality adjustment', *American Anthropologist* 67:372–93.

Cobb, S. 1976. 'Social support as a moderator of life stress', *Psychosomatic Medicine* 38:300–14.

Colson, E. 1971.*The Social Consequences of Resettlement: The Impact of the Kariba Resettlement upon the Gwembe Tonga*. Manchester: Manchester University Press.

Conley, W. 1973. 'The Kalimantan Kenyah: a study of tribal conversion in terms of dynamic cultural themes'. PhD dissertation, Fuller Theological Seminary. Ann Arbor: University Microfilms.

Davis, K. 1940. 'The sociology of parent–youth conflict', *American Sociological Review* 5:523–35.

De Vos, G.A. (ed.). 1976. *Responses to Change: Society, Culture, and Personality*. New York: Van Nostrand.

Dohrenwend, B.S., and Dohrenwend, B.P. (eds). 1974. *Stressful Life Events: Their Nature and Effects*. New York: John Wiley & Sons.

Dunn, F.L. 1972. 'Intestinal parasitism in Malayan aborigines (Orang Asli)', *Bulletin of the World Health Organization* 46:99–113.

Eder, J.F. 1985. 'Agricultural development and social equity in the upland Philippines'. In G.N. Appell (ed.), *Modernization and the Emergence of a Landless Peasantry: Essays on the Integration of Peripheries to Socioeconomic Centres*, pp. 243–61. Williamsburg, VA: College of William and Mary.

Engel, G.L. 1968. 'A life setting conducive to illness: the giving up-given up complex', *Annals of Internal Medicine* 69:293–300.

——— 1977. 'The need for a new medical model: a challenge for biomedicine', *Science* 196:129–36.

Frankl, V.E. 1973. *The Doctor and the Soul: From Psychotherapy to Logotherapy* (2nd edn.). New York: Vintage Books.

Fried, M. 1969. 'Grieving for a lost home: psychological costs of relocation'. In J.Q. Wilson (ed.), *Urban Renewal: The Record and the Controversy*, pp. 359–79. Cambridge, MA: The MIT Press.

Gunderson, E.K.E. and Rahe, R.H. (eds). 1974. *Life Stress and Illness*. Springfield, ILL: Charles C. Thomas.

Gurr, T.R. 1970. *Why Men Rebel*. Princeton: Princeton University Press.

Henderson, S. 1977. 'The social network, support and neurosis: the function of attachment in adult life', *British Journal of Psychiatry* 131:185–91.

Kahn, R.L. *et al.* 1964. *Organizational Stress: Studies in Role Conflict and Ambiguity*. New York: John Wiley & Sons.

Kaplan, B.H., Cassel, J.C. and Gore, S. 1977. 'Social support and health', *Medical Care* 15: 47–58, supplement No. 5.

Kelman, H.C. 1973. 'Violence without moral restraint', *Journal of Social Issues* 29(4):5–61.

Lynch, J.J. 1977. *The Broken Heart: The Medical Consequences of Loneliness*. New York: Basic Books.

Marris, P. 1974. *Loss and Change*. London: Routledge and Kegan Paul.

Mayer, J. 1986. 'Indonesian corruption seen as obstacle to stronger economic ties with U.S.', *Wall Street Journal* (1 May):36.

Mazer, M. 1965. 'The human predicaments of an island population', *Science and Psychoanalysis* 3:159–70.

——— 1976. *People and Predicaments*. Cambridge, MA: Harvard University Press.

Menninger, K. 1963. *The Vital Balance*. New York: Viking Press.

Miller, D.T. 2001. 'Disrespect and the experience of injustice', *Annual Review of Psychology* 52:527–53.

Parkes, C.M. 1972. *Bereavement: Studies of Grief in Adult Life*. New York: International Universities Press.

Ploeg, A. 1971. 'The Situm and Gobari ex-servicemen's settlements', *New Guinea Research Bulletin* 39:1–136.

Rabkin, J.G. and Struening, E.L. 1976. 'Life events, stress, and illness', *Science* 194:1013–20.

Robertson, H. 1970. *Reservations Are For Indians*. Toronto: James Lorimer.

Saler, B. 1993. *Conceptualizing Religion: Immanent Anthropologists, Transcendent Natives, and Unbounded Categories*. Leiden: Brill.

——— 1999. 'Family resemblance and the definition of religion', *Historical Reflections* 25:391–404.

Schmale, A.H. and Engel, G.L. 1967. 'The giving up-given up complex illustrated on film', *Archives of General Psychiatry* 17:135–45.

Scott, J.C. 1985. *Weapons of the Weak: Everyday Forms of Peasant Resistance*. New Haven: Yale University Press.

——— 1998. *Seeing Like a State: How Certain Schemes to Improve the Human Condition Have Failed.* New Haven: Yale University Press.

Tibbles, T.H. 1957. *Buckskin and Blanket Days: Memoirs of a Friend of the Indians.* Lincoln: University of Nebraska Press.

Vaillant, G.E. 1977. *Adaptation to Life.* Boston: Little, Brown.

Wallace, A.F.C. 1968. 'Anthropological contributions to the theory of personality'. In E. Norbeck, D. Price-Williams and W.M. McCord (eds), *The Study of Personality: An Interdisciplinary Appraisal*, pp. 41–52. New York: Holt, Rinehart and Winston.

Wintrob, R.M. 1968. 'Acculturation, identification and psychopathology among Cree Indian youth'. In N.A. Chance (ed.), *Conflict in Culture: Problems of Developmental Change Among the Cree*, pp. 93–104. Ottawa: Canadian Research Centre for Anthropology, Saint-Paul University.

——— 1969. 'Rapid socio-cultural change and student mental health: part 1', *McGill Journal of Education* 4(2):1–10.

——— 1970. 'Rapid socio-cultural change and student mental health', *McGill Journal of Education* 5(1):1–9.

Contributors

Rogaia Abusharaf: Professor of Anthropology, Georgetown University in Qatar.

George Appell: Firebird Foundation for Anthropological Research.

Laura Barber: Formerly research student at the London School of Economic and Political Science.

Jean Comaroff: Professor of African and American Studies and of Anthropology, Harvard University.

John Comaroff: Professor of African and American Studies and of Anthropology, Harvard University.

Emma Gilberthorpe: Associate Professor, School of International Development, University of East Anglia.

Roxanne Hakim: Social Development Cluster Leader, World Bank, Washington D.C.

Mark Jamieson: Senior Lecturer in Anthropology, University of East London.

Robert Layton: Emeritus Professor of Anthropology, University of Durham (UK).

Thanuja Mummidi: Head of Centre for the Study of Social Exclusion and Inclusive Policy, School of Social Sciences and International Studied, Pondicherry University.

Kwesi Sansculotte-Greenidge: Peace and Development Advisor, United Nations Development Programme (UNDP), Ethiopia.

Noriko Sato: Former Urgent Anthropology Fellow at the University of Durham.

Index

9 781912 385225